COMPARATIVE PSYCHOLOGY

Alan Clamp and
Julia Russell

Hodder & Stoughton

A MEMBER OF THE HODDER HEADLINE GROUP

Order queries: please contact Bookpoint Ltd, 39 Milton Park, Abingdon, Oxon
OX14 4TD. Telephone: (44) 01235 400414, Fax: (44) 01235 400454. Lines are
open from 9.00–6.00, Monday to Saturday, with a 24 hour message answering
service. Email address: orders@bookpoint.co.uk.

British Library Cataloguing in Publication Data
A catalogue record for this title is available from The British Library

ISBN 0 340 69703 2

First published 1998
Impression number   10 9 8 7 6 5 4 3
Year   2003 2002 2001 2000

Copyright © 1998 Alan Clamp and Julia Russell

Typeset by Wearset, Boldon, Tyne and Wear.
Printed in Great Britain for Hodder & Stoughton Educational, a division of
Hodder Headline Plc, 338 Euston Road, London NW1 3BH by Redwood Books,
Trowbridge, Wilts.

CONTENTS

Part 3: *Kinship and social behaviour*

Part 4: *Behaviour analysis*

Contents

DEDICATION

To Helen, with love. A.C.

To Stuart, love always. J.R.

ACKNOWLEDGEMENTS

We would like to acknowledge the help and guidance given to us by Tim Gregson-Williams and Marie Jones at Hodder & Stoughton. We would also like to thank Richard Gross and Rob McIlveen for their constructive comments.

Thank you to my sister, Jackie, for her support, encouragement and patience. (J.R.)

PREFACE

Our aim in this book is to provide an introduction to the area of comparative psychology. In order to do this, we have divided the book into four parts. The first, *Evolutionary determinants of behaviour*, comprises three chapters. In Chapter 1, we consider the evolution of behaviour in non-human animals. Chapter 2 deals with competition for resources. Chapter 3 looks at predator–prey and symbiotic relationships.

Part 2, *Reproductive Strategies*, consists of four chapters. Chapter 4 discusses the importance of sexual selection in evolution. Chapter 5 considers parental investment in the rearing of the young, while Chapter 6 looks at mating strategies and social organisation. Chapter 7 is concerned with the issue of parent–offspring conflict.

Part 3, *Kinship and social behaviour*, comprises four chapters. Chapter 8 deals with apparent altruism, while Chapter 9 considers sociality in non-human animals. In Chapter 10, we deal with imprinting and bonding, and Chapter 11 discusses signalling systems in non-human animals.

Part 4, *Behaviour analysis*, consists of four chapters. Chapter 12 is concerned with classical and operant conditioning, while Chapter 13 discusses foraging and homing behaviour. Chapter 14 considers the issue of animal language. The final chapter, Chapter 15, examines evolutionary explanations of human behaviour.

We believe that this book covers the major aspects of comparative psychology as it would be taught on most courses, including A level and undergraduate courses. While the sequence of chapters and much of the content is based on the revised AEB A level syllabus, the general issues and major theories that are discussed represent the core of this central and influential area of psychology. For the purposes of revision, we have included detailed summaries of the material that is presented in each chapter. Although we have not included a separate glossary, the Index contains page numbers in **bold** which refer to definitions and main explanations of particular concepts for easy reference.

PART 1
Evolutionary determinants of behaviour

EVOLUTION OF BEHAVIOUR IN NON-HUMAN ANIMALS

Introduction and overview

Comparative psychology may be defined as the study of the behaviour of animals with a view to drawing comparisons (similarities and differences) between them. It also involves studying non-human animal behaviour in order to gain a better understanding of human behaviour. The basis of comparative psychology is the evolutionary relationship between all living organisms. According to Charles Darwin and Alfred Russel Wallace (Darwin, 1859), all species are biologically related and so behaviour patterns are also likely to be related. Comparative psychologists believe that most of the differences between animals are quantitative rather than qualitative. It is important to note, however, that the degree to which investigations of non-human animal behaviour are applicable to humans is questionable, and that there may be critical qualitative differences to be considered.

The first part of this book (Chapters 1, 2 and 3) considers the evolutionary determinants of behaviour and examines the evolution of behaviour in non-human animals, competition for resources, and predator–prey and symbiotic relationships. Chapter 1 considers evolutionary concepts as explanations of the behaviour of non-human animals. This will involve an examination of how, and to what extent, evolutionary processes can explain the behaviour of a wide range of species. In many ways, the evolution of behaviour is what this whole book is about, and this chapter should be viewed as an introduction to what follows.

Evolution

Evolution is the process by which new species arise as the result of gradual changes to the genetic make-up of existing species over long periods of time. The father of evolutionary theory was Charles Darwin, and an understanding of his theory of evolution by natural selection is fundamental to the study of comparative psychology. Although far reaching in its effects, this theory is actually quite simple and can be summarised as shown in Box 1.1.

> **Box 1.1   A summary of Darwin's theory**
>
> **1** All species tend to produce very many more offspring than can ever survive. For example, Darwin calculated that after 750 years, the descendants of one pair of elephants could number more than 19 million. However, the size of populations tends to remain more or less constant, meaning that most of these offspring must die. It also follows that there must be competition for resources such as mates, food and territories (see Chapter 2).

1

Therefore, there is a 'struggle for existence' among individuals.

2 Individuals within a species differ from one another (**variation**). Much of this variability is inherited (**genetic variation**).

3 Competition for resources, together with variation between individuals, means that certain members of the population are more likely to survive and reproduce than others. These individuals will inherit the characteristics of their parents and evolutionary change takes place through natural selection. Over a long period of time this process may lead to the considerable differences now observed between living organisms. It is important to remember that for natural selection to drive evolutionary change, the environment must select certain individuals *and* the differences between individuals must be (to some extent) inherited. Without these two factors, evolution is not likely to occur.

Nature versus nurture

How much of the variability within a species is due to genetic factors and how much depends upon the influence of the environment? This *nature* (inherited characteristics) versus *nurture* (acquired characteristics) debate has been hotly contested in biology and psychology. However, although certain features may fall neatly into one of these two categories, the question of whether learning or evolution underlies any given behaviour is largely meaningless. Any behaviour, however simple or complex, has an element of both inheritance and learning about it (the interaction of which is known as *penetrance*). The only point of debate is over the relative importance of the contributions made to a behaviour by *phylogeny* (inherited, species-specific behaviour patterns) and *ontogeny* (behaviour patterns acquired during the lifetime of the individual which are not shared with every member of the species). The importance of this, as far as the present chapter is concerned, is that most animal behaviour appears to have some genetic component, and is therefore capable of being influenced by the processes of evolution.

What causes genetic variation?

One of the major sources of genetic variation is the process of sexual reproduction. In species which reproduce sexually, offspring inherit 50% of their genetic information from the male parent and 50% from the female parent. This genetic information is in the form of discrete units, known as genes. Offspring of the same parents are genetically different from each other, and from their parents, because they all inherit different combinations of genes (unless they happen to be monozygotic or 'identical' twins). This process means that humans have the potential to produce a *minimum* of 70,000,000,000,000 (7×10^{13}) genetically different offspring.

A second source of genetic variation, which could increase the potential number of different offspring indicated above, is *mutation*. A mutation is defined as any sudden change in the genotype (genetic make-up) of an organism. Mutations are relatively rare, occurring at a natural rate of one per 100,000 genes in each generation. However, this rate may be increased by so-called *mutagens*, which include ionising radiation such as X-rays or ultraviolet light, or chemicals such as caffeine. Most mutations are deleterious (a disadvantage), but a few confer a selective advantage on the individual and may spread through populations. Other potential sources of genetic variation include *genetic drift* (random fluctuations in gene frequency which usually only occur in small populations), *non-random mating* (an individual animal does not have an equal chance of mating with any other individual due to differences in competitive ability, attractiveness or locality) and *migration* into or out of populations.

The evidence for evolution

Darwin's theory of evolution by natural selection is supported by evidence from four main areas. These are shown in Box 1.2.

In addition to the evidence cited above, it is also possible to observe evolution in action over relatively short time periods. Classic examples of this include the

Box 1.2   The evidence supporting Darwin's theory

1 Palaeontology Fossil records indicate clear evidence for evolution, particularly for the vertebrates (animals with backbones). The most convincing evidence is found in cases where, in successive rock layers from the same locality, a series of fossil exhibits gradual change.

2 Comparative anatomy When the anatomy of one group of animals is compared with that of another, resemblances are generally more obvious than differences. One example of this is the pentadactyl ('five-digit') limb, which is found in various forms in all mammals. Comparing the physiology or embryology (development of the embryo) of species also provides evidence for evolution by natural selection.

3 Geographical distribution Places with the same climatic conditions in different regions of the world do not always possess the same animal forms. Elephants, for example, live in India and Africa, but not in South America. This phenomenon is best explained by assuming that existing animals are the descendants of extinct populations which were of a more generalised type. These ancestors were dispersed from their place of origin, became geographically isolated (for example by sea or mountains), and evolved along different paths, becoming adapted to their new environments.

4 Artificial selection Modern varieties of domesticated animals are very different from their ancestors. They have evolved as a result of humans choosing examples with the most desirable qualities through selective breeding. Artificial selection is essentially the same as natural selection except that it is very much quicker and the features selected may not be of survival value in natural populations.

Box 1.3   The evolution of industrial melanism in the peppered moth

The peppered moth exists in two genetically determined forms: a light-coloured peppered form (*Biston betularia typica*) and a dark form (*Biston betularia carbonaria*). The first melanic moth (dark type) was reported in Manchester in 1849. By 1900 it had almost replaced the typical mottled form. Clearly, evolution (a change in gene frequency) had occurred.

The most significant selection pressure for peppered moths is visual predation by birds, which remove them from trees when they rest during the day. H.B.D. Kettlewell's (1955) famous experiments involved releasing moths in various locations and investigating what happened to them. He found that more moths were eaten by birds if they were conspicuous against their background than if they were camouflaged. In polluted industrial areas (e.g. Manchester), the melanic form was better camouflaged and predation was largely restricted to the mottled form. In areas not polluted by soot, the reverse was true and the mottled form predominated.

Industrial melanism appears to be a classic example of evolution in action. However, Hailman (1992) has argued that the evidence is far from conclusive. It is not clear whether anyone has actually observed the ratio of peppered to melanic forms change over time. Data from the mid-nineteenth century come from amateur moth collections, not scientific samples. Hailman also claims that it is unlikely that birds eat sufficient numbers of moths to shift the ratio. Furthermore, the correlation between melanic moths in industrial areas and peppered moths elsewhere is far from clear. Without further experiments, industrial melanism may be considered a myth of evolutionary biology.

development of antibiotic resistance in populations of bacteria and the evolution of industrial melanism in the peppered moth (*Biston betularia*) as described in Box 1.3.

Types of selection and other evolutionary forces

NATURAL SELECTION

All animals are subjected to selection according to the environmental conditions that exist at the time (known as the *selection pressure*). There are three types of natural selection. *Stabilising selection* occurs during periods of minimal environmental change, when most variations from the norm are likely to be harmful. The organisms most likely to reproduce successfully are those which are close to the average, with selection pressure acting against extreme versions. The fossil record of sharks suggest that they have the same structure today as they did tens of millions of years ago, representing a good example of stabilising selection (Figure 1.1a).

Directional selection occurs when environmental change favours a new form (phenotype) of an organism (Figure 1.1b). This has been demonstrated by industrial melanism in populations of the peppered moth, as described in Box 1.3. *Disruptive selection* occurs when selection favours forms representing the extremes of the range of phenotypic variation (the reverse of stabilising selection). The effect of disruptive selection is to eliminate phenotypes in the middle of the range, producing a bimodal distribution (Figure 1.1c).

SEXUAL SELECTION

Natural selection cannot explain all evolutionary processes. Certain behaviours or anatomical structures appear to *reduce* the probability of survival. The tail of the peacock (*Pavo cristatus*), for example, appears to have the dual disadvantage of attracting predators and impeding efficient flight, making escape difficult. Such features may be explained by sexual selection. According to Darwin (1871), sexual selection 'depends upon the advantage which certain individuals have over others of the same sex and species solely in respect of reproduction'. In the case of the peacock, female preference for longer tails has outweighed any disadvantages involved in owning such a cumbersome appendage. A detailed discussion of sexual selection is provided in Chapter 4.

ADAPTED OR ADAPTABLE?

At any one time, each *species* (group of organisms capable of interbreeding to produce fertile offspring)

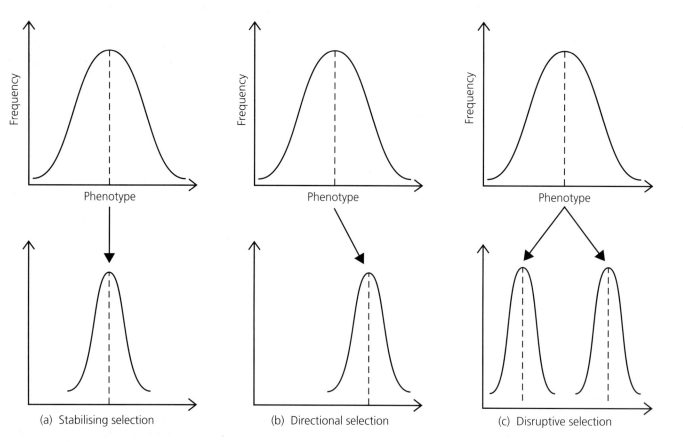

(a) Stabilising selection   (b) Directional selection   (c) Disruptive selection

Figure 1.1   The three types of natural selection

occupies a particular *ecological niche* (place of the organism within an ecosystem, including its habitat, diet and behaviour). Only one species can occupy a particular niche at any one time. For example, lions (*Panthero leo*) and elephants (*Loxodonta africana*) occupy different niches even though they live side by side. Selection pressure ensures that each species is particularly adapted to its niche. However, if the environment changes, it is important that species possess sufficient genetic variability to be able to adapt to the new conditions, otherwise they will become extinct. Therefore, there is a critical balance to be struck between *adaptation* (characterised by genetic stability) and *adaptability* (characterised by genetic change).

The environment is constantly changing and organisms must be adaptable in order to survive, although they must also be well adapted to the new environment in order to compete successfully with other species. Conversely, too much change may threaten survival. Offspring should be as similar as possible to their parents to ensure that they will be well adapted to their environment and that mating will be possible. Stable environments will favour adaptation, whereas more changeable environments will favour adaptability. Most species, therefore, seek a compromise between being adapted and being adaptable (Figure 1.2).

It is important to be aware of the distinction between *evolutionary adaptation*, which takes place as species adjust genetically to changes in their environment, and *phenotypic adaptation*, in which animals adjust during the course of their lifetime through processes such as maturation and learning (see Chapter 12). The extent to which an individual animal is genetically adapted to its particular niche, therefore surviving and reproducing successfully, is known as the *fitness* of the animal.

FITNESS

Darwin's theory of evolution by natural selection has often been summed up by the phrase 'survival of the fittest'. However, this is an oversimplification. Fitness is not a quality that individuals possess, such as size or speed, but is closely linked with evolutionary success and may be defined as a measure of the ability of an individual to leave behind offspring. The relative fitness of the offspring is also important. It is likely that at least some of this fitness is genetic in nature and therefore determined by natural and sexual selection.

More recent examinations of Darwin's work have tended to replace the term 'fitness' with '*inclusive fitness*' (Dawkins, 1989). Inclusive fitness may be defined as the total number of an animal's genes present in subsequent generations. These genes will be present in direct offspring *and* in the offspring of close relatives, such as brothers and sisters. The use of the term 'inclusive fitness' may solve one of the problems of Darwin's theory, that being the existence of *altruistic behaviour* in certain species (see Box 1.4).

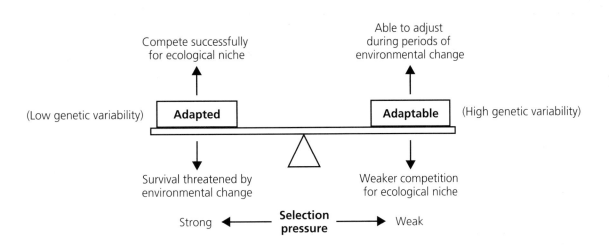

Figure 1.2   Natural selection generally favours a compromise between being adapted (to a particular niche) and being adaptable (in conditions of environmental change)

Box 1.4   The paradox of altruism

Altruistic behaviour refers to any act which increases the survival potential of others at a potential risk to the altruist's survival. Animals sometimes draw a predator's attention to themselves to divert it from their mate, nest or offspring. Army ants (*Eciton burchelli*), for example, sacrifice their own lives to form bridges across small streams so that others may cross in safety. Such behaviour is difficult to explain by natural selection because it reduces the survival chances of the altruistic individual. On this basis, altruism would be expected to diminish with each successive generation because all individuals displaying this behaviour would be selected against. This is because genes for altruism will *reduce* the survival chances of the owner and so not get passed on to the next generation. The existence of altruism becomes less of a problem to explain if we think in terms of inclusive fitness. A good example of this can be seen in Florida scrub jays (*Aphelocoma coerulescens*) (Figure 1.3). These

Figure 1.3   The Florida scrub jay. Helpers provide food for the young and defend the nest against predators such as snakes. This altruistic behaviour may be explained by the concept of inclusive fitness

birds are communal breeders, the parents being assisted by up to six non-breeding helpers, 75% of which are offspring of a previous brood. It has been found that nests with helpers produce more fledglings than nests without (Woolfenden & Fitzpatrick, 1984). Although they produce no young of their own, the inclusive fitness of helpers is not zero because they increase the survival rates of close genetic relatives. Altruistic behaviour in non-human animals is discussed in detail in Chapter 8.

The evolution of behaviour

BACKGROUND

As noted in the introduction and overview to this chapter, our main aim is to consider evolutionary concepts as explanations of the behaviour of non-human animals. With this in mind, evolution may be more specifically defined as the processes by which animal *behaviour* is altered by means of adaptation through natural selection. It is important to remember that natural selection works by differential reproduction. When examining animal behaviour, therefore, we should usually ask, 'How does that behaviour enable that animal to produce more offspring?', or 'Why would an animal that performed a different behaviour pattern leave fewer offspring?'

According to Darwin, all species are biologically related to each other through evolution, and so behaviour patterns are also likely to be related. Grier and Burk (1992) suggest that nearly all animal behaviour is influenced by genetic factors to some degree, and that behaviour makes important contributions to an animal's survival and reproductive success. The behaviour of animals must, therefore, be subject to the forces of evolution in the same way as their anatomy and physiology.

One important question which needs to be addressed is, how do *new* behaviours arise? It is important to realise that most behaviour patterns do not suddenly appear as a whole, especially if they are complex. They probably originate as very small modifications of ancestral behaviour which conferred a slight but significant advantage (perhaps due to a mutation). This behaviour pattern would then spread by natural selection. New behaviour patterns can also arise by combining preexisting behavioural units (single observable acts) in novel forms.

INSTINCTIVE AND LEARNED BEHAVIOUR

The 'nature' versus 'nurture' debate mentioned on page 2 may also be applied to animal behaviour. In this case, nature traditionally represents *instinctive* behaviours and nurture represents *learned* behaviours. As will be seen, this is an oversimplification because instincts are not purely genetic and learning is not purely environmental.

Instinctive behaviour evolves gradually and is modified

by natural selection in order to adapt animals to fit a fixed and unchanging environment. Such behaviours are advantageous for animals that have short lifespans and little or no parental care. These animals have little opportunity or need for learning. Learned behaviour enables animals to discover which responses give the best results in certain circumstances and to modify their actions accordingly. The ability to learn gives animals an adaptive advantage in that it gives them a greater potential for changing their behaviour to meet changing circumstances within their own lifetime. However, few behaviours can be said to be entirely dominated by either inheritance or learning, and an interaction between the two is the norm.

Seligman (1970) has suggested that animals are biologically prepared to learn some things more readily than others. Some associations, such as taste avoidance, may be more biologically useful (or have greater survival value) than others and are therefore learned more quickly and are more resistant to *extinction* (see Chapter 12). Research on bird song has demonstrated the importance of both instinct and learning, as shown in Box 1.5. Although most male birds inherit the basics of their song, they need to experience singing and listening to the songs of other birds before they can produce the final form (Kirn & DeVoogd, 1989). Similar genetic and environmental factors appear to play a role in the opening of milk bottle tops by blue-tits. In this case, the physical ability to remove strips of material is instinctive, but its application to the foil tops of milk bottles is learned (Sherry & Galef, 1984).

EVIDENCE FOR THE EVOLUTION OF BEHAVIOUR

Explanations of the evolution of behaviour are essentially the same as those of the evolution of anatomy and physiology. However, evidence for the evolution of behaviour is not as easily obtained. For example, behaviour is not easily fossilised. However, fossil records may provide evidence of particular anatomical features which *imply* certain behaviours. The role of head ornaments in dinosaurs, such as the horns of *Triceratops*, has been inferred from the behaviour of animals such as deer and certain beetles that have head ornaments today (Molnar, 1977).

By far the best evidence for the evolution of animal behaviour comes from interspecies comparisons (which is what comparative psychology is all about). To make these comparisons we need a phylogenetic tree (Figure 1.4) which shows the ancestral relations of modern

---

Box 1.5   The role of genetic and environmental factors in the development of bird song

In the normal course of development, young male white-crowned sparrows (*Zonotrichia leucophrys*) do not start to sing until about 2 months of age. At this point, the sounds the birds produce are called *subsong*. At around 4 months, the variable sounds of subsong 'crystallise' into the final adult song characteristic of this species.

If a young male is isolated from other white-crowned sparrows during the sensitive period (days 1–50), he produces subsong but it does not crystallise into the proper adult version. This appears to suggest that the ability to produce subsong is instinctive, but that learning is required to develop the correct adult song. Further evidence for the interaction of genetic and environmental factors comes from white-crowned sparrows exposed only to the song of the song sparrow (*Melospiza melodra*) during the sensitive period. These birds learn neither the related species' song nor their own (Ridley, 1995).

---

forms based on anatomical and physiological evidence. If we know the evolutionary relationship between a group of species, we can infer whether common behaviour patterns are *homologous* (species share a common ancestor) or *analogous* (similar behaviour patterns evolved in unrelated organisms due to similar environmental pressures).

If similar behaviours evolve independently in a number of unrelated species, this is known as *convergent evolution*. The social insects represent a good example of convergent evolution, with termites (*Amitermes hastatus*) and the social hymenopterans (ants, bees and wasps) developing this distinctive behaviour independently. If, however, different behaviours are observed among related species, this is known as *divergent evolution*. An example of this is courtship behaviour in ducks, which is typically a distinctive pattern of vocalisations and head and tail movements (Lorenz, 1958). In this case, the behaviour is probably advantageous in ensuring that individuals do not waste time and effort courting members of a different species.

Convergent and divergent evolution form the basis of two approaches to studying comparative psychology.

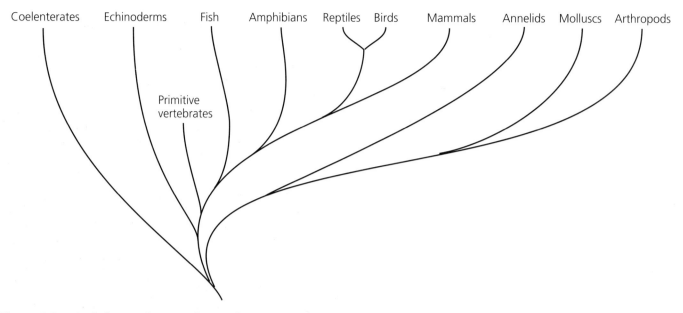

Figure 1.4   A phylogenetic tree of some large groups of animals

The first considers the function of analogous behaviours among unrelated species and attempts to explain what caused these behaviours by searching for similar environmental factors. The second looks at differences among closely related species to investigate the evolutionary changes undergone by a particular behavioural unit based on phylogenetic relationships. A comparison of closely related species living in different habitats can often reveal those aspects of behaviour which are particularly important in adapting the animal to its environment. It is also possible to combine these two approaches for a detailed study of the evolution of a particular behaviour.

Phylogenetic trees based on behavioural similarities can be constructed and compared to those based on anatomical and physiological evidence. Konrad Lorenz (1958) did this with ducks and geese and found that the grouping of species according to their behaviour is similar, but not exactly identical, to groupings based on anatomical similarity.

Several experimental studies have shown that differences in behaviour can result from differences in genes. For example, Seymour Benzer (1973) induced genetic mutations that changed behaviour in the fruit fly *Drosophila*. One example of this is the 'amnesiac fly', which learns normally but forgets very rapidly. The physiological basis of these altered behaviour patterns

has been investigated and shown to be due to a mutation in a specific gene (Dudai, 1989). Artificial selection experiments have also demonstrated that genetic factors are important in calling behaviour in crickets (*Gryllus integer*) (Cade, 1981).

When examining the evolution of behaviour, it is important to consider two main points. First, when we talk about genes for a particular behaviour it does not mean that one gene alone codes for the trait. It is much more likely that several genes are involved. However, a difference in behaviour between two individuals may be due to a difference in a single gene. Second, just because it can be shown that genes influence behaviour, this does not imply that genes alone produce the behaviour, or even that the behaviour can be divided up into genetic and environmental components. The way in which behaviour develops is the result of a complex interaction between genes and the environment.

Sociobiology

Sociobiology was introduced by Hamilton (1964) and Wilson (1975) and can be defined as the systematic study of the biological basis of all social behaviour, including altruism, aggression and sexual behaviour. Sociobiology differs from classical studies of animal

8

behaviour (known as *ethology*) in that it generally considers the set of genes, rather than the individual, as the basic unit of evolution. In other words, it is not as important for individuals to survive as it is for their genes to do so. Sociobiologists have suggested that this may explain the existence of altruism (Dawkins, 1989). What appears as an altruistic act is actually selfish at the gene level (see Box 1.4 on page 6).

Sociobiology has been criticised for oversimplifying explanations of behaviour and overemphasising the role of genetic factors. It has also been suggested that the extension from non-human animal to human behaviour is doubtful because genetic evolution has been overtaken by cultural evolution, a point which will be returned to shortly.

Evolutionarily stable strategies

An evolutionarily stable strategy (ESS) is a behaviour pattern which, if most of the population adopt it, cannot be bettered by any other strategy and will therefore tend to become established by natural selection. It is an optimum strategy dependent on the circumstances in which it is used. This means that an individual cannot successfully behave differently from the others in a population, even if it appears that there would be a short-term gain by doing so. A good example of this is described in Box 1.6.

Using a concept known as *game theory*, mathematicians such as David Wise (personal communication) have calculated the outcomes of various different strategies and determined theoretical ESSs. These ESSs have then been compared with the actual behaviour observed in the animals concerned, and this idea is discussed further in Chapter 2.

Cultural evolution

Cultural evolution may be seen as analogous to genetic evolution. *Cultural behaviour* is that which is passed on from one generation to the next, leading to a process of evolutionary change. Those behaviours which are suc-

---

Box 1.6   An evolutionarily stable strategy

Consider a species in which *both* parents are required to raise the young. If a male of this species had a mutant gene which made it take no part in parenting, it would be able to mate with a greater number of females. The short-term gain, in evolutionary terms, is that it would produce many offspring and, therefore, many copies of its own genes. However, the success of the male's strategy depends on the behaviour of the female. In this case, she is incapable of raising the young alone and none of them would survive. The male would not benefit from breaking away from the ESS and his mutant gene would not survive to change the behaviour of later generations. (Like most mutations, the effect would prove to be deleterious in a well-adapted species.) Although this is an oversimplified example, it serves to illustrate the idea that the evolutionary success of one behaviour pattern depends on the behaviour of others.

---

cessful or adaptive will be imitated (*selected*) and passed on to future generations (*inherited*). Cultural transmission is more powerful and flexible than its genetic equivalent, mainly because it is considerably faster (Brown, 1986).

Although examples of cultural evolution are most readily available for humans, examples of non-human animal culture also occur. In 1952, Kawamura undertook studies of Japanese macaques (*Macaca fuscata*). He left sweet potatoes on the beach for the monkeys, one of whom (Imo) 'invented' the idea of washing the sand off the potatoes in the sea. Soon other monkeys imitated her (Ridley, 1989). Another example of non-human animal culture involves the removal of foil tops of milk bottles, and drinking of the milk, by blue-tits (Sherry & Galef, 1984) (Figure 1.5).

Although examples of cultural transmission have been observed in non-human animals, it is still genetic factors which play by far the largest role in determining behaviour. In humans, however, much of our behaviour is due to cultural rather than genetic determinants (see Chapter 15). It is for this reason that many psychologists are hesitant to apply the same insights to humans as to non-human animals.

Figure 1.5   Blue tits opening milk bottle tops and drinking the milk. This behaviour appears to be influenced by both environmental and genetic factors, and represents an example of cultural evolution

Box 1.7   Some limitations of the evolutionary approach

1 Behaviour is always an interaction between genes and the environment, never purely genetic. The further an animal is up the phylogenetic scale, the more its behaviour is determined by experience. Therefore, evolution can only provide a limited understanding of behaviour.
2 Behaviour is also culturally transmitted, even in non-human animals.
3 Sociobiology has been accused of being extremely selective in the examples of behaviour which it considers, ignoring numerous examples of both non-human animal and human behaviour which do not fit the theory (Hayes, 1994).
4 There is currently little scientific evidence to support the theoretical arguments. However, this assumes a simple relationship between genes and behaviour, which is probably not the case. Furthermore, a lack of scientific evidence in favour of an approach is *not* the same as evidence against this approach.

Limitations of the evolutionary approach

The evolutionary approach to studying animal behaviour has a number of potential problems. These are summarised in Box 1.7.

Conclusions

In general, comparative psychologists use an evolutionary approach to explain the behaviour of non-human animals. They ask questions about how particular behaviour patterns contribute to an animal's chances of survival and its reproductive success. The appeal of the evolutionary approach is that it is based on a logical concept (Darwinian natural selection) and produces plausible hypotheses, many of which can be tested. There is a wide range of evidence for the evolution of behaviour, based on both comparative and experimental studies. However, there are also limitations to the evolutionary approach and alternative ways of explaining animal behaviour may be required.

SUMMARY

• **Comparative psychology** may be defined as the study of the behaviour of animals with a view to drawing comparisons between them. It also involves studying animal behaviour in order to gain a better understanding of human behaviour. The basis of comparative psychology is the evolutionary relationship between all living organisms.
• **Evolution** is the process by which new species arise as the result of gradual changes to existing species over long periods of time. Evolution results from **superior genetic variants** having an advantage in the **struggle for existence**. These individuals are more likely to **survive** and **reproduce**, resulting in a change in the **gene frequency** of a population. This process may gradually lead to the considerable differences now observed between living organisms.
• There is considerable debate as to how much of

the variability within a species is due to genetic factors (**nature**) and how much depends on the influence of the environment (**nurture**). However, all behaviour has an element of both inheritance *and* learning about it, the interaction between which is known as **penetrance**.

- Genetic variation arises as a result of **sexual reproduction, mutation, genetic drift, non-random mating** and **migration** into or out of populations.
- Darwin's theory of evolution by natural selection is supported by evidence from **palaeontology, comparative anatomy, geographical distribution** and **artificial selection**. It is also possible to observe evolution in action over relatively short time periods. An example of this is the evolution of **industrial melanism** in the peppered moth.
- There are three types of natural selection: **stabilising selection, directional selection** and **disruptive selection**.
- **Sexual selection** depends on the advantage which certain individuals have over others of the same sex and species solely in respect of **reproduction**. It is a specialised form of natural selection, used to explain the existence of behaviours or anatomical structures which appear to *reduce* the probability of survival, such as the tail of the peacock.
- Most species seek a compromise between being **adapted** to their environment and being **adaptable**. The extent to which an individual animal is genetically adapted to its environment, therefore surviving and reproducing successfully, is known as the **fitness** of the animal.
- **Fitness is a measure of the ability of an individual to leave behind offspring**. This term has generally been replaced by **inclusive fitness**, which may be defined as **the total number of an animal's genes present in subsequent generations**. These genes will be present in direct offspring *and* in the offspring of close relatives. The concept of inclusive fitness may solve one of the problems of Darwin's theory, that being the existence of **altruistic behaviour** in certain species.
- It appears that nearly *all* animal behaviour is influenced by genetic factors to some degree and that behaviour makes important contributions to an animal's survival and reproductive success. The behaviour of animals must, therefore, be subject to the forces of evolution in the same way as their anatomy and physiology.
- Behaviour may be divided into **instinctive** (predominantly genetic) and **learned** (predominantly environmental). Few behaviours can be said to be entirely dominated by either inheritance or learning and an interaction between the two is the norm. Research suggests that animals are **biologically prepared** to learn some things more readily than others. These associations may have survival value and are therefore learned more quickly and are more resistant to extinction.
- The best evidence for the evolution of animal behaviour comes from **interspecies comparisons**. Phylogenetic trees based on behavioural similarities are generally similar to those based on anatomical and physiological evidence. In addition, several experimental studies have shown that **differences in behaviour can result from differences in genes**.
- **Sociobiology** is the systematic study of the biological basis of all social behaviour. It differs from classical ethology in that it generally considers the set of genes, rather than the individual, as the basic unit of evolution. Sociobiology has been criticised for oversimplifying explanations of behaviour and overemphasising the role of genetic factors.
- An **evolutionarily stable strategy (ESS)** is a behaviour pattern which, if most of the population adopt it, cannot be bettered by any other strategy and will, therefore, tend to become established by natural selection.
- **Cultural evolution** may be seen as analogous to genetic evolution. Although examples of cultural transmission have been observed in animals, it is still genetic factors which play by far the largest role in determining behaviour. In humans, however, much of our behaviour is due to cultural rather than genetic determinants. It is for this reason that many psychologists are hesitant to apply the same insights to humans as to animals.
- The evolutionary approach to studying animal behaviour has a number of potential problems. These include the influence of the environment and cultural transmission upon behaviour, the apparent existence of behaviours which cannot be explained by sociobiology, and the lack of empirical evidence supporting the theoretical arguments.

COMPETITION FOR RESOURCES

Introduction and overview

Chapter 1 outlined Charles Darwin's theory of evolution by natural selection. This theory suggests that the majority of animals have to compete for resources such as mates, food and territories. Individuals which are successful in attaining these resources are more likely to survive and reproduce than their less successful counterparts. The aim in this chapter is to consider the nature of competition for resources. This will involve an examination of the exploitation of resources, resource defence, and potential conflict arising from competition between animals.

Exploitation of resources

THE IDEAL FREE DISTRIBUTION

Competition by exploitation occurs when competitors are distributed between different habitats according to the quality of resources available in each. Consider two separate habitats, a rich one containing a lot of resources (such as food) and a poor one containing few resources. Assuming that there is no territoriality or aggression, animals which are free to choose would be expected to select the richer habitat. However, the resources in this habitat would gradually become depleted as they were shared among more and more individuals. Eventually, a point would be reached at which any new animals would do better by choosing the poorer quality habitat where, although the resources are in shorter supply, there would be less competition. Theoretically, the two habitats would be filled in such a way as to ensure that each animal has the same resources, regardless of which habitat it occupies. This is known as an *ideal free distribution* (Fretwell, 1972) (Figure 2.1). This distribution can be observed in grazing animals such as sheep and cattle, as well as in bird colonies.

The ideal free distribution model was tested experimentally by Manfred Milinski (1979), as described in Box 2.1.

UNEQUAL COMPETITION

In Milinski's experiment described in Box 2.1, it seems likely that some fish will be better competitors than others. At each end of the tank there could be one or two large fish taking most of the prey. The ideal free distribution could come about because of the way the weaker competitors (*subordinates*) distribute themselves in relation to the stronger competitors (*dominants*). In fact the dominants are probably part of the habitat to

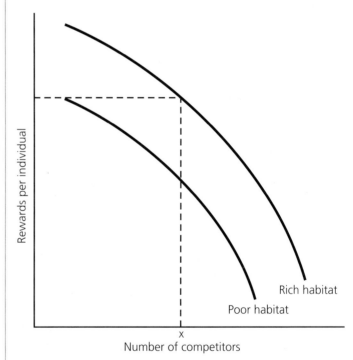

Figure 2.1 The ideal free distribution. The first arrivals will select the rich habitat. The resources become depleted in this habitat as they are shared among more and more competitors. At point x, any new arrivals will do just as well in the poor habitat. Thereafter the habitats are filled so that each animal has the same resources

Box 2.1   Milinski's research into the ideal free distribution

Six sticklebacks (*Gasterosteus aculeatus*) were put into a tank, and prey (waterfleas) were dropped into the water from a pipette at either end. The prey were dropped into the tank twice as fast at one end (A) as at the other (B). The best place for an individual fish to go depends on where all the others go. Milinski found that the fish distributed themselves according to the food supplies, with four fish at end A and two at end B. This arrangement represents the only stable distribution under ideal free conditions.

Milinski's laboratory experiments have been supported by Mary Power's (1984) field studies on armoured catfish (*Ancistrus spinosus*). However, in both these cases there was a continuous supply of food, the density of which did not change with time. While this may be true in some natural environments, more often the supplies are likely to be gradually depleted. The predictions of the ideal free model are more complicated in this situation (Kacelnik et al., 1992).

Figure 2.2   The Chinese giant panda (*Ailuropoda melanoleuca*). Overexploitation of food supplies means that this species may face extinction in the near future

which the subordinates respond when deciding where to search (Milinski, 1984). In many cases, it may be difficult to distinguish between the simple ideal free distribution with equal competitors and one with unequal competitors (Parker & Sutherland, 1986).

A good example of the ideal free distribution with unequal competitors is shown by the gall aphid (*Pemphigus betae*). These aphids feed on plant sap from leaves. The largest leaves provide more resources and result in the greatest reproductive success. As expected, the large leaves are quickly occupied and so additional aphids have the problem of whether to settle on large leaves and share the resources or occupy smaller leaves alone. Whitham (1979) has shown that the average reproductive success is equal on all leaves, supporting the prediction of the ideal free model. However, within the leaf habitat not all individuals get equal rewards. The best place to feed is on the mid-rib at the base of the leaf blade. Aphids occupying this position have greater reproductive success and females fight each other for these prime positions. Thus, although numerical analysis of the leaves appears to support the simple ideal free distribution, closer examination reveals the effects of unequal competition typical of resource defence (see below).

DEPLETION OF RESOURCES

As populations increase, so do the demands made upon food resources. In many populations, such exploitation may deplete a resource altogether, with potentially catastrophic effects. One animal currently facing such a crisis is the Chinese giant panda (*Ailurpoda melanoleuca*) (Figure 2.2). Pandas only eat one particular type of bamboo shoot and require large amounts each day. Exploitation of this resource has led to a reduction in bamboo supplies. Furthermore, there has also been large-scale deforestation of the pandas' natural habitat, so that the total food available has diminished drastically. The number of pandas is decreasing rapidly and the extinction of this species appears to be inevitable.

Resource defence

THE DOMINANCE DISTRIBUTION

Resource defence refers to the situation in which animals are not free to choose a habitat, but are forced to accept the best available territory. Consider the same two habitats as described on page 12, one rich in resources and one poor. The first animals will choose the better quality habitat and defend their resources by establishing territories. Animals arriving later will be forced to occupy lower quality habitats even though

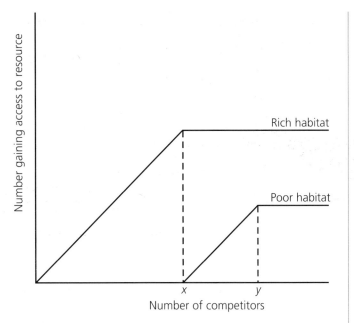

Figure 2.3   Resource defence. Competitors occupy the rich habitat first of all. This becomes full at point *x* and new arrivals will be forced to occupy the poor habitat. At point *y*, the poor habitat is also full and further competitors are excluded completely. Based on Brown (1969)

Box 2.2   Competition by resource defence

In Wytham Woods, near Oxford, England, the optimal breeding habitat for great tits (*Parus major*) is in oak woodland. This is quickly occupied by dominant birds in the spring and becomes completely filled with territories. Subordinates are excluded from the oak wood and have to occupy the hedgerows nearby, which have less food and so are a lower quality breeding habitat. If great tits are removed from the oak woodland, new birds rapidly move in from the hedgerows to occupy the vacant territories (Krebs, 1971). A similar situation occurs in **resource defence polygyny**. In this case, males attempt to gain access to as many females as possible. They do this by fighting for control of a harem (see Chapter 4), or by maintaining a territory containing resources such as nest sites or food (Emlen & Oring, 1977).

they do less well there than the individuals in the rich area. Eventually these habitats will become full and any further animals will be excluded completely. In this way, some animals gain access to the best-quality resources, some have to put up with lower quality resources, and others are excluded altogether (Figure 2.3).

The first observations of dominance hierarchies were made in hens (Schjelderup-Ebbe, 1935). When a group of hens is first placed together, they fight amongst themselves, but they soon learn which is stronger and give way rather than risk injury. Dominance confers feeding and mating advantages, and also reduces aggression. It is not entirely clear what causes some animals to become dominant over others. Many factors appear to influence the dominance of an individual, including size, strength, sex, health and age (Ridley, 1995).

Competition by resource defence is very common in nature, as shown in Box 2.2.

INTERFERENCE

Interference refers to the situation in which competitors are less successful in exploiting a resource due to the time and energy spent in competitive bouts. For example, an animal may be unable to take advantage of a rich source of food because it is constantly trying to deter competitors which are attracted to the area by the abundant resources. Although interference is a measure of the loss that each individual suffers as a result of competition, the stronger competitor will tend to lose less of the resource than the weaker one.

Energy losses caused by interference may be reduced by maintaining an exclusive territory from which all others are deterred. Although there is still a regular cost in defending an area, food resources within it can be more effectively maintained and exploited (Gill & Wolf, 1975). This strategy can be observed in strongly territorial species such as the European robin (*Erithacus rubecula*) (Figure 2.4). The decision to engage in territoriality depends on the relative costs and benefits involved and requires an examination of the economics of resource defence.

THE ECONOMICS OF RESOURCE DEFENCE

In order to examine the economics of resource defence, it is important to understand the concepts of economic defendability and optimal territory size.

Economic defendability

The idea of economic defendability was first introduced by Jerram Brown (1964). Resource defence has

Figure 2.4   The European robin, a strongly territorial species

both costs (energy expenditure and risk of injury) and benefits (access to resources). Selection pressure would be expected to favour territorial behaviour whenever the benefits are greater than the costs. This has been demonstrated in the field using the golden-winged sunbird (*Nectarinia reichenowi*), as described in Box 2.3.

If resources in an area are very scarce, the benefits of excluding competitors may not be sufficient to pay for the costs of territorial defence and the animal may abandon the territory. At the other end of the scale, when resources are abundant in an area, territoriality may not be economical due to increased defence costs (rich areas will attract more intruders) and an inability to make efficient use of all the additional resources. Therefore, it appears that territoriality is only favoured over a certain range of resource availability (Figure 2.5).

Optimal territory size

Although the idea of economic defendability is a useful one, it lacks flexibility. Instead of maintaining or abandoning a territory, depending on resource availability, an individual animal could simply alter its territory size. Expansion of a resource-poor territory could be problematic because it may involve encroachment onto other territories, and the extra energy required to maintain the larger area may not be compensated for by the additional resources gained. A reduction in territory size in a resource-rich area appears to pose fewer prob-

Box 2.3   Economic defendability in the golden-winged sunbird

The metabolic cost of various activities undertaken by the sunbird was measured under laboratory conditions.

Resting	1.68 kJ/h
Foraging for nectar	4.2 kJ/h
Territory defence	12.6 kJ/h

Field studies showed that the birds need to spend less time collecting the energy required for survival when the flowers contain more nectar.

Nectar per flower (µl)	Time to get energy (h)
1	8
2	4
3	2.7
4	2

By maintaining an exclusive territory, the bird increases the amount of nectar available in each flower. It therefore saves foraging time and can spend longer resting (which requires less energy). For example, if territory defence results in an increase in the nectar level from 1 µl to 2 µl per flower, the bird saves 4 hours' foraging time per day. It therefore saves:

$$(4.2 \times 4) - (1.68 \times 4) = 10.08 \text{ kJ}$$
foraging   resting

However, this saving has to be weighed against the cost of defence. Field measurements suggest that the birds spend about 0.28 hours per day on defence. This time could otherwise be spent resting, so the cost of defence is:

$$(12.6 \times 0.28) - (1.68 \times 0.28) = 3.06 \text{ kJ}$$
defence   resting

In other words, the flowers are economically defendable when the nectar levels are raised from 1 µl to 2 µl as a result of defence. This is not the case, however, if nectar levels are raised from 3 µl to 4 µl (energy *gain* = 1.76 kJ, but energy *loss* = 3.06 kJ). Gill and Wolf (1975) found that most of their sunbirds were territorial when the flowers were economically defendable. (Based on Krebs and Davies, 1993.)

lems. Less energy would be required for patrolling the smaller area (which may be less attractive to intruders) and ample resources would still be available.

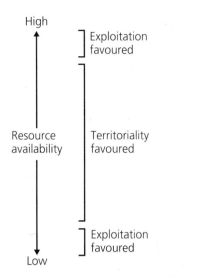

Figure 2.5   The idea of economic defendability suggests that territorial behaviour is only favoured over a certain range of resource availability

These arguments have led to the concept of optimal territory size. Rufous hummingbirds (*Selasphorus rufus*), for example, appear to adjust territory size to maximise weight gain (Carpenter et al., 1983) (Figure 2.6).

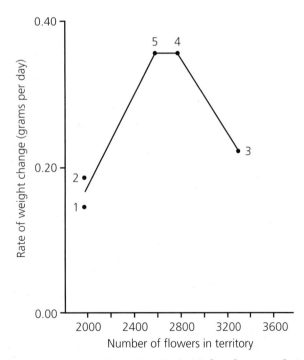

Figure 2.6   Rufous hummingbirds (*Selasphorus rufus*) appear to adjust territory size to maximise weight gain. The five points represent five consecutive days and suggest that the bird has an optimum territory size of 2600–2800 flowers

SHARED RESOURCE DEFENCE

It is not uncommon for two or more competitors to share the same territory. Typically, sharing individuals are a mated pair. European robins, for example, share a territory for the breeding season. This shared resource defence is related more to mating and parental duties than to economic efficiency. However, there are examples of shared defence occurring because of economic considerations. Pied wagtails (*Motacilla alba*) share territories in pairs under certain conditions. The additional bird takes some of the food from the territory, but also helps to defend it against intruders. If food is abundant, the cost of sharing is relatively small. On days when the intrusion rate is high (many competitors attempt to exploit the territory), the benefit of sharing is relatively large. Under these conditions (abundant food and high intrusion rate), shared resource defence would be expected to occur. This theoretical model has been supported by observations of pied wagtails in the field (Davies & Houston, 1981).

Conflict over resources

Competition between animals for resources may lead to conflict. A good example of such conflict is seen in sticklebacks. If a male stickleback (A) swims into the territory of another male (B), the owner (B) attacks the intruder (A) and drives it off. However, if stickleback B trespasses onto A's territory, the roles are reversed. The *site dependence* of which fish attacks and which one flees has been demonstrated experimentally by Niko Tinbergen (1951). This territorial behaviour only occurs when males are in the reproductive state. This state appears to be controlled by a high level of gonadal hormone and is signalled externally by a bright red belly (representing an invitation to females and a territorial warning to other males). When the hormone level drops, the red belly fades and the fish ceases to be territorial.

It is not totally clear why it should be that the owner usually wins. Suggestions have been made that owners are stronger (that is why they own a territory in the first place) or that the owner will fight harder because it is worth more to him. However, in many species, there appears to be an 'owner wins' convention (perhaps to reduce aggressive conflict). Davies and Houston (1984) tested this idea using the speckled wood butterfly (*Pararge aegeria*). After an intruder had lost a contest,

16

they removed the owner and waited for the intruder to occupy the vacant territory. They then reintroduced the original owner and found that the new owner won the contest. It appears that intruders automatically back down when meeting owners.

Conflict between animals (for example over food) could be resolved by sharing the resource. The probability of sharing rather than fighting will be influenced by the relative costs and benefits to the animals concerned. Hungry animals are more likely to fight each other, as are unrelated individuals (see Chapter 1, page 5). However, embarking upon a protracted battle with a rival may require more energy than would be gained by winning the resource. It may pay to give up and look elsewhere for food. Certain resources, however, seem to be worth fighting for, whatever the circumstances. Typically, these battles are between males, competing for females, in *polygynous species* (in which one male mates with several females) (see Chapter 6). The battles may be particularly aggressive, even though the absence of a mate would not threaten an individual's survival. Alaskan moose bulls, for example, may fight to the point of death or serious injury over ownership of a harem (Davies, 1996).

Most animal fights are restrained or ritualised, such as that observed between rattlesnakes (*Crotalus viridis*). When fighting an opponent, rattlesnakes do not use their poison fangs. Instead the two snakes 'wrestle' one another and each attempts to push the other to the ground. The loser retreats once he has been floored and both contestants come out of the fight relatively uninjured. Other conflict rituals may be entirely non-contact. One example of this is when cats face each other, arching their backs, erecting their fur and spitting at one another to signal (and exaggerate) their size and readiness to fight.

Why do animals perform their restrained ritual contests rather than direct fighting straightaway? According to John Maynard-Smith (1993), one reason for this is that there is an equilibrium between the risks of injury if fighting is common and the advantage of winning if fighting is rare. In other words, fighting is a good strategy when there are few fighters in the population, but not when there are many. *Game theory* is a useful way to analyse animal contests, because the best fighting strategy for one animal to adopt depends on what others in the population are doing. Natural selection is

expected to lead to an evolutionarily stable strategy, or ESS (see Chapter 1, page 9).

Box 2.4 describes a relatively simple situation involving competition between two animal strategies. Individuals which display when entering a territory, but always back down if they are challenged, are known as *doves*.

Box 2.4   An analysis of the hawk–dove model

Let us suppose that two animals compete for a resource that is worth X points to the winner and zero to the loser. Let us also suppose that the serious injuries inflicted by hawks when they fight cost Y points. If a hawk meets a dove, the hawk wins X points and the dove scores zero. If a dove meets a dove, they engage in a brief ritualised contest that each has an equal chance of winning. Therefore, on average, a dove will win X/2 from conflict with other doves. Finally, when a hawk meets another hawk, there will be an unrestrained fight. The winner will gain X points and the loser will suffer serious injury, costing it Y points. If a hawk has an equal chance of winning or losing, its average payoff will be (X − Y)/2. The four payoffs can be summarised as below (written from the viewpoint of contestant 1).

		Contestant 2	
		Hawk	Dove
Contestant 1	Hawk	(X − Y)/2	X
	Dove	0	X/2

In a population mainly consisting of doves, the hawk strategy will be favoured because its average payoff will be twice as high (X > X/2). In a population consisting mainly of hawks, a dove would win zero and a hawk would win (X − Y)/2. Which strategy is favoured depends on the relative values of X and Y.

X > Y   Hawk is the best strategy and restrained fighting does not evolve.

X < Y   Hawk is best when dove is common, but dove is best when hawk is common.

Calculations have shown that if the gain from winning is half the cost of losing (X = Y/2), we should expect the population to contain 50% hawks and 50% doves. The strategy that natural selection produces is the ESS. If only hawks are present, it is known as a 'pure' ESS. If both hawks and doves are present, it becomes a 'mixed' ESS.

Those which will always fight if faced with another animal in competition are known as *hawks*. In the game theory model, we calculate the effect of dangerous fighting (hawks) or restrained fighting (doves) on the number of offspring an individual produces. We can then work out which strategy (or combination of strategies) natural selection will favour at equilibrium.

The model shown in Box 2.4, however, is highly simplified, and many other strategies may exist. One example is the *bourgeois strategy*, which states 'play hawk if owner, and play dove if intruder'. This appears to be what happens in the case of the speckled wood butterfly, referred to earlier in this chapter. If the bourgeois strategy is added to hawk-and-dove strategies in a population, it does better than either of them. Bourgeois is, in fact, the only ESS in a population initially consisting of hawk, dove and bourgeois strategies. The hawk–dove model assumes that the contestants are equally matched. In reality, this is rare and contests are usually asymmetric. In this case, *conditional strategies* (which are adjusted to the circumstances) are more successful. For example, the strategy adopted by female funnel-web spiders (*Agelenopsis aperta*) depends upon their relative weights. If the territory holder is larger, the intruder plays dove and immediately retreats. However, if the intruder is larger, she plays hawk and escalates the confrontation (Riechert, 1978). Asymmetries can exist in resource value (e.g. great tits), fighting ability (e.g. red deer, *Cervus elaphus*), or both (e.g. spiders).

Another, perhaps more important, reason why fighting is restrained is that animals differ in strength. Weaker animals will be selected to avoid fights with stronger adversaries. If a mere display of strength is able to scare off an opponent before any fighting commences, it is in both parties' interests to engage in such displays. The opportunity to 'weigh up' opponents during ritualised preliminary bouts, and possibly withdraw, reduces the risk of wasting energy, suffering injury and possibly death (Figure 2.7). Many behaviours which were once the first stages of an aggressive act have become a signal of threat, avoiding the need for further action. Many other signals also exist to prevent escalation of aggression, such as dominance, submission and appeasement.

Finally, it is possible that many rituals succeed as mere bluff. This behaviour is often seen in prey species facing their predator and is discussed in more detail in Chapter 3.

(a)

(b)

(c)

Figure 2.7   The three stages of a fight between two red deer stags (*Cervus elaphus*). In (a) the harem holder is roaring at the challenger. In (b) the pair size each other up during a parallel walk. Most encounters (75%) stop before the third stage (c), in which the stags interlock antlers and push against each other

Competition for resources in humans

Arguments relating to the nature of competition for resources may apply to humans. Many natural resources are being overexploited by our species and total depletion of some of these in the near future is a real possibility. Unlike non-human animals, we have the ability to take a long-term view and should be capable of safeguarding vital resources for the future of all species. However, sociobiologists may argue that the selfish way in which certain humans exploit resources is a function of our evolutionary past. Putting ourselves first, at the expense of others in the world (and future generations), may be determined by our genes (see Chapter 15).

Human societies employ resource defence and many countries appear to be prepared to engage in conflict over territorial disputes. It has been suggested that humans have lost the natural means of stopping aggression because we lack ritualised fighting and dominance behaviour. Co-operation, rather than conflict, may be the key to the long-term success of all species on our planet (Axelrod, 1990).

Conclusions

Animals frequently compete for resources such as access to food, water and mates. They may compete by pure exploitation, resource defence, or a combination of the two. Useful concepts when considering whether it pays to be territorial are those of economic defendability and optimal territory size. The likelihood of animals fighting over a resource is partly determined by the relative costs and benefits to each animal. Territoriality, dominance and ritualised fighting all result in less aggression being observed in nature than the theoretical maximum.

SUMMARY

- Most animals have to compete for resources such as food, water and mates. Those which are successful in attaining these resources are more likely to survive and reproduce.
- **Competition by exploitation** occurs when competitors are distributed between different habitats according to the quality of resources available in each. Theoretically, habitats will be filled in such a way as to ensure that each animal has the same resources. This is known as an **ideal free distribution**. This theoretical distribution has been supported by experimental studies and can be observed in a variety of species.
- The ideal free distribution may also come about because of the way **subordinates** (weaker competitors) distribute themselves in relation to **dominants** (stronger competitors).
- Exploitation may deplete a resource altogether, with potentially catastrophic effects. This is the situation currently facing the Chinese giant panda.
- **Competition by resource defence** occurs when animals are not free to choose a habitat, but are forced to accept the best available territory. Some animals gain access to the best-quality resources,

some have to put up with lower quality resources and others are excluded altogether. Competition by resource defence is very common in nature.
- **Interference** refers to the situation in which competitors are less successful in exploiting a resource due to the time and energy spent in competitive bouts. Energy losses caused by interference can be reduced by maintaining exclusive territories.
- **Economic defendability** relates to the costs and benefits of resource defence. Selection pressure would be expected to favour territorial behaviour whenever the benefits are greater than the costs. It appears that territoriality is only favoured over a certain range of resource availability.
- Many species appear to adjust the size of their territories according to the availability of resources. Each animal may therefore have an **optimal territory size**.
- It is not uncommon for two or more competitors to share the same territory, a strategy known as **shared resource defence**. This may be related to mating and parental duties (if the sharing individuals are a mating pair), or economic efficiency. In the latter case, we would predict that shared

resource defence should occur under conditions of **abundant food** and **high intrusion rate**. This prediction has been supported by observations in the field.

- Competition between animals for resources may lead to **conflict**. However, most animal fights are **restrained** or **ritualised**. One reason for this is that there is an equilibrium between the **risks of injury** if fighting is common and the **advantage of winning** if fighting is rare. Another reason for ritualised fighting is that animals differ in strength and weaker animals will be selected to avoid fights with stronger adversaries. The opportunity to weigh up opponents during ritualised preliminary bouts reduces the risk of wasting energy, suffering injury and possibly death.

- Animal contests can be analysed using **game theory**. The best fighting strategy for one animal to adopt depends on what others in the population are doing. One example of the use of game theory is the **hawk–dove** model. The behaviour patterns produced by natural selection represent an **evolutionarily stable strategy**.

PREDATOR–PREY AND SYMBIOTIC RELATIONSHIPS

Introduction and overview

It is important to consider the influence of interactions between animals when attempting to explain the existence of certain behaviour patterns. Many animal behaviours are concerned with eating and/or avoiding being eaten. These behaviours have obvious survival value. An examination of *predator–prey relationships* is therefore fundamental to an understanding of comparative psychology. Another significant type of relationship between animals is *symbiosis*. In this case, different species form temporary or permanent associations, each influencing the other's behaviour.

This chapter considers the effects of predator–prey and symbiotic relationships on the evolution of behaviour patterns. This will involve an examination of behavioural adaptations in predators for detecting, capturing and consuming prey, together with counteradaptations in the prey. The influence of symbiosis upon animal behaviour is also discussed.

Seeing and not being seen

During evolution, we would expect natural selection to increase the efficiency of predators at detecting prey. However, we would also expect selection to improve the prey's ability to detect the presence of a predator. The sensory systems of both will therefore co-evolve. Each becomes increasingly well adapted in its ability to detect the other, through sight, sound or smell. Furthermore, both predators and prey will attempt to avoid being detected. In the battle for survival, the trick is to see without being seen.

DETECTING PREY

In daylight, the predominant sense used in predator–prey detection is vision. This would be expected to lead to the evolution of improved visual acuity (ability to detect pattern and movement), particularly in predators. Counteradaptation in prey would favour the use of camouflage and polymorphism (see below).

Nocturnal animals (those which are active at night) tend to use hearing and smell to detect the presence of others. Therefore, predators tend to approach slowly and stealthily from a downwind position. Another adaptation for the detection of prey is the ability to locate animals by their body heat. This is seen in female mosquitoes (Herter, 1962) and in many species of snakes. Other methods of detecting prey include vibrations, as used by the sand scorpion, and electric fields, as used by the duck-billed platypus.

CAMOUFLAGE

Species which use camouflage evolve to resemble their background (Figure 3.1). The behavioural strategy is to be immobile and try to be invisible. Of course, many

Figure 3.1   A camouflaged lizard, which blends in beautifully with its background

predators detect prey using their sense of smell. In this case, animals may be camouflaged by being either odourless or similar in odour to their background (Edmunds, 1974). It is important to remember that an animal is only camouflaged if it settles in the right place. The European grasshopper (*Acrida turrita*) exists in both green and yellow forms. In nature, the green forms tend to live in green habitats and the yellow forms in yellow habitats (Ridley, 1995). Similarly, Kettlewell's (1955) studies on the peppered moth (*Biston betularia*) have shown that prey that is hard for predators to detect survives longer than those which are easy to find (see Chapter 1, page 3). It should be remembered that predators will also have an advantage if they are camouflaged. The spotted coat of leopards (*Panthera pardus*), for example, makes them difficult to see on low tree branches because they blend in with light patterns created by sunlight penetrating the foliage. Some predators also have markings which disguise them as a harmless species, enabling them to get close to their prey. One such example is the blennid fish (*Aspidontus taeniatus*), which looks and behaves like a harmless cleaner wrasse (*Labroides dimidiatus*), but which will attack if the opportunity arises (Wickler, 1968).

Some animals improve their chances of survival by modifying the background upon which they normally rest. Insectivorous birds appear to use leaf damage as a clue to the location of camouflaged caterpillars. Several species of caterpillars avoid attracting these birds by removing partially eaten leaves at the end of a feeding session (Heinrich, 1979). Other animals achieve camouflage by carrying parts of their environment around with them. Many species of spider crabs, for example, decorate themselves with algae, barnacles and sponges, becoming virtually indistinguishable from the ocean floor (Wicksten, 1980).

Although it may pay to be camouflaged as a defence against predators, this may conflict with the advantage of being conspicuous for other activities. These include territory defence (see Chapter 2, page 13) and mate attraction (see Chapter 4, page 36). Many species of birds attempt to resolve this problem by males being brightly coloured in the mating season but moulting into duller, female-like plumage after breeding.

Any strategy that a predator can use to increase its ability to detect its camouflaged prey will be beneficial. One method which has been suggested is the formation of a *search image*, in which the predator learns characteristic features of prey and searches for these when hunting. The idea of search image formation has been supported by experimental studies (Dawkins, 1971). Predators may develop a search image for a particular camouflaged species and systematically seek out and consume remaining individuals. However, if the prey are widely spaced, predators will rarely encounter them and may soon forget the search image. A wide distribution of individuals is therefore an advantage to prey species.

POLYMORPHISM

Many camouflaged species get around the problem of predators forming search images by occurring in several different shapes and/or colour forms. This is known as polymorphism. Industrial melanism in peppered moths (see Chapter 1, page 3) is one such example of polymorphism. However, not all polymorphic species use camouflage. Many rely solely on their diverse appearance to evade detection by predators, permitting them to occur at higher densities. These species avoid suffering increased mortality from predators which search for individuals with a specific appearance (Moment, 1962).

Attacking and not being attacked

After detecting the presence of prey, the next stage for the predator is attack. However, many species of prey are adapted to induce predators not to attack. Several of these species contain toxins that make them poisonous. Some use sprays, secretions, injections or repellents to discourage potential consumers. Many of these dangerous species use warning colouration, as described in Box 3.1. Others assume the appearance of unpalatable or poisonous species, a phenomenon known as *mimicry*.

MIMICRY

Mimicry refers to the resemblance of one species of prey (the mimic) to another (the model) such that the two are indistinguishable to a predator. The model is usually an unpalatable or poisonous species. Therefore the mimic, which is normally edible, is avoided by predators. This gives the mimic a selective advantage,

Box 3.1   Warning colouration

The aim of warning colouration is to communicate the message to predators that the prey is dangerous in some way. The distinctive black and white colouration of skunks warns of their ability to produce a noxious repellent, and the painful sting of the wasp is indicated by its boldly patterned yellow and black body. Another example of the use of bright warning colours is found in the monarch butterfly (*Danaus plexippus*). The wings of this insect contain powerful heart-stopping poisons known as cardiac glycosides.

The advantage of poisonous prey being brightly coloured is that it probably helps predators learn to avoid them more quickly. This idea has been supported by experimental evidence. Chicks were fed with blue or green breadcrumbs, which had been made distasteful by dipping them in quinine sulphate and mustard powder. Four groups of chicks were then presented with:

(a)   blue crumbs on a blue background;
(b)   green crumbs on a blue background;
(c)   blue crumbs on a green background;
(d)   green crumbs on a green background.

Overall, the camouflaged crumbs were consumed in the greatest quantities (Figure 3.2). This suggests that it does indeed pay a distasteful prey to be conspicuous (Gittleman & Harvey, 1980).

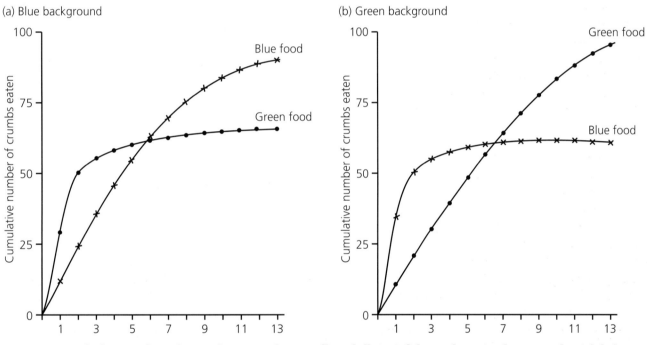

Figure 3.2   Cumulative number of conspicuous and camouflaged distasteful crumbs eaten in successive trials by chicks. In (a) the blue food is camouflaged, in (b) the green food is camouflaged. In both experiments, the distasteful crumbs are eaten more when they are camouflaged

which may account for the evolution of this trait. The two main types of mimicry are known as Batesian mimicry and Mullerian mimicry.

Batesian mimicry involves the use of a *dishonest* signal to predators (Figure 3.3). The edible mimic is avoided because of its physical similarity to a more dangerous or noxious model, as shown in Box 3.2. Although mimics normally copy other animals, they may also mimic plants and other objects. For example, stick insects resemble twigs that are inedible to their predators. In addition, mimicry does not have to be visual, but may be olfactory (smell) or acoustic (sound). This is seen in the burrowing owl (*Speotyto cuniculana*), whose hissing call resembles the rattle of a rattlesnake (*Crotalus viridis*) (Rowe et al., 1986).

The usefulness of Batesian mimicry depends upon a

Figure 3.3 The snake-mimicking caterpillar, an example of Batesian mimicry

number of factors, such as noxiousness of the model and availability of alternative prey. If the mimics significantly outnumber the models, predators are more likely to encounter them before they encounter the model. Therefore, as their first experience was not with the noxious model, predators will search for the mimics rather than avoid them. This will increase the risk of the model being attacked by predators, resulting in a selection pressure to divert from the original form. (Of course, the predators will then have to learn that this new model is unpalatable or poisonous, which will necessitate the consumption of a few.) One further point to consider is that many species of noxious prey advertise their unpalatability by bright colours and/or markings. For a palatable mimic to model itself on such a distinctive species is a high-risk strategy.

Mullerian mimicry is an example of an *honest* signal to predators. In this case, a number of noxious species share similar warning signals (usually based on the most unpalatable of the group) and every mimic benefits because predators avoid them all. An example of Mullerian mimicry can be seen in South American butterflies of the genus *Heliconius*. Two species, *Heliconius erato* and *Heliconius melpomene*, bear a strong resemblance to each other and are both poisonous to birds.

Occasionally, predators may also use mimicry (known as *aggressive* mimicry). In this case the model is usually a species which is harmless to the prey. This enables the mimics to get close to their victim in order to attack. As mentioned previously, the blennid fish mimics the colour and markings of the cleaner wrasse. Unlike the model, however, which cleans larger fish of parasites (which benefit from the service and so do not attack the cleaner), the mimic uses its opportunity to take a bite out of the bigger fish.

Catching and not being caught

ADAPTATIONS IN PREDATORS

Predators have various strategies for hunting mobile prey. One tactic is simply to move faster than the intended victim. In this case, the environment would be expected to select predators with well-developed motor skills, such as speed and agility. For example, a cheetah (*Acinonyx jubatus*) will usually stalk its prey so that it can get to within a few hundred metres. It then

---

Box 3.2   An experimental demonstration of the effectiveness of mimicry

Two groups of Florida scrub jays (*Aphelocoma coerulescens*) were fed a particular species of butterfly. The control group was given palatable viceroy butterflies (*Limenitis archippus*) (the mimics) and the experimental group was given the noxious monarch butterflies (the models).

The jays were then offered viceroys and the number of trials in which they avoided the butterflies, or pecked at them, was recorded. The results are shown in the table below (based on Brower, 1958).

Mean number of trials in which jays avoided or pecked viceroys

	Control group	Experimental group
Avoided viceroys	2.5	10.5
Pecked viceroys	22.5	4.5

Box 3.3   Stotting behaviour in Thomson's gazelles

It appears that gazelles stott to let cheetahs know that they have been detected. As the prey is ready to escape, the probability of capture is sharply reduced. Therefore it may be in the best interests of the predator to give up the hunt. (Based on Caro, 1986.)

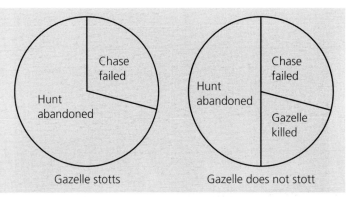

chases its quarry, running at speeds of up to 70 miles per hour. One counteradaptation observed in prey to deal with an attack by a cheetah is stotting behaviour in Thomson's gazelles (*Gazello thomsoni*). Stotting involves the animal leaping a metre or two in the air by bouncing along on all four legs. Box 3.3 shows that stotting appears to be a fairly effective escape strategy.

Many predators hunt in groups. This has the dual advantage of enabling them to surround the prey and permitting them to hunt animals larger than themselves (Figure 3.4). Lions (*Panthera leo*) hunting in groups have been shown to be more successful than those hunting alone. They can also hunt kinds of prey that

they could not catch by themselves, such as buffalo (*Syncerus caffer*) (Ridley, 1995). Occasionally, lions may employ an ambush strategy for acquiring prey. This involves hiding, motionless, until the prey draws near enough to attack. Lions using this tactic often wait by water holes for thirsty prey to appear (Schaller, 1972).

Finally, some predators are able to trap their prey, as seen in the spider's web. Often the traps involve a lure of some type. For example, the female angler fish (*Lophius piscatorius*) has a long, fleshy appendage attached to the top of her head. This is luminous and attracts curious fish within reach of her jaws (Wickler, 1968).

ADAPTATIONS IN PREY

The aim of prey is to make capture less likely. Individual animals use a variety of strategies to achieve this aim, including startle mechanisms and intimidation. Social animals also have a range of antipredator behaviours that are not available to solitary individuals.

Startle mechanisms involve sudden and conspicuous changes in the appearance or behaviour of prey that can cause confusion or alarm in a predator. The sudden presentation of a visual stimulus (such as large eyespots), or a loud auditory stimulus may startle the predator into hesitating just long enough for the prey to escape (Figure 3.5). This idea has been examined in studies of underwing moths (*Catocala cerogama*). When a resting moth is seized by a blue jay (*Cyanocitta cristata*), it suddenly exposes its brightly coloured hindwings. This appears to startle jays, which sometimes gape involuntarily, allowing the moth to escape (Schlenoff, 1985). Some animals employ intimidation tactics when dealing with potential predators. These

Figure 3.4   Co-operative prey capture by lions

Figure 3.5   The emperor moth (*Saturnia pavonia*) displaying two large eyespots. This startle mechanism may cause a predator to hesitate long enough for the moth to escape

serve to make the animal appear larger and/or well defended, encouraging the predator to retreat. For example, a cat hunches its back, erects its fur and displays its teeth when confronted by a dog.

One of the main strategies used by prey to avoid capture is group defence. Generally, predators experience less success when hunting grouped rather than single prey. This is because of the superior ability of groups to detect, confuse and repel predators. In addition, an individual within a group has a lower probability of being caught during a predator attack. The tactics used by groups of prey include improved vigilance, alarm signals, flocking and mobbing.

Early detection of a predator can often lead to escape for prey. Groups of animals are usually superior to individuals in their ability to spot predators (more eyes, ears and noses for the detection of danger). Furthermore, as a result of the enhanced vigilance associated with groups, an individual can often spend more time feeding and less time on the lookout for predators. Powell (1974) has shown that the average 'escape time' of a single starling (*Sturnus vulgaris*) faced with a dummy hawk was significantly slower than that of a bird in a group. This was despite the fact that single birds spent about four times as long looking around for danger as a bird in a flock.

In order for group vigilance to be effective, individuals must be able to communicate the danger to the rest of the group. This may simply consist of taking flight, encouraging others to follow, or may involve the use of alarm signals. Alarm signals may be communicated by sight, sound or smell, and usually serve to enlist support in confronting the attacker (see below) or inspire retreat to a safe location. A good example of the use of alarm signals is seen in Belding's ground squirrels (*Spermophilus beldingi*). When one of the squirrels sees a hawk or falcon, it emits a high-pitched whistle and dashes for cover. This causes the other squirrels instantly to run for the nearest shelter, creating a brief moment of chaos as large numbers of the animals dash in all directions (Sherman, 1985).

Within a group of animals, individuals located centrally appear to be safer than those at the edges. Animals can therefore reduce their chances of being attacked by obtaining a central position within the group. This antipredator behaviour is known as the *selfish herd* (Hamilton, 1971). Although a group appears to consist of members that co-ordinate their escape efforts, it is actually composed of selfish individuals, each trying to maintain a central position within the group.

One example of the selfish herd is seen in Adélie penguins (*Pygoscelis adelic*). These birds gather in groups at the edge of the ocean and then jump in the water together to swim out to the feeding areas. Each time they do this, there is a risk of being attacked by a leopard seal (*Hydrurga leptonyx*). However, the seal can only capture and kill a small number of penguins in a short time. By swimming out in a group through the danger zone, most penguins will escape while the seal is busy catching one or two unfortunate individuals. This phenomenon is known as the *dilution effect*, because individuals within a group have a smaller chance of being a victim than solitary animals (Alcock, 1993).

Occasionally, prey will attack predators. This is known as *mobbing* and usually involves visual and vocal displays as well as direct attacks on the predator. Mobbing appears to function by confusing and discouraging the predator as well as alerting others to the danger (Curio, 1978). Most evidence suggests that mobbing is usually a selfish act performed by individuals attempting to protect themselves and their relatives (Tamura, 1989).

Eating and not being eaten

A captured animal is not necessarily doomed. Several strategies exist in prey for avoiding being eaten by predators. These include the use of chemical deterrents, misdirecting the attack of predators, and attracting competing consumers. A wide variety of animals can discharge noxious chemicals when they are captured. Some of these chemicals are powerful toxins or irritants. For example, the assassin bug (*Platymeris rhadamantus*) defends itself by spitting large quantities of saliva in the direction of the attacker. The fluid causes intense local pain when it comes into contact with membranes of the eyes or nose, often enabling the bug to escape (Goodenough et al., 1993).

Several species of prey attempt to misdirect the attack of predators away from the vulnerable head region. Although they may still be damaged in some way, the injuries are often minor and the strategy permits a chance of escape. One tactic is to induce predators into attacking false heads on the posterior part of the animal's body, which can be sacrificed without incurring a fatal wound. Hairstreak butterflies (*Theda togarna*), for example, possess a false head, complete with dummy antennae, at the tips of their hindwings. Experiments have shown that false heads increase the possibility of escape for captured prey (Wourms & Wasserman, 1985) (Figure 3.6). A second strategy used by prey is to tempt the predator to make its initial strike at a non-vital part of the body. This is seen in lizards, which lure predators into attacking their brightly coloured twitching tails. When the tail is seized by an attacker, it breaks off (without harming the animal), giving the lizard a few extra seconds to escape (Dail & Fitzpatrick, 1983).

A final tactic to avoid being eaten is to attract competing consumers. When a rabbit is being attacked, it sometimes produces very loud, piercing screams. The function of this behaviour may be to attract other predators to the scene. These animals may interfere with the original captor, possibly enabling the rabbit to escape in the confusion (Hogstedt, 1983).

Predator–prey arms races

During evolution we would expect natural selection to increase the efficiency of predators at detecting and capturing prey. However, we would also expect selection to improve the ability of prey to avoid detection and to escape. The complex adaptation and counteradaptation of predators and prey suggest that this 'arms race' has been taking place for a very long time (Box 3.4).

The reason that predators do not drive prey to extinction is probably that prey are always one step ahead in the arms race. Dawkins and Krebs (1979) have called this the *life–dinner principle*. Rabbits run faster than foxes because the rabbit is running for its life, while the fox is only running for its dinner. Therefore, selection pressure will have been stronger on improving the ability of rabbits to escape than the ability of foxes to catch

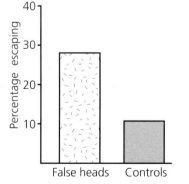

Figure 3.6   False heads increase the possibility of escape from predators. In an experiment, blue jays mishandled captured cabbage butterflies with artificial false heads more often than unaltered controls

Box 3.4   Adaptations and counteradaptations in predators and prey

	Predators	Prey
Detection	Improved sensory ability	Camouflage
	Use of a search image	Polymorphism
Attack	Avoidance of dangerous or noxious prey	Warning colouration or mimicry
Capture	Stealthy or very rapid approach	Vigilance and alarm signals
	Hunting in groups	Group defence
Eating	Consumption begins at head	Misdirection of attack
	Avoidance of dangerous foods	Chemical deterrents

them. However, this does not explain why prey do not become so efficient at escaping as to drive their predators to extinction. One suggestion to account for this is that, as predators become rare (because of increased prey efficiency), they exert little selection pressure on the prey for further improvement.

Symbiosis

Symbiosis may be defined literally as 'living together'. It is a term used to describe the relationships that exist between different species. Although there are many such relationships, they can be conveniently assigned to one of three categories: *commensalism*, *parasitism* or *mutualism*, as defined in Box 3.5. The species involved in a symbiotic relationship exert a selection pressure on each other, which may include influencing each other's behaviour. In many ways, symbiotic associations are similar to those between predators and prey. (Indeed, many biologists classify predator–prey relationships as a form of parasitism.) Therefore, many of the principles discussed previously under the heading of predator–prey relationships are also relevant when examining symbiotic associations.

COMMENSALISM

This association is characterised by one species (the *commensal*) benefitting from the relationship, while the other (the *host*) remains unaffected. For example, trum-

pet fish sometimes join groups of yellow sturgeon fish and take advantage of the camouflage provided to attack smaller prey fish. The trumpet fish dart out from among the sturgeon and seize the prey. The sturgeon remain unaffected by the relationship, and there appears to be no communication between the two species (McFarland, 1996).

The most common type of commensalism occurs when one species feeds off the scraps left by another (commensalism literally means 'feeding at the same table'). Remoras, for example, attach themselves to sharks and ride along to pick up scraps of food from the animals when they feed. Occasionally, the chain becomes more complex. Birds will follow army ants (*Eciton burchelli*) to eat insects flushed out by the ants, and ant-butterflies will follow the birds to feed on their droppings. In other words, the butterflies follow the birds, following the ants (Grier & Burk, 1992).

Another commensal relationship which occurs frequently in nature is the use of one species as a source of transport by another. This is known as *phoresy*. The riders simply use the animal to get from one place to another, do not cause the carrier any harm, and ride at virtually no cost. For example, several species of mites that live in dung ride on dung beetles (*Kheper aegyptiorum*) to get from one pat to another. The beetles and mites live and reproduce separately in the dung, but co-evolution has led to their life cycles becoming synchronised (Wilson, 1975).

PARASITISM

Host–parasite relationships are discussed in detail in several chapters of this book. For example, parasitism as a cost of sociality is addressed in Chapter 9 (page 87), and the influence of parasites upon foraging efficiency and mate choice is examined in Chapter 13 (page 126) and Chapter 4 (page 38) respectively. These issues will not be repeated here, but instead two further types of parasitic relationships will be concentrated on: *manipulated altruism*, which is the control of behaviour by parasites (as discussed in Box 3.6), and *brood parasitism*, which is the exploitation of parental care by unrelated individuals.

Brood parasitism

Several bird species, such as the European cuckoo (*Cuculus canorus*), are brood parasites (Figure 3.7). A female cuckoo locates the nest of another bird species during the egg-laying and incubation period, lays an

---

Box 3.5   Symbiotic relationships

Commensalism is a relationship between two species which results in benefit to one (the commensal) without affecting the other (the host).
Parasitism is an association in which one organism (the parasite) lives in or on another organism (the host), deriving benefit from the relationship and causing harm to the host.
Mutualism is an interspecific interaction in which both species benefit.

Symbiotic relationship	Species A	Species B
Commensalism	Gains	Unaffected
Parasitism	Gains	Loses
Mutualism	Gains	Gains

Box 3.6   Manipulated altruism: the control of behaviour by parasites

Natural selection normally makes animals behave in their own selfish interests. Even when it favours altruistic behaviour, it is only in the interest of some broader form of selfishness (see Chapter 8). However, parasites may exploit their hosts, forcing them to behave in ways which do not benefit the hosts (or their genetic relatives). For example, the parasitic fluke (flukes are small, flattened, worm-like animals) *Dicrocoelium dendriticum* lives in sheep, but uses ants as an intermediate host (in order to get from one sheep to another). The ants become infected with *Dicrocoelium* from sheep droppings, but how does the fluke get from an ant into another sheep? Ants normally avoid being eaten by sheep, staying in the soil. However, an ant infected with *Dicrocoelium* changes its behaviour. One of the flukes burrows into the ant's brain and causes the ant to climb a blade of grass and fasten its jaws to the top of the blade. The ant stays in this position until eaten, hopefully (for the parasite) by a sheep.

Box 3.7   Brood parasitism by the European cuckoo

Brood parasitism (laying eggs in the nests of other species) is one of the most fascinating, and largely unresolved, mysteries of animal behaviour. The European cuckoo has about ten favourite host species, but individual cuckoos specialise on just one particular host. The birds lay distinctive eggs which usually mimic those of their hosts. It is not yet known how these various forms within the cuckoo species are maintained. One possibility is that daughter cuckoos lay the same egg type as their mother and come to parasitise the same species of host that reared them, perhaps learning the host characteristics through imprinting (Krebs & Davies, 1993)

The cuckoo gains a benefit, namely its young are raised for free, while the host suffers the cost of raising unrelated young. We would expect such a relationship to develop into an evolutionary arms race. For example, cuckoos may be expected to produce eggs which mimic those of their host as closely as possible. A counteradaptation by the host may enable it to discriminate more finely between its own eggs and those of the brood parasite. The cuckoos may eventually lose the race with a particular host species, but they then switch to a new host species and begin a new arms race (McFarland, 1996).

egg and disappears. (Often the egg will resemble those of the host species, an example of mimicry.) When the nest owner returns, it usually accepts the addition to its clutch and incubates the parasitic egg until it hatches. The hatchling cuckoo may instinctively eject some of the other eggs in the nest, enabling it to monopolise the food supply from its foster parents. Despite usually being much larger than the hosts' offspring, the foster parents continue to feed the cuckoo, often having to work very hard to satisfy the parasite's large demands. Parasitism by cuckoos is discussed further in Box 3.7.

Why do foster parents exhibit this (apparently) maladaptive response? One answer could be that the accepting species have only recently come into contact with the parasite and so may not have had sufficient time to evolve an adaptive response. Alternatively, the foster parents may be employing a rule which states 'incubate the eggs that appear in our nest'. This will be generally adaptive because these eggs are usually those of the incubator, but will occasionally be maladaptive when care is given to parasites. However, the response of the accepting species may not be truly maladaptive when the costs and benefits of removing the parasitic

Figure 3.7   A European cuckoo (*Cuculus canorus*) begs for food from its smaller foster parent, a hedge sparrow

egg are considered. Host species are usually smaller than parasite species, and so they have great difficulty removing a parasitic egg. If the costs are significantly high, such as abandoning the nest and building a new one, acceptance of the parasite could be the adaptive response. This cost–benefit approach to brood parasitism has been supported in studies by Burgham and Picman (1989) on yellow warblers (*Phylloscopus inornatus*) nesting in southern Canada. Individuals parasitised by cowbirds (*Molothrus ater*) near the start of the short breeding season were significantly more likely to abandon their nests and try again than were birds whose nests were afflicted with cowbird eggs late in the season. In the latter case, too little time was left to start from scratch and succeed in rearing a new brood, and acceptance of the parasite was the better option.

Brood parasitism is one example of *social parasitism*, which is considered to be a more advanced form of this symbiotic relationship because it generally involves more than just feeding. This type of association has also been identified among a number of social insects, as described in Box 3.8.

MUTUALISM

Mutualism refers to a relationship between two individuals of different species in which each animal derives benefit from the association. For example, the cleaner wrasse mentioned earlier (see page 24) is a small reef-dwelling fish which exists in a mutualistic relationship with larger predatory fish. The wrasse eats parasites from the scales of the other fish, thereby gaining a source of food. The host fish (which does not attempt to eat the cleaner) also benefits by the removal of health-threatening parasites. Indeed, experiments have shown that, in the absence of cleaners, there is a rapid decline in the health of host fish (Davies, 1996). Other mutualists (organisms in a mutualistic relationship) may actually associate permanently, such as a hermit crab (*Eupagurus berhardus*) and a sea anemone (*Stomphia coccinea*). The crab gains camouflage and protection from the anemone which lives on its shell and the anemone gains scraps of food dropped by the crab.

A particularly complex example of mutualistic behaviour has been reported by DeVries (1990). In this case, certain butterfly caterpillars form relationships with various species of ants. The ants feed on proteins and sugars secreted by the caterpillars. In return, the ants vigorously defend the caterpillars from predatory wasps. However, what makes this example of mutualism interesting is that the caterpillars appear to attract the ants by performing a kind of tap-dance on the leaves and stems of plants. According to DeVries, the function of the tap-dancing sound (which is transmitted through the plant) is to prevent the ants returning to their nest. Tap-dancing encourages the ants to stay, providing the caterpillars with a bodyguard. The importance of this protection can be seen when caterpillars are placed on plants where there are no ants. Under these circumstances, very few of the caterpillars survive without their minders.

Another example of communication between mutualists can be observed in the honey guide (*Indicator indicator*) and honey badger (*Mellivora capensis*). When the bird discovers a hive of wild bees, it searches for a badger and guides it to the hive by means of a special display. Protected by its thick skin, the badger opens the hive with its large claws and feeds on the honeycombs. The bird feeds upon the wax and bee larvae, to which it could not gain access unaided (McFarland, 1996).

It is important to note that mutualistic behaviour is not truly altruistic, but is based on the self-interest of the individuals concerned. Each gains from the relationship with no thought as to what happens to the other. Mutualism, therefore, appears to be an adaptation resulting from selfish behaviour.

Box 3.8   Social parasitism in insects (Hölldobler, 1971)

Highly advanced symbiotic relationships often involve the use of one species' signals by another (see Chapter 11). One well-known example is the beetle *Atemeles pubicollis*, which is a social parasite in colonies of ants. The beetles initially locate the ants by the airborne odours of the colonies. When they first encounter a worker ant, they present an appeasement gland, located at the tip of the abdomen. This calms the worker, and the beetle then presents its adoption gland, which the ant licks. The ant then picks up the beetle and carries it into the colony. Once inside, the beetles communicate with the ants by tactile (touch) signals and are fed by the ants. In addition, the larvae of the beetles emit a scent that causes the ants to pick them up and place them with the ants own larvae, which the beetle larvae then eat.

The evolution of symbiotic relationships

Thompson (1982) suggested that commensalism and mutualism arose from encounters between species that were inevitable and unavoidable. In such cases, selection favoured individuals which had traits causing the interaction to have less of a negative effect upon them, providing the basis for the evolution towards commensalism or mutualism. For example, burying beetles (*Nicrophorus orbicollis*) and *Calliphora* flies are competitors over dead mice, on which they both lay their eggs and the larvae develop. The flies are the superior competitors, and when flies are present, the beetle larvae do not survive. However, the beetles have developed a mutualistic relationship with a particular species of mite. The mites are provided with transport by the beetles and, in turn, eat fly eggs and permit the beetle larvae to survive (Springett, 1968).

Davies et al. (1989) considered parasitism as an evolutionary arms race, in which each of the two opposing sides must keep up with (or get ahead of) the other side if it is to survive the interaction. Davies et al. also suggested that social parasitism is relatively rare because the benefits rarely exceed the costs, and that only birds

and social insects exhibit the required behaviour patterns for this type of parasitism to evolve.

Conclusions

Predator–prey relationships have had a significant influence upon the evolution of behaviour patterns. Predators exhibit anatomical and behavioural adaptations for detecting, capturing and consuming prey. Counteradaptations in prey species include: the use of camouflage to avoid being seen; warning colouration and mimicry to avoid being attacked; group defence strategies to avoid being caught; and chemical deterrents to avoid being eaten. The complex adaptation and counteradaptation of predators and prey reflect the results of an arms race over evolutionary time.

Another important influence upon the evolution of animal behaviour is symbiosis. The three main types of symbiotic relationship are commensalism, parasitism and mutualism. Evolutionary explanations of parasitism are similar to those involved in predator–prey relationships. Explanations of commensalism and mutualistic associations appear to be more complex. In the case of mutualism, behaviour has probably evolved for selfish reasons which are advantageous to both the animals concerned.

SUMMARY

- During evolution we would expect natural selection to increase the efficiency of predators at detecting prey. This may be through improvement in **visual**, **auditory** or **olfactory senses**.
- Prey species will be adapted to avoid detection by predators through the use of **camouflage** or **polymorphism**. Species which use camouflage evolve to resemble their background. Although it may pay to be camouflaged as a defence against predators, this may conflict with the advantage of being conspicuous for activities such as territory defence and mate attraction. Polymorphic species rely on their diverse appearance to evade detection by predators which use a standard **search image**.
- Many species of prey are adapted to induce predators not to attack. Several of these species benefit from the use of **warning colouration**,

while others **mimic** the appearance of unpalatable or poisonous animals.
- The aim of **warning colouration** is to communicate the message to predators that the prey is dangerous in some way. The advantage of bright colouration is that it helps predators quickly learn to avoid the prey.
- **Mimicry** refers to the resemblance of one species of prey (the **mimic**) to another (the **model**) such that the two are indistinguishable to a predator. This gives the mimic a selective advantage, which may account for the evolution of this trait.
- The two main types of mimicry are **Batesian** mimicry and **Mullerian** mimicry. Batesian mimicry involves the use of a **dishonest** signal to predators. The edible mimic is avoided because of its physical similarity to a more dangerous or noxious model. Mullerian mimicry is an example of an

honest signal to predators. In this case, a number of noxious species share similar warning signals and every mimic benefits because predators avoid them all.

- Predators have various adaptations for hunting prey, such as **speed, ambush** or the use of **traps**. **Hunting in groups** has the dual advantage of enabling predators to surround the prey and permitting them to hunt animals larger than themselves.

- Individual prey use a variety of tactics to make capture less likely, such as **startle mechanisms** and **intimidation**. Startle mechanisms involve sudden and conspicuous changes in the appearance or behaviour of prey that can cause confusion or alarm in a predator. Intimidation tactics serve to make the animal appear larger and/or well defended, encouraging the predator to retreat.

- One of the main strategies used by prey to avoid capture is **group defence**. Generally, predators experience less success when hunting grouped rather than single prey because of the superior ability of groups to detect, confuse and repel predators. Tactics used by groups include **improved vigilance, alarm signals, flocking** and **mobbing**.

- **Flocking** behaviour occurs because individuals seek to obtain the safer, central positions within a group. This is known as the **selfish herd**. Individuals within a group have a smaller chance of being killed by a predator than solitary animals, a phenomenon known as the **dilution effect**. **Mobbing** involves attacking predators and appears to function by confusing and discouraging them, as well as alerting others to the danger.

- Several strategies exist in prey for avoiding being eaten by predators. These include the use of **chemical deterrents, misdirecting the attack of predators** and **attracting competing consumers**.

- During evolution we would expect natural selection to increase the efficiency of predators at detecting and capturing prey. However, we would also expect selection to improve the ability of prey to avoid detection and escape. The complex adaptation and counteradaptation of predators and prey reflect the results of an **arms race** over evolutionary time.

- **Symbiosis** is a term used to describe the relationships that exist between different species. Although there are many such relationships, they can be conveniently assigned to one of three categories: **commensalism, parasitism** or **mutualism**. The species involved in a symbiotic relationship exert a selection pressure on each other, which may include influencing each other's behaviour.

- **Commensalism** is characterised by one species (the **commensal**) benefiting from the relationship, while the other (the **host**) remains unaffected. Two common types of commensalism are: one species feeding off the scraps of another, and the use of one species as a source of transport by another.

- A **parasite** is an organism which lives in or on another organism (the **host**), deriving benefit from the relationship and causing harm to the host. Parasites may influence host behaviour in a number of ways, including **foraging efficiency** and **mate choice**. An example of interspecific parasitism in birds is **brood parasitism**.

- **Brood parasitism** is the exploitation of parental care by an unrelated individual, as seen in the European cuckoo. The foster parents may be exhibiting maladaptive behaviour because they have not had time to evolve an adaptive response, or because caring for eggs and hatchlings in the nest usually enhances fitness. However, when a cost–benefit analysis is applied, acceptance of the parasite may actually be the best possible option.

- **Mutualism** refers to a relationship between two individuals of different species in which each animal derives benefit from the association. This behaviour is not truly altruistic, but is based on the self-interest of the individuals concerned.

- It has been suggested that commensalism and mutualism arose from encounters between species that were inevitable and unavoidable. Under these circumstances, the evolution of a co-operative relationship would be expected. The relationship between parasites and their hosts is probably an example of an evolutionary arms race, similar to that seen between predators and prey.

PART 2
Reproductive strategies

SEXUAL SELECTION IN EVOLUTION

Introduction and overview

The second part of this book (Chapters 4–7) looks at reproductive strategies in a wide range of animals. It examines sexual selection in evolution, parental investment in the rearing of the young, mating strategies and social organisation, and parent–offspring conflict. This chapter considers the nature and consequences of sexual selection in evolution, including mate choice and mate competition.

Sexual selection

Chapter 1 described the extent to which the behaviour of non-human animals could be explained by evolutionary concepts. The general assumption in this approach was that evolution works almost exclusively through natural selection. However, Darwin himself was aware that natural selection could not explain all evolutionary processes. One major problem was to explain the evolution of certain behaviours or anatomical structures which appeared to *reduce* the probability of survival. The most often quoted examples of this are altruistic behaviour (Cronin, 1991) and the peacock's impressive tail. The former is discussed in Chapter 8 of this book, but the latter is examined in detail in the present chapter.

The tail of the peacock (*Pavo cristatus*) appears to have the dual disadvantage of attracting predators and impeding efficient flight, making escape difficult

(Figure 4.1). If it was the case that such tails really increased fitness in some non-obvious way, one would expect them to be present in females also. As natural selection seemed to be unable to explain the existence of such a structure, Darwin proposed the theory of *sexual selection*. Sexual selection is a process which perpetuates certain genes within a species, while eliminating others. In this regard, it may be seen as a special case of natural selection. However, whereas natural selection operates through the process of differential mortality, sexual selection achieves its effects via differential reproductive potential.

Figure 4.1   A peacock (*Pavo cristatus*) displaying his extravagant and cumbersome tail. The existence of such a structure is more readily explained by sexual selection than by natural selection

According to Darwin (1871), sexual selection 'depends on the advantage which certain individuals have over others of the same sex and species solely in respect of reproduction'. This advantage usually accrues through competition between males for females (*mate competition*), or through choice by females of particular types of male (*mate choice*), although these sex roles may be reversed. Often the two kinds of selection act at the same time. Males which are adept at fighting off rivals, and attracting females, will pass their genes on to the next generation, while unsuccessful males will not. Because the result of sexual selection is not death to the unsuccessful competitor, but few or no offspring, Darwin viewed this type of selection as less vigorous than natural selection.

Sexual selection appears to suggest that anything that increases reproductive success will spread at the expense of anything that does not, even if it threatens survival (Ridley, 1993). Numerous examples have been observed of the conflict between natural and sexual selection. In certain cases, sexual selection may dominate, as observed in salmon (*Salmo salar*), which may starve to death while breeding. However, in a particular population of the three-spined stickleback (*Gasterosteus aculeatus*) found in North America, the males have evolved a black protective colouration to avoid predators, rather than the more common (and more attractive to the female stickleback) red colouration. Here we can see that natural selection, in the form of predator selection, may override the effects of sexual selection.

Female choice

Why should it be that females are the choosers and males the suitors? There are examples for which the roles are reversed, such as the jacana (*Jacana spinosa*) (a bird that walks on the leaves of water lilies). In this case, the males are responsible for nest building, incubation and care of the young. The females are larger, more brightly coloured, defend territories against each other and compete for the attention of males (Maynard-Smith, 1993). A similar situation occurs in sea horses. However, such examples are rare, and in the overwhelming majority of cases the competition is between males.

Sexual reproduction creates a social environment of conflict and competition among individuals, as each tries to maximise its genetic contribution to subsequent generations (Alcock, 1989). A male can potentially fertilise hundreds of females, and his gene pool is best served by ensuring that he does so to the maximum. Any adaptation in a male which enables him to copulate with more females will be strongly favoured by natural selection. Females are limited in their mating by the rate at which they produce eggs and young. They therefore invest more in the outcome of each fertilisation and each time must select the 'fittest' mate. Natural selection will thus favour discrimination in females.

In simple terms, it appears that males invest less and seek many females, while females invest more and wait for the right male. This results in competition between males for the attention of females, one consequence of which is great variability in the reproductive success of males (Trivers, 1985). This competition may be particularly marked when females come in to breeding condition at different times, as there is an opportunity for a small number of males to control many females, one after the other. Among elephant seals (*Mirounga angustirostris*), for example, one large dominant male may possess a group of up to fifty females. A typical female may weigh 650 kg and produce a pup weighing 50 kg. During the first five weeks of lactation the mother may lose as much as one third of her bodyweight in feeding the pup. Contrast this situation with the male, who contributes just a few hours' production of sperm cells (gametes), and may therefore father a large number of such pups (Cartwright, 1996).

A similar situation occurs in the common European fruit fly (*Drosophila subobscura*). The females mate only once, acquiring enough sperm to fertilise all the eggs (about 1000) they can lay in a lifetime. Males, on the other hand, can mate about six times a day. A female's breeding success is limited by the number of eggs she can lay, and would not be increased if she mated repeatedly. However, a male that mates twice as often will leave twice as many descendants (Maynard-Smith, 1993) (Figure 4.2).

However, it is an oversimplification to say that males invest little in the reproductive process. Biological and parental investments are often low, but the cost to males of fighting opponents, securing a territory, or providing resources can be very high. Similarly, females are not always passive participants in the mating game. They are often very active in selecting males, commonly using courtship behaviour as an opportunity to

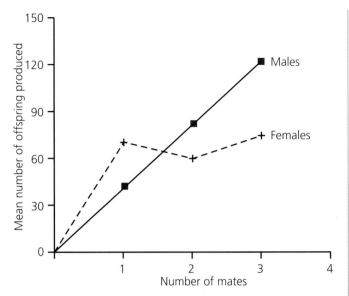

Figure 4.2   The relationship between number of matings and reproductive success in the European fruit fly (*Drosophila subobscura*). The number of matings strongly influences the reproductive success of a male, but not of a female

test males for the required qualities. Box 4.1 identifies some of the expected characteristics of low-investing males and high-investing females (Cartwright, 1996).

Is sexual selection equally important for all species?

The intensity of sexual selection depends on the degree of competition for mates, and would be expected to be weakest when competition is minimal and there is little or no parental care. There would appear to be little point in fathering lots of offspring and deserting them if they are vulnerable in terms of food requirements or attacks from predators. In such a case, the offspring are likely to die before reaching reproductive age, representing a genetic 'dead end'. However, many fish and amphibian species do just this. They desert their fertilised eggs, many of which are eaten by predators. Their strategy is to produce such an overwhelming number of fertilised eggs that a few will survive to sexual maturity in order to ensure continuity of the genetic line.

In monogamous species, therefore, in which both parents care for the young (e.g. swans, gibbons and humans), there are likely to be elements of both competition and choice among both sexes. In parrots and puffins, both males *and* females exhibit colourful plumage, which may represent cases of mutual sexual selection (Ridley, 1993). The importance of sexual selection in humans is addressed at the end of this chapter and the influence of parental investment in the choice of sexual partners is discussed in detail in Chapter 5.

Sexual dimorphism

It has been suggested that sexual selection helps to explain many aspects of sexual dimorphism (the differences between the male and female sexes of the same species). Darwin (1859) believed that 'when the males and females of any animal have the same general habits of life, but differ in structure, colour, or ornament, such differences have been mainly caused by sexual selection'. Unlike males, females usually do not need to compete with rivals. Therefore they do not need weaponry for psychological or physical advantage, or physical attributes to make them more attractive to the opposite sex. One striking example of sexual dimorphism is the antlers of male elks (*Alces alces*). These antlers, which are present only in the breeding season, can reach a span of around 4 metres, and have been known to weigh as much as 27 kg. It has been claimed that the evolution of such extravagant male structures is more readily explained by sexual selection than by natural selection. However, evidence suggests that most of the differences between the sexes are actually the result of natural selection (due to the asymmetry of the roles

---

Box 4.1   Expected characteristics of low-investing males and high-investing females. Based on Cartwright (1996)

Males	Females
• Seek many females	• Wait for right male
• Compete with other males for access to females	• Less competition
• Prefer polygyny (one male bonded with several females)	• Will accept polygyny under certain conditions
• Sexual response easily triggered	• Generally more coy than males and may require elaborate courtship
• High variation in reproductive success	• Reproductive success less varied

of the two sexes), such as those characteristics to do with parental care (e.g. breasts in human females).

Mate competition

Mate competition is usually the male strategy, to compete with rival males, and is also known as *intrasexual selection*. Males may dispute over direct access to females or over places where females are likely to go, as, for example, when male speckled wood butterflies defend patches of sunlight. As might be expected, mate competition is most pronounced during the breeding season. An example of this is shown in Box 4.2.

Mate competition may take more indirect forms than fighting or threatening behaviour. Males of species with internal fertilisation can never be absolutely sure that they have fathered the children of their mate. Courtship may allow males to assess whether or not females have previously mated with others. Male barbary doves (*Streptopelia risoria*) will reject females who appear too eager in their courtship, perhaps taking it as a sign that they have been previously courted, and therefore mated (Erickson & Zenone, 1976). The risk that a male's sperm will be superseded by those of a rival has led to many postcopulatory traits. For example, in some invertebrates the male cements up the

female's genital opening after copulation to prevent fertilisation by other males. The males of *Moniliformes dubius*, a parasitic worm in the intestine of rats, take this one step further by also mating with rival *males*, applying cement to their genital region and preventing any further copulation (Abele & Gilchrist, 1977). Postnatal competition occurs in the Langur monkeys (*Presbytis entellus*) of India, the males of which will kill a mother's offspring by another male with the aim of making her available to themselves (Jones, 1993). (See Chapter 7, page 67 for a discussion of infanticide.)

It has been argued that *all* sexual selection is due to mate competition. Whilst this seems plausible for the antlers of red deer stags or the tusks of the male walrus, it is difficult to envisage in the case of the peacock's tail. Some biologists have suggested that almost all ornaments and ritual displays are for intimidating other males, but when two peacocks fight, or when one runs away from a predator, the tail is kept carefully folded away. Therefore, for a complete examination of sexual selection, we must investigate the concept of mate choice.

Mate choice

Mate choice is usually the female strategy, to select the best (fittest) in the opposite sex, and is also known as *intersexual selection*. According to Darwin (1871), the function of the peacock's tail is to 'stimulate, attract and charm' the peahen. Females appear to prefer males who possess the longest and most brightly coloured tails. The original choice of this feature may have been arbitrary, or may have been linked to some survival value. In each generation such males will be selected for mating, and thereby pass on the genes for this long, bright tail to their male offspring. The short-tailed males would be relatively unsuccessful in the mating game, and therefore subsequent generations would contain increasing proportions of long-tailed peacocks. It is important to realise that the genes causing the long-tail preference in females will also be passed on to female offspring, thereby driving the selection process for longer and longer tails as generations pass. This assumes that female preference is transmitted genetically, something which has yet to be shown by experiment for the peahen. A similar tendency for female ladybirds to prefer mates with a certain colouring has apparently been shown to be a heritable trait (Sigmund, 1993), although female preference appears

Box 4.2   Mate competition in red deer

Each year, just prior to the mating season, the stag of the red deer (*Cervus elaphus*) develops antlers for fighting and threat display. The males compete and fight one another for the ownership of harems. The competition for females is, therefore, a direct one between the males, as the antlers are used for threat and fighting and not for wooing of the females. In this respect, mate competition differs from mate selection, but the antlers clearly confer reproductive advantage in that those with larger antlers serve more females. Apart from this advantage, the antlers appear to contribute little to survival. The females do not possess them, nor do stags outside the breeding season. Moreover, they constitute a considerable drain on the stag's metabolism, requiring large quantities of materials such as calcium salts and phosphorus for their growth each year.

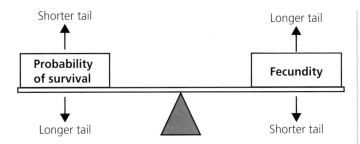

Figure 4.3 **The opposing forces of sexual and natural selection acting upon the length of the peacock's (*Pavo cristatus*) tail. The actual length represents a compromise between optimal fecundity and maximum probability of survival**

Figure 4.4 **A male East African widowbird (*Euplectes progne*) with its distinctive long black tailfeathers**

to be learned by imprinting (see Chapter 10) in snow geese (Diamond, 1992).

Sexual selection of the long tail must outweigh the effects of natural selection due to reduced mobility and attractiveness to predators. The actual length of the tail thus represents a compromise between optimal fecundity and maximum probability of survival. Peacocks need to survive long enough to reach sexual maturity (which will be more likely with a shorter tail), but also need to be attractive to peahens (who prefer a longer tail) in order to reproduce (Figure 4.3). It is also possible that females may not have a strict preference for males with the longest tails, but there may be a genetically programmed 'search image' for an ideal length (Sigmund, 1993).

Sexual selection has been demonstrated experimentally by Andersson (1982). Male East African widowbirds (*Euplectes progne*) have 45 cm long black tail feathers, which they whirl in spectacular displays visible for a kilometre (Figure 4.4). Andersson cut some of the males' tail feathers short and stuck the cut sections on to other males' tails. He found that males with artificially extended tails attracted four times as many females as those with normal tails or those whose tails were cut short. Similar results have been found for swallows (Møller, 1988).

The major debate about mate choice centres upon the question of whether females select males with extravagant features purely for aesthetic reasons (the 'good taste' hypothesis), or whether such features somehow signify a high level of genetic fitness (the 'good genes' hypothesis). These hypotheses are discussed in Box 4.3. If we accept that the aim of the female is to ensure that

the 'best' genes are mixed with her own (to enhance the likelihood of the survival of her genes), she may choose an attractive mate to improve her chances of producing attractive male offspring, who will reproduce and pass on her genes. Alternatively, she may select a healthy mate to improve her chances of having offspring which survive to reproductive age, or she could opt for a combination of health and beauty. For example, female satin bower birds (*Ptilonorhynchus violaceus*) select males on the basis of the decorative state of their bowers (Borgia, 1985). A male who builds a particularly impressive bower may be attractive because his sons may inherit his decorative skills (and therefore attract females in the future, continuing the genetic line), because the decoration reflects his competitive ability, which may indicate a healthy set of genes, or a combination of both factors.

The handicap principle mentioned in Box 4.3 may be the basis of elaborate courtship behaviour in some animals. Courtship provides the female with an opportunity to assess the male's fitness. In the European fruit fly, for example, females perform an elaborate dance, with which the male must keep up if he is to be allowed to mate. Old or inbred males usually fail in

Box 4.3   Mate choice: good taste or good genes?

Good taste: The geneticist R.A. Fisher (1930) has argued that male attractiveness will be selected for because it is a useful feature in itself. A female's advantage in choosing males with long tails consists in having her sons inherit the sex appeal of their father, an idea which has been nicknamed the *sexy son hypothesis*. If a female went against the trend, and mated with a male with a short tail, her sons would tend to have short tails and get few or no matings. Hence a female that bucked the trend would leave fewer descendants. The tendency for developing a characteristic in this way through evolution is known as a *runaway process*. In Fisher's (1930) words:

The two characteristics affected by such a process, namely plumage development in the male and sexual preference in the female, must thus advance together, and so long as the process is unchecked by severe counterselection, will advance with ever-increasing speed.

Mathematical research has since shown that Fisher's process can work (Lande, 1981).

Good genes: The 'good genes' hypothesis suggests that beauty may be more than skin deep. Females may select males whose genes will enhance the viability of their offspring and therefore choose peacocks with the longest tails *because* of the difficulties they have overcome in owning these cumbersome appendages (thus proving that they are robust individuals). This is known as the *handicap principle* (Zahavi, 1975). The longer the tail, the greater the handicap and so the better that male must be as a survivor. It is the capacity of the male to survive, despite the handicap, that attracts the female to him, rather than his attractiveness directly (Davies, 1995).

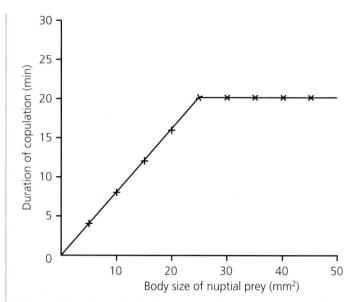

Figure 4.5   Female choice for good resources. Female hanging flies (*Hylobittacus apicalis*) will mate with a male only if he provides a large insect for her to eat during copulation. The larger the insect, the longer the male is allowed to copulate and the more eggs he fertilises. From Thornhill (1976)

The larger the insect, the longer the male is allowed to copulate and the more eggs he fertilises (Figure 4.5). Similarly, in the common tern (*Sterna hirundo*) there is a correlation between the ability of the male to bring food during courtship feeding and his ability to feed the chicks later in the season. Pairs often break up during the courtship feeding period and it is possible that females are assessing their mates and rejecting poor-quality partners (Nisbet, 1977). An experimental study on the 'good genes' hypothesis was conducted by Linda Partridge (1980). This is described in Box 4.4.

It was in 1889 that Alfred Russell Wallace first hinted at a 'good genes' explanation of sexual selection by suggesting that birds with more robust plumage were generally stronger individuals, and perhaps they were really being selected for their vigour, not their beauty. Recently, it has been found that species of songbirds plagued by high levels of blood parasites tend to be those with bright, displaying males, and that the males with the brightest plumage tend to have the highest resistance to parasites. It seems that bright plumage in males may signal vigour to females by acting as a type of 'health certificate'.

Male sticklebacks have a bright red belly, but if they get

their attempts, and are consequently rejected. By avoiding such males (whose lack of vigour may have a genetic basis), a female may make it more likely that her offspring will survive (Maynard-Smith, 1993). Similarly, males may use gifts of food, or the possession of a territory, to convince potential mates of the quality of their genes. A female hanging fly (*Hylobittacus apicalis*), for example, will mate with a male only if he provides a large insect for her to eat during copulation.

Box 4.4   An experimental study on the 'good genes' hypothesis. Based on Partridge (1980)

Partridge's experiment suggests that females are able to increase the survival of their offspring by choosing good genes in their mates. However, the results could also be explained in part by intrasexual competition (in the 'choice' experiment the males that mated may have been superior competitors against other males).

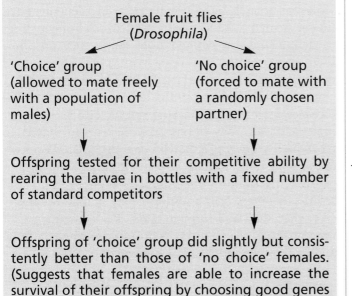

Female fruit flies
(Drosophila)

'Choice' group (allowed to mate freely with a population of males)

'No choice' group (forced to mate with a randomly chosen partner)

Offspring tested for their competitive ability by rearing the larvae in bottles with a fixed number of standard competitors

Offspring of 'choice' group did slightly but consistently better than those of 'no choice' females. (Suggests that females are able to increase the survival of their offspring by choosing good genes in their mates.)

infected by a ciliate parasite, they develop white spots which make the belly appear less red. Female sticklebacks prefer the redder males, and thus select for less-infected mates. If their aquarium is illuminated by a green light, however, they stop caring one way or another, because they can no longer see the red. It must be the colour, therefore, which guides their choice, rather than the presence or absence of parasites as such (Sigmund, 1993). It is possible that females may originally pick males for reasons of 'good genes', but that this initial selection then becomes a runaway process (the selection of beauty for beauty's sake). On this basis, Wallace and Darwin could both have been correct in their assumptions about sexual selection.

Critics of the handicapping theory have suggested that males who have been injured but survived would be perceived by females as being robust individuals. However, this handicap would not be heritable, and

may even act detrimentally as those individuals that are injured might be less 'fit' than their counterparts. It is also possible that, in some cases, parasites have found ways to manipulate their hosts' appearance by making them look healthier and more colourful than their rivals – that is, faking good health (Dawkins, 1989). This coevolution of parasite and host (adaptation and counteradaptation) further complicates the issue of sexual selection. However, Dawkins himself believes that cheating is unlikely, as females would be able to see through such trickery. In addition, Zahavi's verbal ideas on the 'handicap principle' have been translated into a mathematical model which suggests that it actually works. (See Dawkins (1989) for a full explanation.)

Vanishing variation: the paradox of sexual selection

If peacocks are constantly being selected for longer and longer tails, we might expect to reach the point when *all* peacocks will have the longest tail that the genes available can code for, and variation in tail length no longer exists. With natural selection, this problem does not occur because the environment, the selecting force, is itself constantly changing. The same is not necessarily true, however, for female preference and hence for sexual selection.

One solution to this paradox is mutation (Lande, 1981). However, controversy exists as to whether mutation rates are fast enough to maintain variation in the face of strong sexual selection. A more plausible explanation is that the necessary variation is provided by the constant adaptation and counteradaptation involved in the battle between parasite and host. W.D. Hamilton (1990) believed that hereditary disease resistance in males is the most important criterion by which females choose their partners. As the definition of the 'best' animal is always changing, there will always be something important for females to choose between when they examine males. As parasites never let up, so females cannot let up in their relentless search for healthy males. The variation amongst males will, therefore, always be present enabling sexual selection to continue (Dawkins, 1989).

Sexual selection in humans

According to Ridley (1993), 'People are attracted to people of high reproductive and genetic potential – the healthy, the fit and the powerful.' In general, women would be expected to attempt to increase their reproductive success by choosing males of high status, with sufficient resources to care for the offspring. As male fertility in humans is less age dependent than that of females, it would also be predicted that age should be less important for women than for men as an indicator of attractiveness. These ideas have been supported by studies on human mate choice, as described in Box 4.5.

Evidence suggests that humans are a sexually selected species, and that many of our traits such as fat distribution, hair colour and eye colour are designed to make us appear more attractive to the opposite sex. This may be particularly true for facial features, which may be

---

Box 4.5   Human mate choice

Dunbar (1995) studied the 'Lonely Hearts' columns of magazines and newspapers and found that men predominantly offer resources and seek attractiveness. The reverse is usually true in females (see the examples below). Buss (1989) found that the preference among women for power and earning capacity held across thirty-seven different cultures, regardless of the status and financial position of the women concerned.

'Professional male (37) looking for attractive female (25–30) to share weekends in his country cottage.'

'Attractive female (27) seeks professional male for friendship and romance.'

A man can increase his reproductive success either by taking many wives or by choosing a woman who is fertile and demonstrates the potential to be a good mother. On the basis of the latter option, we would expect men to prefer women in a relatively narrow age band of peak reproductive potential to ensure maximum fertility. In addition, we would expect human males to use physical attractiveness as a guide to age and reproductive ability. Again, these ideas have broad support from the evidence on human mate choice referred to above.

---

selected for their inherent attractiveness, or which could be a clue to genetic quality or personality. This appears to lend support to Darwin's (1871) original ideas about sexual selection explaining hairlessness in humans, as well as many differences in inter-racial morphology.

The evolution of human behaviour may also have been influenced by sexual selection. It is probable, for example, that men's more competitive nature is a consequence of such selection. It has even been suggested that men may take alcohol, tobacco or stronger drugs to demonstrate to women how tough they are, how their constitutions can cope with mistreatment and how they might make excellent fathers as a result (Jones, 1993). Ridley (1993) believes that the human intellect itself is a product of sexual, rather than natural, selection. Big brains may have contributed to reproductive success either by enabling men to outwit other men (and women to outwit other women), or because big brains were originally used to court and seduce members of the opposite sex. It may be, therefore, that the large human brain is a consequence of mutual sexual selection (as seen in parrots and puffins) and that 'clever people are sexy people'.

Conclusions

Charles Darwin introduced the term sexual selection to explain the evolution of certain secondary sexual characteristics in animals which natural selection could not account for, such as the peacock's tail. Whereas natural selection operated through differential survival, sexual selection depended on the struggle between individuals of one sex (normally the males) for the possession of individuals of the opposite sex. The relative importance of natural and sexual selection in the evolutionary process is still the subject of much debate in the present day.

Darwin conceived of sexual selection operating in two ways: mate competition (intrasexual selection) and mate choice (intersexual selection). Furthermore, mate choice may be made on the basis of attractiveness (the 'good taste' hypothesis), perceived genetic quality (the 'good genes' hypothesis), or a combination of both. The role of sexual selection in human evolution remains unclear. However, it seems likely that such selection can account for at least some of the differences between men and women.

SUMMARY

- **Natural selection** cannot explain all evolutionary processes. Certain behaviours or anatomical structures appear to **reduce** the probability of survival. The tail of the peacock, for example, appears to have the dual disadvantage of attracting predators and impeding efficient flight, making escape difficult. Such features may be explained by **sexual selection**.

- Sexual reproduction creates a social environment of **conflict** and **competition** among individuals, as each tries to **maximise its genetic contribution** to subsequent generations. Natural selection will favour **discrimination** in females and adaptations in males which enable them to copulate with more females.

- In simple terms, it appears that **males invest less and seek many females**, while **females invest more and wait for the right male**. This results in **competition** between males for the attention of females, as seen in elephant seals and many other species.

- It is an oversimplification to say that males invest little in the reproductive process. **Biological** and **parental investments** are often low, but the cost to males of **fighting opponents, securing a territory** or **providing resources** can be very high. Similarly, females are often very active in selecting mates, commonly using **courtship behaviour** as an opportunity to test males for the required qualities.

- The **intensity** of sexual selection depends upon the degree of competition for mates, and would be expected to be weakest when competition is minimal and there is little or no parental care. In **monogamous** species, in which both parents care for the young, there are likely to be elements of both competition and choice among both sexes, which may result in **mutual sexual selection**.

- It has been suggested that sexual selection helps to explain many aspects of **sexual dimorphism** (the differences between the male and female sexes of the same species). However, evidence suggests that *most* of the differences between the sexes are actually the result of natural selection.

- According to Darwin, sexual selection operates in two ways: **mate competition (intrasexual selection)**, and **mate choice (intersexual selection)**. Often these two kinds of selection act at the same time.

- **Mate competition** is usually the male strategy, to compete with rival males, and is also known as **intrasexual selection**. This differs from mate choice in that the competition is a direct one between the males, and does not involve wooing the females. Often this means that only the strongest animals get to reproduce.

- **Mate choice** is usually the female strategy, to select the best in the opposite sex, and is also known as **intersexual selection**. Peahens appear to prefer peacocks who possess the longest and most brightly coloured tails. This has led to increasing proportions of long-tailed peacocks in each generation. Sexual selection of the long tail must outweigh the effects of natural selection due to reduced mobility and attractiveness to predators. The actual length of the tail thus represents a compromise between **optimal fecundity** and **maximum probability of survival**.

- The **'good taste' hypothesis** suggests that male attractiveness will be selected for because it is a useful feature in itself. The **'good genes' hypothesis** suggests that extravagant male features somehow signify a high level of genetic fitness. This is known as the **'handicap principle'**. It is the capacity of the male to survive, despite the handicap, that attracts the female to him, rather than his attractiveness directly.

- Species of songbirds plagued by high levels of blood parasites tend to be those species with bright, displaying males, and the males with the brightest plumage tend to have the highest resistance to parasites. A similar situation occurs in sticklebacks, and it seems that male displays may signal vigour to females by acting as a type of **'health certificate'**.

- **Courtship** also provides the female with an opportunity to assess the male's genetic fitness. Males may perform elaborate **displays**, possess **territories** rich in resources, or use **gifts of food** to convince potential mates of the quality of their genes.

- The influence of sexual selection upon a species would appear to be limited by the quantity of **genetic variation** available. However, it appears that the necessary variation is provided by the constant **adaptation** and **counteradaptation** involved in the battle between **parasite** and **host**. **Hereditary disease resistance** in males is probably the most important criterion by which females choose their partners.

- Recent evidence suggests that **humans** are a

mutually sexually selected species. There appears to be a universal tendency for men to **seek attractiveness** and **offer resources**, and for women to do the reverse. It seems that many of our traits such as fat distribution, hair colour and eye colour are designed to make us appear attractive to the opposite sex. Furthermore, it may be that sexual selection is partly responsible for the evolution of the large human brain.

PARENTAL INVESTMENT IN THE REARING OF THE YOUNG

Introduction and overview

As seen in Chapter 4, sexual selection can lead to differences in behaviour between males and females because they promote their individual fitness in different ways. The aim of this chapter is to examine parental investment in the rearing of the young, looking in detail at the differential investments of males and females in the rearing process.

Males and females: speed versus size

In primitive organisms, such as single-celled animals, sexual reproduction involves the fusion of *gametes* (sex cells) of identical size (*isogamy*). In less primitive organisms, such as fungi, + and − strains exist in which gametes from the + strain always move to gametes of the − strain. The principles explored in Chapter 4, and those in this chapter, however, are dependent on the existence of 'males' and 'females'. These sexes need not be physically or behaviourally different, as is the case in humans (who are *sexually dimorphic*), they are simply required to produce gametes of differing sizes (*anisogamy*). 'Males' produce small motile gametes called *sperm*, and that is what makes them male. 'Females' produce large immobile gametes called *eggs* which have a store of energy (Figure 5.1) which serves to assist the embryo in its development. Sperm are produced in very large numbers, each individual sperm having the capacity to fertilise an egg, although very few will do so. Eggs are more costly to produce, so females make fewer in a lifetime, and release them in significantly smaller numbers than males produce sperm. Overall, males and females put the same amount of energy into making gametes, they simply spread that energy out differently.

In terms of evolution, once it became possible for a gamete to move, selection pressures began to operate to produce smaller, faster-moving sperm. Such sperm would be better able to compete with other motile sperm to find and fertilise static eggs, which were few in number. This represents the beginnings of male competition due to scarce female resources. Similarly, those gametes that were static would be exposed to selection pressure to be bigger, since greater size would enhance the probability of fertilisation and chances of survival.

Specialisation is necessary to perform a given role efficiently. Male and female gametes achieve that specialisation for successful fertilisation in different ways. Baylis (1981) suggested that ease of replacement, rather than motility, was the key to the evolution of separate

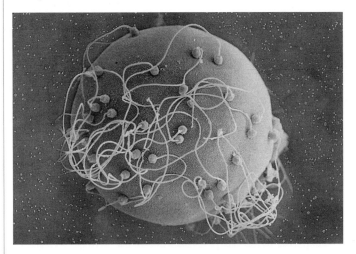

Figure 5.1   For any species, each gamete (sperm or egg) contains the same amount of genetic information. Eggs, however, are very much bigger so require greater investment, hence females can afford to produce fewer gametes than males

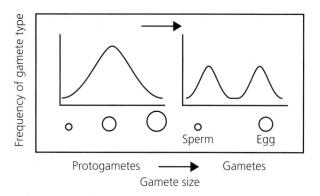

Figure 5.2   Evolution has resulted in specialisation of gametes. Small motile cells which could be produced in large numbers and large static cells which had sufficient energy to survive and to nourish the initial growth of the zygote would both have had advantages over medium-sized gametes. (This is an example of disruptive selection, which is described in Chapter 1, page 4.)

gametes. Males can replace sperm quickly, at a rate of about 100 million per day in humans, and so can 'waste' them on chance copulations. However, egg supply is very limited, because eggs are released at a rate of only one per month in human females. Egg survival is increased by having resources to last longer, whilst sperm success is increased by being able to travel further. Therefore, gametes at either extreme have an advantage over those 'stuck in the middle' (see Figure 5.2). Having arisen, the differences in gamete size and motility would be perpetuated, as would the discrepancy in expenditure on each sex cell by males and females. This difference in investment by the parents in offspring (females exceeding males from the outset) is central to the theme of this chapter, and is returned to later.

Males and females: conflicting interests

Evolution is survival by success. It produces adaptive structures and behaviours. Dawkins and Krebs (1979) describe the battle between two evolving lines as an *arms race* (see Chapter 3, page 27), with each line attempting to develop more successful *strategies* (behaviour patterns employed by individuals which raise their fitness). The battle may be between predator and prey as seen in Chapter 3 or, in this case, between males and females. However, it is not fought between the sexes,

but between individuals in competition for the goal of fertilisation. Males are competing with other males and, to a lesser extent, females with other females.

It is also important to recognise that we are not implying that any animal is conscious of these strategies, or that they 'develop' in any sense other than by evolution. Those individuals inheriting a less successful strategy are less likely to reproduce, so genes controlling such a strategy are lost. This is, of course, somewhat simplistic. Whole behavioural patterns are not controlled by single genes. It is, however, convenient to think in these terms, whilst recognising that a single gene governing the inheritance of a strategy in each sex probably does not exist.

As mentioned previously (see page 43), the production of eggs requires a bigger investment than the production of sperm, and eggs are produced in correspondingly small quantities. In humans, for instance, a woman is only likely to produce about 450 viable eggs in her lifetime. A man, by contrast, will release in the order of 120,000,000,000,000 (or 12×10^{13}) sperm, which is enough to fertilise all the women in the world! A human female is able to produce fertile gametes for only a short proportion of her life span, and during this time she is only *fertile* (carrying an egg which can be fertilised) for two days in every month. Once the egg is fertilised, the woman will then be pregnant for nine months, during which time she will release no further eggs. Excluding factors such as contraception and the inhibitory effect of lactation on *ovulation* (the release of eggs), a woman who became pregnant at every opportunity would only be fertile for about 900 days in total. Men, by contrast, are fertile for decades. Therefore, females bearing fertile eggs are a *scarce resource*, but fertile males are common. This is one of the reasons why females are usually the choosers in the mating game (see Chapter 4, page 34).

Parental investment as a consequence of sex

In the previous section, we saw how the difference in size of sperm and eggs results in different reproductive strategies for males and females. Receptive females, by their scarcity, are able to 'choose' between males. What do the males offer which the females can use as a basis for choice? As discussed in Chapter 4, one reason a female may choose a particular male is for his genes. His successful male status will be passed on to her sons (the 'sexy son hypothesis'). However, good genes are not the only advantage one male may have over another. A male who is prepared to invest more (assisting the female by providing food or protection, or helping to teach the young) might be preferred by females, because he would raise the chances of her offspring surviving.

STAYING OR STRAYING

Females would be best served by a strategy in which males were faithful, staying to help rear the offspring. For the female, each breeding attempt represents a significant proportion of her total breeding capacity, and so each potential offspring is more 'valuable' to her. Females should, therefore, either court males to ascertain their parenting skills, such as their ability to forage and defend the young, or try to prevent them deserting to fertilise other females. A good male who deserts his female not only deprives her of his caring services, but also donates his good genes to her competitors or the competitors of her offspring. Males, on the other hand, would benefit from seeking females who will raise their young alone, enabling the males to mate again. The sexes are in conflict because their optimal strategies are opposed to one another. Females want males who will stay, males want females who will let them stray.

SELECTING THE 'BEST' MALE

Chapter 4 discussed the behaviour of peahens and their choice of peacock, using his appearance and display as indicators of his genes. The heritability of a male's courtship display ensures that the fitness of the female is raised by this strategy via 'sexy sons'. A display may only indicate sexiness, or it may provide informative about valuable assets, such as the suitability of the mate in terms of his vigour or abilities. Hamilton (1971) has suggested that the maintenance of a peacock's tail could indicate resistance to infestation by parasites, so a bigger tail means a healthier male. Halliday (1976) observed that in smooth newts (*Triturus vulgaris*), who perform complex displays under water, male reproductive success is related to the length and intensity of their display (Figure 5.3). Females may use the display as a test of endurance, males who can perform under water for the longest being considered the fittest. Vigorous males such as these, however, only provide 'fit genes' and 'fit bodies'. The 'best' males would additionally supply parental assistance.

To maximise her fitness, a female should select a mate on the basis of good genes *and* parental investment. Like many avian (bird) courtship displays, that of the common tern (*Sterna hirundo*) requires the male to provide food for the female (see Chapter 4, page 38), enabling her to assess the parenting skills of a prospective mate (Figure 5.4). Protracted courtship of this kind demands such an investment of resources by the male that, even if he were to desert subsequently, he would be unlikely to have the time or energy to find and court another unpaired female. Females may therefore 'trap' males into staying. Similarly, female weaverbirds (*Ploceus cucullatus*) also use parenting skills as a guide to selecting a mate. Captive males, displaying on freshly woven green nests, attract more mates than those on old brown nests. This is clearly advantageous for females, as they can select a mate which will build a safe new nest in which they can raise their offspring.

Parental investment theory

Trivers (1972) introduced the idea of *parental investment*, defining it as 'any investment by the parent in an individual offspring that increases the offspring's chance of surviving (and hence reproductive success) at the cost of the parent's ability to invest in other offspring'. He states that this investment should include the 'metabolic investment' in gametes, and behaviours which assist the survival of the young such as feeding or guarding from predators. He excludes effort expended on finding a mate or repelling competitors, since such investment does not affect the survival of the resulting offspring and is not, therefore, *parental* investment.

At the time of conception, the female has already made a greater investment in each gamete than has the male (because eggs are bigger). As a result, she has more to lose by the failure of any particular breeding attempt. It is, therefore, in her interests to continue to invest once she has begun. This results in two evolutionary consequences: firstly, she should be more reluctant to begin any investment (that is, be more selective in her choice of mate), and secondly, once committed, she should be less likely to abandon her goal.

The disparity in early investment between the sexes is accentuated in birds and mammals, as these females are inescapably committed to a long and costly investment in the development of eggs, or in gestation. The inequality of investment is, therefore, in part depen-

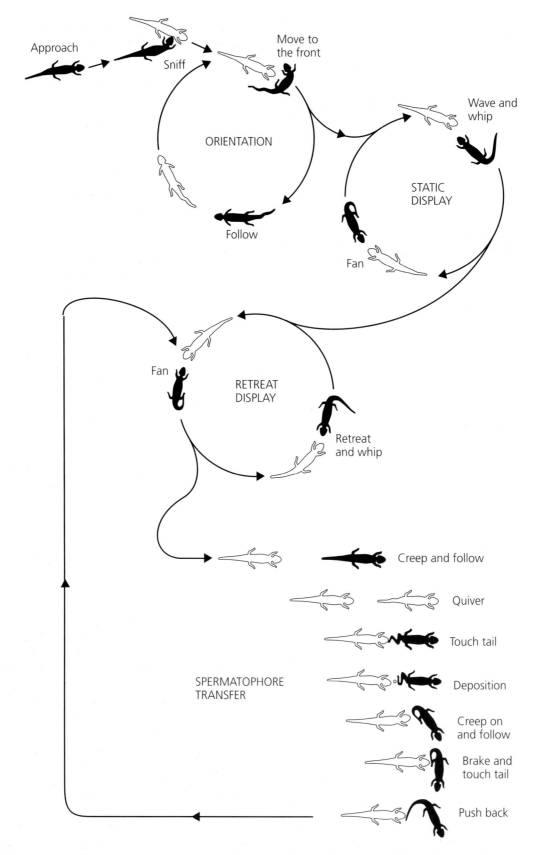

Figure 5.3   The reproductive success of male newts is related to the intensity of their display. More vigorous males mate more often

Figure 5.4   A male common tern (*Sterna hirundo*) demonstrates his parenting skills to his potential mate by offering her food

dent upon *phylogeny* (the evolutionary history of the species). For instance, once a female bird's eggs have been fertilised, she is unavoidably committed to foraging sufficiently to ensure their development until they are laid. Obtaining sufficient food and water to sustain developing eggs is energetic. In the same way, a female mammal bears the cost of nourishing the embryo, and possible costs of increased susceptibility to predation during pregnancy if her agility is reduced. Finally, a female mammal is endowed with the capacity to suckle her young (via mammary glands). She is therefore capable of making a significant contribution to the survival of her offspring, which the male cannot make.

Female birds and mammals commit to one breeding opportunity to the temporary exclusion of others. Consequently, at hatching, or birth, a much greater parental investment has been made by the female than by the male. A female has less time and energy, as well as fewer gametes, to invest in a new breeding attempt, so is less likely to abandon her offspring. Females are more likely to continue to invest, because of their small chances of success if they begin again.

By contrast, males can desert when the female has made a sufficient contribution to 'tie' herself to the offspring. As the post-fertilisation investment of males is generally smaller, they are less vital for offspring survival. A male's departure may not significantly reduce the survival chances of his existing offspring, but could enhance his future reproduction through new reproductive attempts (for which he has ample energy and gametes). Even so, when males desert, females left alone are likely to suffer reduced reproductive success (see Box 5.1).

The reasons for, and consequences of, desertion are discussed in detail in the 'Mating Strategies' section of the next chapter. Species in which both sexes care for the young are unusual (except amongst the birds), and species in which the female deserts, such as the jacana, and stickleback, are very rare. The implications of parental investment for strategies of parental care are discussed in the last section of Chapter 6 (see page 58). It should be noted that the sex of the parent is not the only factor which affects the level of investment in the young. Box 5.2 identifies some of the other factors influencing parental investment, factors which are amplified in the rest of this chapter.

Altricial versus precocial young

If the offspring are able to fend for themselves, there is little to be gained by assisting them. In terms of reproductive success, the parents' efforts would be better spent embarking on new breeding attempts. *Altricial young*, those born relatively undeveloped (such as being unable to walk, without fur, or with their eyes closed) require more care than *precocial young*, born at a relatively advanced state of development. For example, polar bear cubs (*Thalarctos maritimus*) are born unable to walk or feed themselves. They are tended by the mother for more than two and a half years before they disperse to survive alone (Stirling & Latour, 1978). Young wildebeest (*Connochaetes gnou*), by contrast, are able to walk almost from birth and whilst (like all mammals) they suckle, they quickly begin to graze. As a consequence, young wildebeest require relatively little parental care.

r and K selection

Cases in which parental investment is absent can sometimes be explained by the inability of the parents to offer any significant assistance to their offspring. Whilst mammals provide milk for their young, and a dung beetle (*Scarabaeus semipunctatus*) lays its egg beside a carefully rolled ball of dung, a housefly (*Musca domestica*) can do very little for its offspring. Parental care is characteristically absent from the behavioural repertoire of many insects. These insects, ill prepared to provide for their young, have a low offspring survival (as a percentage of eggs laid). This can only be countered by producing offspring in huge numbers. Species in which

this strategy has evolved are described as *r-selected* (like rabbits). By having many offspring, they can best ensure the survival of some, despite the absence of care. In such species, there is little difference between the level of investment of males and females.

K-selected species, by contrast (such as kangaroos), have fewer offspring but offer extended care. These species may give food, protection, warmth and instruction to their offspring to enhance their survival prospects. The attention of K-selected parents to their offspring helps to raise the probability of the progeny reaching reproductive age, thus enhancing both parents' individual fitness. K-selection is more likely to arise when food is scarce or when offspring can be produced in only relatively small numbers. In particularly demanding environments, two parents, rather than one, significantly increase the probability of finding enough food to ensure survival. Therefore, food availability, more than any other factor, increases the participation of males in rearing. (Chapter 6, page 58, offers a fuller discussion of parental care.)

Being biologically prepared for caring

Parental investment theory predicts that females will invest more in their offspring postnatally (after birth) because they have invested more prenatally (before birth). In mammals, at least, that inescapable responsibility continues with the exclusive ability of females to lactate and therefore nourish the young. There are, however, a small number of cases in birds, fish, amphibia and reptiles for which it is the males who invest more after hatching. This again illustrates that early investment in gametes is not a sufficient criterion to dictate subsequent parental investment in all cases.

In species dependent upon *external fertilisation* (where the female spawns (lays eggs) and the male sheds his sperm onto them so fusion of the gametes occurs outside the body), there is no unavoidable obligation for the female to continue to invest in the young. She, like the male, has the option to desert as she is not 'trapped' by the internal development of eggs or embryos. The additional amount she has invested in her egg, compared to his sperm, is small compared to the forthcoming cost of caring for the developing young. In animals such as seahorses, the three-spined stickleback

Box 5.3 Paternal care in the three-spined stickleback

Sticklebacks (*Gasterosteus*) have a complex courtship which culminates with the female spawning and the male following to fertilise the eggs. The male can therefore be certain that the offspring are his own (there is high *paternity certainty*). The male has consumed time and energy defending a territory, building a nest and courting females. He has therefore already made a large investment. As he sheds his sperm after the female has spawned, he is literally 'left' with the fertilised eggs. (The female deserts immediately). The male stickleback, like females bearing viviparous young (developing *inside* the body), is left 'holding the baby' because of the cost of his own efforts. The male stickleback stays to fan the eggs, providing them with oxygen, and defends his territory to protect them from predators (Tinbergen 1951).

(*Gasterosteus aculeatus*) (see Box 5.3) and the midwife toad (*Alytes obstetricans*), it is the female who deserts and the male is left to tend the fertilised eggs. In seahorses, the male has a 'brood pouch' where the eggs are protected until hatching. He, like a female mammal, is predestined by his physical structure to invest an unequal share in the care of the young.

Role reversal, and sharing of roles, can occur in species in which neither sex is committed (by its anatomy, physiology, or instinctive behaviour) to parental investment. For example, both male and female wood pigeons (*Columba palumbus*) can produce 'crop milk', a secretion used to feed the nestlings. Males can (and do) assist in rearing the young and enhance their chances of survival. The tasks of incubation and feeding are shared equally between the sexes.

The role of non-parents and the social group

For species in which all the essential components of the behavioural repertoire are innate, the need for parental care is minimised. For example, the cuckoo (*Cuculus canorus*) lays her egg in another bird's nest (see Chapter 3, page 29) and the foster parent cannot instruct the young cuckoo in areas of species-specific behaviours. These behaviours, such as food begging, migration, calling for a mate, mating and egg laying, must all be inherited. This genetic endowment replaces the necessity for parental investment in teaching and allows the cuckoo to continue its parasitic lifestyle. Clearly, this is an extreme example of lack of social interaction with the parents, and for many species this dereliction of duty is not possible.

Higher primates and carnivores have complex behavioural repertoires in which their responses and strategies are too varied, and situation specific, to be inherited. These species must acquire their behavioural responses whilst under the guidance of their parents during a period of infancy. Where the feeding strategy is complex it must generally be learned, for instance in social foraging or hunting. Gibbons (*Hylobates concolor*), for example, live in close family groups and both parents assist in care. The female devotes her attention to young infants as she alone can produce milk to nourish them. Juvenile offspring are taught to forage by the male, since he has time to devote to their instruction. Teaching of the young is common when potentially life-threatening behaviours, such as the ability to hunt, must be acquired. Here, parents can make a significant contribution. By providing relatively safe learning environments, their efforts allow the offspring to acquire essential skills to enhance their own fitness without impairing survival chances. They can learn to kill without being killed. This is described in Box 5.4

A similar pattern to that observed in lions and cheetahs (Box 5.4) is seen in meerkats (*Suricata suricatta*), whose young need to learn to find, and deal with, 'tricky' food like scorpions (Figure 5.5). Here again the kits (young meerkats) are 'tutored' by adults (Ewer, 1963). Interestingly, these tutors may *not* be the parents, so 'parental' investment is not the only driving force in investing in young. Similarly, Rood (1978) observed that a female mongoose (*Helogale parvula*) who was unrelated to any members of her group made a greater contribution to rearing the young than the mother, father or any other relative. This may have been the product of selection pressure towards social behaviour (only 'helping' individuals are allowed in the group), a consequence of group or kin selection (see Chapter 8), or an investment for the individual in terms of acquiring parenting skills.

Box 5.4 The acquisition of hunting skills by lions and cheetahs

Lions (*Panthera leo*) are dangerous beasts, yet spend up to a year 'learning the ropes'. By watching and following the pride, and through play, lion cubs develop the strength and strategies required for successful hunting (Schaller, 1972). Cheetahs (*Acionyx jubatus*) are also powerful hunters, but they are smaller than lions and hunt alone. The cost of failure as a predator is greater for cheetahs as errors carry the cost not only of starvation (as they cannot share kills) but also of injury. A threatened wildebeest, for example, can easily harm a young cheetah. In raising their cubs, cheetah mothers invest time and energy, as well as risk to themselves, in the active 'teaching' of their offspring. They catch and disable prey, such as young gazelles, giving the cubs an opportunity to practise hunting in relative safety (Eaton, 1970). By making this costly contribution, the mother raises her overall fitness by enhancing the prospect of her offspring reaching reproductive age.

Figure 5.5 Meerkats must learn to deal with difficult food, such as scorpions

Parental investment in humans

Observations and explanations discussed in this chapter enable comparisons to be made between the different strategies displayed by non-human animals and our own parental behaviour. Humans, like all anisogametic species, are exposed to selection pressures as a consequence of the difference in gamete size and frequency between the sexes. From this difference in investment, and of course the phylogenetic consequences of being mammalian (such as the possession of mammary glands), greater parental investment would be expected in women. In most societies, it is predominantly the women who are engaged in child care. It is still rarely the father who ceases work to look after the children, and it is usually women who run nurseries and who are primary school teachers. Should this, however, be taken as evidence for lack of investment by males? Until recent generations, the contribution made to the offspring by the father was simple, but highly significant. As the breadwinner, his wages enabled his wife to care for their exceedingly altricial children. The importance of this role is discussed in Box 5.5. Whilst not endorsing the use of evolutionary theory to justify inequalities, it can be used to see how differences in behaviour may have arisen.

Box 5.5 The male as a bread winner

If some males were able to offer material benefits, females would prefer them as partners as this investment would increase the survival chances of the young. In our society, courting males are required to demonstrate their ability to provide for the family. Females want males who will stay, and ensure provision for them and their young.

Why do girls want to be taken out to expensive Italian restaurants? Perhaps because, although many present-day primates live in food-rich areas, we may not have evolved in such areas. Early humans, living on the savannah, would have struggled to find sufficient food, as do baboons (*Papio anubis*) in the same environment. It is therefore unsurprising to observe that male baboons are involved in the care of their young. Here again, they can make an important contribution to survival, and do so. Unlike baby baboons, a human infant cannot cling to its mother. This means that females with newborn babies would have been restricted in their ability to forage, thus further increasing the importance of the male in providing food to ensure the survival of both the lactating female and, therefore, his child.

THE ROLE OF THE MALE IN PARENTING: HUSBANDS AND FATHERS

In humans, the males contribute more to parenting than most other higher primates. Why should this be the case? People are mammals who give birth to very altricial young. Human babies are utterly dependent on adult care for several years. As a consequence, males who invested in helping their females would reap significant benefits in terms of offspring survival. This would also be true before the birth of the offspring as human females require relatively more care during the long gestation period than other primates. Imagine a woman who was eight months pregnant performing the acrobatics required by a gestating gibbon just to feed herself.

Alcock (1993) suggests that, in the course of human evolution, women may have received food from consort males who guarded them during oestrus (the fertile period). If so, then by hiding the exact time of ovulation from the man, the woman could gain greater assistance in terms of food. If the guarding period were extended in this manner, the male might gain the relatively permanent status of 'husband'. The best strategy from the male's point of view would then be to expend further resources on the offspring (which he could relatively safely assume were his own). The male, therefore, ends up making greater parental investment than would have been the case in a 'receptive stage only' guarding strategy.

In the only other pair-bonded higher primate, the gibbon, the pair defend a territory in which the family remain together. Like humans, the babies are altricial, requiring constant care initially, and only dispersing after five to six years. The female looks after the young while they are suckling, and once they are weaned the male takes over. He instructs the juvenile in foraging techniques, whilst the female is preoccupied with the next, newborn, sibling. As the reproductive success of the male is increased by 'freeing' the female to care for the younger offspring, he can fulfil a useful role. His investment in the older sibling raises the survival chances of both that individual in its own right, and of the younger sibling by ensuring it has the full attention of the mother, the only parent who at that time can care for it. Care by the male in this instance makes a significant contribution to increasing his individual fitness.

In terms of return on investment, humans may be better compared to most birds than to primates. Both parents can contribute and so often do. Contribution in both cases can take many forms, including caring for the pregnant, suckling or incubating parent, feeding and protecting defenceless, immobile young, and care of fledglings in the danger zone between total parental protection and independence.

Conclusions

This chapter has explored how, and why, males and females show parental investment, or avoid it. Early in each breeding attempt, females invest more, relative to males, because eggs are bigger than sperm. This imbalance tends to reduce the likelihood of females deserting. This difference, combined with the specialisations of the females of some species (such as lactation in mammals), results in females typically offering more parental care than males.

SUMMARY

- In primitive organisms, sexual reproduction involves the fusion of **gametes** (sex cells) of identical size (**isogamy**). However, most animals are **anisogametic**, they produce gametes of different sizes. **Males** produce many, small, motile **sperm**, **females** produce few, large, static **eggs**. Therefore, investment per gamete is higher in females. This inequality has implications for later parental investment.
- Females bearing fertile eggs are a **scarce resource**, so males compete for them. Because of their rarity, females can be **choosy**. A female seeks a male with **good genes** or **good resources** who will help to rear the offspring in which she has already invested. She may use courtship to measure the contribution a male will make to parenting, or to trap him into staying.
- Males, who invest little per breeding attempt, should seek females who will raise the young alone. This will allow males to mate again. The

sexes are in conflict because their optimal strategies are opposed to one another. Females want males who will stay. Males want females who will let them stray.

- **Parental investment** is the effort males and females commit to individual offspring that they could have spent on another breeding attempt. It includes energy spent on gametes, gestation, incubation and parental care. It does *not* include effort expended on finding a mate or repelling competitors, since such investment does not affect the survival of the resulting offspring.

- The more individuals invest, the less they have left in terms of energy and opportunity and the more they have to lose. They are less likely to abandon a breeding attempt if they have contributed a lot to it.

- All females invest in large, nutrient-rich eggs, and many have specialisations dependent upon their **phylogeny** (evolutionary history). This means that females should be more reluctant to *begin* an investment and be more selective in their choice of mate. In **mammals**, the females are committed to prolonged investment, which the male cannot provide, during **gestation** and **lactation**. This early outlay by females results in their costs tending to outweigh those of the male. Consequently, females are less likely to desert and tend to continue to invest more.

- In a few species, such as sticklebacks and seahorses, the male invests more than the female. This is more common when the male has phylogenetic adaptations for care of the young and when **external fertilisation** enables the female to desert after minimal investment (and results in high **paternity certainty** for the male.)

- In addition to the sex of the parent, other factors determine the extent of parental investment. **Altricial** animals are born relatively undeveloped compared with **precocial** ones, and are less able to care for themselves. In **r-selected** species, in which parents can offer little assistance, either because they are to small or short lived, or because the environment is too variable, many offspring are produced but parental care is minimal or absent. In **K-selected** species, living in harsh environments where survival depends on competing successfully against others, parental care is common. Having altricial young and being a K-selected species lead to increased parental care by both sexes.

- **Parental investment theory** predicts that females will invest more in their offspring postnatally (after birth) because they have invested more prenatally (before birth). When males are phylogenetically prepared to provide parental care, they often do so. Both male and female pigeons produce crop milk to feed the young, and male seahorses have a brood pouch in which the young develop prior to hatching. Role reversal and sharing of roles can occur in species in which neither sex is committed (by their anatomy, physiology or instinctive behaviour) to parental investment.

- It is not always the parents who provide care for the young. In cuckoos it is an innocent foster parent, unaware that its parental care is raising an entirely unrelated individual. In this case, the foster parent cannot instruct the young cuckoo in areas of species-specific behaviours. Higher primates and carnivores have complex behavioural repertoires in which their responses and strategies are too varied, and situation specific, to be inherited. These species must acquire their behavioural responses whilst under the guidance of their parents during a period of infancy. In mammals such as lions, co-operative predatory behaviour is learned as part of the group, and in meerkats, individual, unrelated tutors may be responsible for instructing the young in foraging techniques.

- **Human** females, like other mammals, are phylogenetically prepared for parental care. Human males can invest in parental care as children are highly altricial. Males who invest in helping their female would reap significant benefits in terms of offspring survival. Their prolonged investment in the female may have evolved as mate guarding if females disguised the time of their oestrus.

- Male courtship in humans, with an emphasis on indicators of wealth and the ability to provide, may have evolved to enable females to select males who could assist with parental care.

MATING STRATEGIES AND SOCIAL

ORGANISATION

Introduction and overview

A *strategy* is a behaviour pattern which an individual employs to increase his or her fitness. A *mating strategy*, therefore, is the behavioural plan an individual uses to raise fitness through the successful pursuit of a mate. Mating strategies are most easily defined by the number of mates an individual has in one breeding season.

The aim of this chapter is to explain why different mating strategies exist – that is, why some individuals have only one mate whilst others have many. Each strategy has both advantages and disadvantages, and these will be discussed from the view point of males and females. The influence of different mating strategies on social organisation and parental care is also examined.

Mating strategies

We shall define mating strategies by the number of partners each sex maintains, either serially (one after the other) or simultaneously (at the same time). A male could have one mate or many. Similarly, a female could have one mate or many. Thus, there are four basic mating strategies as shown in Box 6.1 *Monogamy* is where one male and one female form a pair which is exclusive of others. All other mating strategies are *polygamous* –

that is, they involve more than one member of one or both sexes. In *polygyny*, one male mates with many females, whilst in *polyandry* one female mates with many males. Where both sexes have multiple partners, the strategy is called *promiscuity*.

Monogamy

As noted above, monogamy is a mating strategy in which each male and female pair is exclusive. The pair may bond for life (*perennial monogamy*) as swans do, or individuals may court a new mate each year (*annual monogamy*), as seen in robins. Where environmental pressures are harsh (through high predation or limited food supply), or where parental care is labour intensive, monogamy is the norm. It is not surprising, therefore, that 90% of bird species are monogamous (Lack, 1968).

Monogamy, however, is not without its problems. Males, who produce vast amounts of sperm to fertilise many females, could benefit from 'cheating'. Females are at risk as they cannot be sure that they are the single mate of any male, or that he will stay to care for the young. Males, by contrast, risk *cuckoldry* (being duped by the female into raising young which they did not father). They are less sure than females which offspring are theirs (as they do not lay the eggs or give birth to the young). To use Trivers' (1972) phrase, males have *low paternity certainty*. However, Gross and Shine (1981) suggest that lack of paternity certainty cannot prevent the evolution of parental care in males, because investing in just a *few* of their own offspring would accrue sufficient genetic benefit for selection pressure to favour such care.

Virtually any care the males offered in a harsh environment would improve reproductive success, but it would also improve the fitness of competitors if a male unwit-

Box 6.1 Possible mating strategies

| | | Number of males in partnership | |
		1	2+
Number of females in partnership	1	Monogamy	Polyandry
	2+	Polygyny	Promiscuity

Mono: = one; poly: = many; andry: = male; gyny: = female.

53

For both sexes, the advantage of monogamy is clear – the young have a better chance of survival with two parents fending for them. Monogamous males should evolve if the increase in offspring survival offsets the cost of cuckoldry. A male can reduce the risk of the female straying by defending a territory in a desirable location, or by denying other males access to her. The latter tactic is seen in the herring gull (*Larus argentatus*). The

Figure 6.1   Threatening postures in territorial herring gulls (*Larus argentatus*)

male herring gull's territory serves initially as an arena for courtship and mating, then as a site for nest building and rearing the young. It contains no useful resources such as food, but is vigorously defended. This protects his female from the attention of other males whilst she is on the nest, but is a behaviour which could be risky. The males only benefit if they survive to help rear their young or to breed again next season. Much of the territorial aggression, therefore, appears as displays (as described in Chapter 2, page 17). 'Grass pulling' and 'upright threat' postures are generally sufficient to deter neighbouring males from incursions into another's territory (Figure 6.1).

tingly reared another male's young. There are therefore two issues facing males: the net gain from an individual helping its own progeny, and the cost of raising the fitness of others by caring for young which are not the individual's own. Box 6.2 explores how males can avoid cuckoldry.

Females also employ tactics to assure the fidelity of their mates. By synchronising their breeding cycles,

they reduce the risk of egg predation (as predator damage is diluted; see Chapter 3, page 26) and the risk of cheating or desertion by their mate. A female is more likely to retain a monogamous mate if she is receptive on the same day as all other females, then there are no fertile neighbours to stray to! Synchronisation of receptivity is brought about in the herring gull by *communal courtship*. Darling (1938) proposed that seeing and hearing birds in the colony courting stimulated sexual activity in other individuals (see Chapter 9, page 82). It is beneficial for each *individual* female for mating to occur simultaneously, to retain her faithful partner, so the *species* is characterised by a monogamous mating system.

Another tactic employed by females to counter the tendency of males to cheat is to demand a vast commitment of time and effort during courtship. The chance of her mate finding and courting another female is then much reduced. A good example of this is shown in Box 6.3.

Among British birds, the great crested grebe (*Podiceps cristatus*) has probably the most extravagant mating display (see Chapter 11, page 103). This monogamous species begins each year with a prolonged period of courtship rituals. The grebe's exotic plumage, with long ear tufts and a ruff, is used to good effect in the postures which form its 'dance routines'. By engaging the continuous attention of the male, the female grebe reduces the risk of his infidelity. The male and female grebe repeat parts of the display throughout the breeding season, reinforcing the pair bond. The males invest heavily in this bond, so are 'trapped' by their efforts into monogamy.

Finally, it should be noted that, whilst the species described in this section are 'socially monogamous', there is some evidence that not all matings are confined to the pair. There may be advantages for both males and females in engaging in extra bond copulations. For example, Birkhead and Møller (1992) suggest that in apparently monogamous species such as the blue-tit (*Parus caeruleus*), sexual promiscuity is common.

Polygyny

Polygamous mating systems involve multiple pairings. As noted earlier, in *polygyny*, one male mates with many females. This may arise as a series of separate meetings (*serial polygyny*), or relatively permanent groups of females may stay with a male (*simultaneous polygyny*). Because the parental investment of males is smaller and often shorter than that of females, they can have simultaneous ongoing breeding attempts. Females, because of phylogenetic specialisations and shortage of gametes (See Chapter 5, page 44), can rarely do this. Since having more mates would enhance male reproductive success, we would expect males to have multiple mates whenever possible, and females to have multiple mates only in exceptional circumstances.

According to Emlen and Oring (1977), polygyny occurs where it is economical for males either to monopolise resources (*resource defence polygyny*) or to monopolise the females themselves (*female defence polygyny*). In other species, males defend a symbolic territory which contains neither resources nor females, but is attractive (perhaps because of the ability of the male to maintain such a territory). Because males compete for these status symbols, this is called *male dominance polygyny*. Finally, in some species, there is no territorial or female defence at all; males compete directly with each other for each female, a strategy known as *scramble competition polygyny*. In this last strategy, it is likely that females, as well as males, have multiple mates, so this may more accurately be described as promiscuity.

RESOURCE DEFENCE POLYGYNY

One attraction of a polygynous mate over a monogamous one is evident in *resource defence polygyny*, where males compete to control scarce environmental resources. Females select mates occupying high-quality areas offering nest sites, protection from predators, or food. Females will tend to congregate at more favourable areas so it is easy for a male to monopolise a group. For example, female impala (*Aepyceros melampus*) will congregate if a male is defending a rich grazing area. The females then remain in his territory, so the male has effectively traded good grass for sex.

FEMALE DEFENCE POLYGYNY

In *female defence polygyny*, males are not competing for environmental resources, but for direct access to females. Males may patrol large areas containing dispersed females, or may locate females which have already congregated. Examples of the latter include female gorillas, who clump to avoid predation, and lionesses, which form groups to enhance hunting success. These ready-made groups are easier for powerful males to monopolise. The females are then either seasonally or temporarily defended by the male, and are referred to as his *harem*.

Female defence polygyny is practised by red deer stags (*Cervus elaphus*), which compete to acquire a harem of hinds (female deer). They then expend effort retaining them and expelling other stags. The risks of such encounters are great, not just from injury but because onlookers may sneak copulations with the hinds whilst the harem master is engaged in defence or mating. The benefits to the male, however, are abundant since he has exclusive access to fertile females, and any costs associated with defending them are countered by the certainty that they will be bearing his offspring.

MALE DOMINANCE POLYGYNY

Male dominance polygyny arises when disputes between competing males occur prior to courtship. Males establish a dominance hierarchy which allows high-ranking individuals preferential access to females. This polygynous strategy is illustrated by the ruff (*Philomanchus pugnax*), a wading bird found on inland waters and meadows in Britain. During the breeding season, the males acquire a 'ruff' of Elizabethan style, which is displayed to attract females. Dominant males defend territories in the middle of a raised area of ground, which is called the *lek*. Here, females watch males court, and select central males if possible. Subordinate males, with pale ruffs, are confined to the outer areas of the lek. However, these 'satellites' wait for females, 'sneaking' opportunities to copulate when dominant males are occupied and a female is unattended.

For females, the benefit of mating with central males is not resource based. These males offer nothing but competitive genes and their sons, too, should occupy central lek sites. Females are therefore selecting dominant males in line with the *'sexy son hypothesis'* (see Chapter 4, page 38). Males will preferentially occupy central sites where they will attract most females. If they cannot occupy these sites, the next best tactic is to attempt sneak copulations. The risk for satellite males is high, because dominant males may attack. However, the gains achieved guarantee survival of satellite male genes.

These two tactics, of dominant and satellite males, coexist at each lek. Both strategies are successfully deployed within the same populations, so this is therefore an example of an evolutionarily stable strategy (see Chapter 1, page 9).

ADVANTAGES OF POLYGYNY FOR MALES

In any polygynous strategy, males will vary in their breeding success. This inequality is well illustrated by the elephant seal (*Mirounga angustirostris*), for which less than 10% of the males may father 90% of the young, whilst some never mate at all. Even greater disparity is seen in the relative success of male turkeys (*Meleagris gallopavo*). For the dominant males, the advantage is clear: they have more mates and increase their individual fitness. When ecological factors permit females to rear offspring alone, polygyny represents a considerably better strategy for males than monogamy. But are there any other advantages, particularly ones which would affect subordinate males? Low-ranking males may gain by sneaking copulations with females which more dominant individuals, or larger groups such as leks, may attract. Box 6.4 suggests some reasons why males may congregate into leks.

ADVANTAGES OF POLYGYNY FOR FEMALES

The advantage of polygyny for (at least some) males is clear – they get to mate more. But what are the advantages for females? In female defence polygyny and male dominance polygyny, females gain access to superior mates. These preferred males demonstrate their supremacy either by defending the females or dominating other males. In resource defence polygyny, a 'popular male' maintains this status because his resources assist in the successful rearing of young, which enhances the females' fitness. A polygynous female must share her superior mate or his resources with others, thus limiting their value, whereas she could have exclusive access to the resources of a less preferable male. What dictates the best strategy for a female facing this choice? Box 6.5 suggests a possible answer.

Polyandry

Polyandry is like polygyny with sex role reversal, because here one female mates with many males. Where courtship occurs in polyandrous species, males choose from displaying females. Males, like females in polygyny, should select mates with good genes and/or resources. In polyandry, it is the males' parental care which is the scarce resource, as it is this that guarantees the survival of the young. The males are investing more, and are therefore more choosy.

Unsurprisingly, polyandry is rare, the most well-known example being the honey bee (*Apis mellifera*) (in which a single queen mates with many drones). This is called a *eusocial system* – that is, one in which individuals other than the mother, including sterile castes, help to rear the young and there are overlapping generations (see Chapter 8, page 74). However, it is an atypical example of polyandry because it is not the father but more often the sisters and other colony members who rear the offspring. Eusociality is uncommon outside of the insects, being restricted to naked mole rats (*Heterocephalus glaber*) amongst the mammals. (Eusociality is discussed further in Chapter 8). A more straightforward example of polyandry is the phalarope, a sea bird found off the coast of Britain. In phalaropes, males select their colourful mate by her courtship behaviour. After mating, the female lays her eggs in a nest built by the male, then leaves to search for another mate. The male, who is speckled for camouflage, incubates the eggs and raises the nestlings alone. Here it is the male, rather than the female, which is specialised for parental care.

In Chapter 4, the activities of polyandrous jacanas were described. Female jacanas, which are the larger sex, compete for small stocky males who, on account of their size, can hide from predators and survive whilst incubating. The female mates with several males and

> **Box 6.4   The advantages of lekking (Krebs & Davies, 1987)**
>
> - Increases efficiency of attracting females
> - Reduces predation (important as courtship displays could attract predators)
> - Display sites may be limited so have to be shared or fought over
> - Preferred display sites, in areas frequented by females, may be limited
> - Females may prefer clumped males, either to assist mate choice or to reduce risk of predation
>
> It should be noted that these advantages of lekking are all *theoretical*. None of the suggestions is, as yet, supported by empirical evidence.

Box 6.5 The polygyny threshold model (Orians, 1969)

This model suggests that, where males possess territories of equal quality, females gain by having a monogamous mate (which would help them care for offspring). However, where males occupy territories of very different qualities, females can achieve greater reproductive success by sharing a good territory with others. They will therefore enter into polygyny and forego the benefit of male parental assistance with the young.

The polygyny threshold model is based on the following assumptions:

a that female reproductive success increases with territory quality;

b that polygynous males occupy better territories; and

c that monogamous males offer more care to the female or her young than polygynous males.

Verner and Willson (1966) surveyed the mating strategies of 291 species of North American birds. They found that only nineteen were generally polygynous or promiscuous, of which thirteen lived in habitats where food was patchy, so territory quality could be very variable. This supports Orians' prediction, because it is only in those species in which some males would be preferable to others that a polygynous strategy is found.

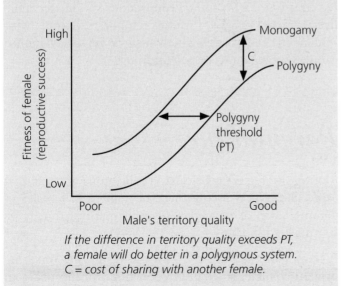

If the difference in territory quality exceeds PT, a female will do better in a polygynous system. C = cost of sharing with another female.

lays her eggs in their nests within her territory. She plays no further part in parenting other than to replace the eggs if they are lost. This polyandrous mating strategy has evolved in response to environmental pressures of high predation and limited nest sites. As many eggs are lost to predators, they need to be replaced quickly. Females must spread eggs around to reduce predation, and generate new eggs quickly, so they need to have many nests and be freed of parental duties to feed themselves. This is achieved by polyandry.

Promiscuity

Promiscuity is where both sexes have many partners. This is superficially most beneficial to males, as their minimal parental investment in each breeding attempt prescribes no limit to the number of offspring they could father. Bateman (1948) has shown that the reproductive success of males in *Drosophila*, the fruit fly, is linked to the number of copulations (see Chapter 4, page 35). Therefore, in male fruit flies, more sex means more offspring, whereas female flies store sperm and so do not need to mate more than once. For a female, unnecessary mating attempts detract from her survival, because they take up extra energy and time when she could be feeding, and she risks damage by vigorous males or from predators. It is therefore a beneficial strategy for female fruit flies to mate only once. The reproductive success of females is not restricted by opportunities to copulate but by their limited resources, initially in terms of eggs and then in terms of the cost of nourishing a growing egg or embryo. A bird's egg may weigh as much as 30% of her body weight (Lack, 1968), yet the weight of a sperm is almost immeasurably small by comparison. However, some females do engage in multiple matings. This may be a strategy to exploit *sperm competition*, as described in Box 6.6.

Social organisation

We must be aware that social organisation (the structure of groups of animals which live together) depends on many factors, such as food source, environmental hazards, and predators. Sociality (living in groups)

Box 6.6   Sperm competition

A possible advantage of having several consecutive mates for females could be *sperm competition*, a kind of internal race in which the most fit sperm wins. This provides the female with a simple and effective strategy for answering the question, which male is best? She simply tries them all and lets their gametes fight it out! Of course, gamete viability is not necessarily related to the vigour or success of adults, but even so, for sons inheriting the capacity to produce fit sperm, it is still an advantage in its own right.

Evidence for sperm competition is provided by Parker's (1978) experiments with dung flies (*Scatophaga sterocoraria*). Male dung flies defend inviting cow pats to entice potential partners. The arrival of a female causes competition between males, and a resident may be dislodged by an intruder, either before or after copulation. From the female's point of view, the aggressor (the second mate) is more attractive. His sons (inheriting his ability to displace competitors) are more likely to pass on their own, and therefore her, genes.

Parker's results showed that if a particular male mated first, his sperm could be displaced, but if he mated second, his sperm would win. Females cannot choose their mates because they cannot avoid the males' attention, but evolution (through sperm competition) ensures their eggs are fertilised by the sperm from the fittest male.

Even in the absence of sperm competition, a female who gathers sperm from a diversity of partners would increase the variability of her offspring, increasing the likelihood of some of them surviving if conditions change. For example, female cuttlefish (*Sepia officinalis*) collect sperm from different males and store them. A female may not be able to recall which sperm was from which male, or to select which ones fertilise her eggs, but she can still gain an advantage through offspring diversity.

being solitary, but this has risks of its own. A single animal must be more vigilant, forage for all its own food and defend its resources. The advantages and disadvantages of sociality are discussed in detail in Chapter 9.

Finding a mate is therefore only one of many needs an animal must satisfy to raise its fitness. Living in a group makes finding a mate easy, but the luxury of mating is one an animal must defer if more basic needs (of food, water, or safety) are unfulfilled. These are life-threatening issues which dictate a level of co-operation or solitude which will maximise survival. None the less, reproduction does have some effect on social groupings. In most species, for at least part of the year, their social organisation is linked to their mating strategy.

Individuals who are monogamous form stable pairs. In species such as the grebe (*Podiceps cristatus*), solitary, dispersed mates may be sought and intensively courted (see Chapter 11, page 103). Other species which pair bond may court in large mixed groups, such as in herring gull colonies (see Chapter 9, page 80). The breeding colony may then remain together to rear the young.

In polygynous and polyandrous species, the 'choosing' sex is drawn to groups of potential mates, to make its choice. Display grounds, such as leks, provide an arena for courtship. In polygynous species, two other groups may form, *bachelor herds* of young, unpaired 'choosers', and *harems*, the females associated with a successful male. Following the birth of the offspring, a third group, the *nursery herd*, may be formed, consisting of the females and their offspring. All three of these groupings are illustrated by species such as zebra and red deer (see Figure 6.2). Promiscuous species generally live in mixed groups, forming temporary liaisons with smaller mating groups which may be relatively monogamous, polygynous or polyandrous.

Parental care

Mating strategies have clear implications for parental care. The typical involvement of males and females in parental care, associated with each mating strategy, is summarised in Box 6.7.

A monogamous male can assure paternity by watching over his female, so that any contribution he makes to rearing the young is certain to increase his own, rather

carries many benefits, such as protection from predators, increased chance of finding and defending a food source, and preservation of a good territory. However, group living also has costs. 'Safety in numbers' may become 'conspicuous to predators', food must be shared, and there is an increased risk of the spread of infectious diseases. These problems may be avoided by

Figure 6.2   The zebra (*Equus zebra*) – a polygynous species

than his competitor's, fitness. Male fidelity is likely because he has committed so much to the pair bond. Any gains which could be reaped by leaving (the possibility of finding another female able to rear his young) are outweighed by the costs of leaving (risk of losing the offspring which already exist). The longer a female can retain her mate, the lower the risk of his desertion, since these costs are amplified.

Interestingly, a female's fidelity is assured by the same logic. Her initial investment is greater, hence her need to prevent early male desertion. Extensive parental care can be seen in monogamous species like the grebe in

Box 6.7	**Mating strategies and parental care**		
		Number of males	
		1	2
Number of females	1	Monogamy Both parents care	Polyandry Males care
	2	Polygyny Females care	Promiscuity Neither cares

The table shows the common patterns of parental care demonstrated by individuals employing each mating strategy.

which the adults take joint responsibility for incubation, feeding and protecting the young and even carry them on their backs. The roles of the male and female only diverge if they raise a second brood. The father than takes responsibility for the first brood whilst the mother cares for the second. The effectiveness of monogamy as a strategy for parental care can be seen by comparing the reproductive success of species which are sometimes polygynous. The number of surviving young is greater, on average, when two parents provide care than when only one does (Askenmo, 1984) (see Chapter 5, page 47).

In polygynous and polyandrous species, parental care is usually offered by the sex which chooses. This is the females in polygynous species and males in polyandrous animals. A polygynous male must ensure that the females he is defending are faithful so that they will offer care to *his* progeny, especially as he is providing them with territory for safety or food, which he is defending at a cost. He achieves this by rigorously protecting them from invading males and by preventing them from wandering. For example, lions (*Panthera leo*) are polygynous, and males will fight off or kill intruders. A new pride male will even kill existing cubs in order to ensure that the lionesses are able to give birth to their young more quickly (see Chapter 7, page 67). Females of the polyandrous phalaropes (sea birds) ensure that the male they hope will raise their young is not copulating with another female by evicting him if he is absent for too long (Trivers 1972)!

Promiscuity tends to reduce the likelihood of care by either sex. The males, and to lesser extent the females, cannot be sure about the parentage of their offspring. A female can at least be certain whether any particular youngster is hers, but cannot guarantee which male sired it. Promiscuous females cannot selectively invest in progeny with the 'best' father, unlike a monogamous mother. Males in this situation cannot begin to ascertain paternity. This uncertainty often leads both sexes to desert. Parental care is minimal and, where it exists, it is offered by the female.

Human mating systems

The difference between male and female reproductive capacity, which underlies the belief that they should attempt to employ different strategies, is supported by studies of humans. The record number of children

Box 6.8   Differences in the sexual behaviour of human males and females (Alcock, 1993)

Trait	Male	Female
Threshold for sexual arousal	Low	High
Desire for sexual variety	High	Lower
Adultery	More frequent	Less frequent
Rape	Occasional	Almost never
Concern for mate's sexual fidelity	Very high	Moderate

fathered by one man is 888, the maximum for a woman is a mere sixty-nine (and was only that high as a consequence of an unusual rate of triplets). Alcock (1993) makes several predictions, based on the difference in restraint on genetic success for males and females, which are shown in Box 6.8.

If male reproductive success depends on the quantity (rather than the quality) of his mates, we would expect males to have been selected to seek a variety of females, since women are fertile at infrequent intervals. This preference for varied mates is readily demonstrated in animals, and is referred to as the *Coolidge effect*. This is named after the American President who, when told that cockerels would only engage in repeated copulations if they were not with the same female, asked for Mrs Coolidge to be told! Symons (1979) suggests that this tendency of males to seek a range of partners, but for females to seek fidelity, is inherited in humans. He defends this with observations of homosexual partnerships. Gay men, according to Symons, tend to have a string of partners, whereas lesbian women form lasting, faithful relationships (see Chapter 15, page 145). Even though homosexuality is not a genetically successful strategy, the underlying genetically driven traits, of variety versus stability, appear to persist. This suggests that males tend toward polygyny while females try to be monogamous.

Western society assumes that, for people, monogamy is the rule. Marriage and the efforts to preserve fidelity and continuity of relationships abound. Even though approximately 30% of marriages fail, people continue to commit to each other, and our expectation is of lasting, faithful relationships. Is this expectation reasonable, based on animal models? Certainly, we have highly altricial young, who demand prolonged care, but does that necessarily demand monogamy? Like herring gulls in colonies, people who live in close proximity to each other are more likely to succumb to extramarital affairs. According to Birkhead and Møller (1992), the incidence of children who are the product of such relationships is 30% higher in high-rise flats than in other accommodation. In this instance, we, like the blue-tits described on page 54, are being socially monogamous but sexually promiscuous.

In some human societies, however, polygyny is the norm. Croutier (1989) describes not just the historical harems of the wealthy in the Ottoman Empire, India and China, but also the ordinary harems of Ottoman, Moslem, and some Jewish and Christian households prior to the twentieth century. She also describes the existence today of legal polygyny in areas of the Middle East, Africa and India, as well as in Mormon families in the USA where *plural marriage* (having more than one wife) is illegal but common.

Conclusions

Mating strategies are adaptive solutions for maximising individual fitness. A male or female is best served by that strategy which will ensure the greatest number of high-quality surviving offspring. This, in turn, depends not just on an animal's species, but on its sex, status and the activities of others. Furthermore, mating strategies can have profound effects upon social organisation and parental care.

SUMMARY

- A **mating strategy** is a behavioural plan for obtaining one or more mates, which has evolved to increase fitness by maximising the reproductive success of an individual. Within a species, most individuals tend to employ the same strategy. This has previously been referred to as a **mating system**.

- Different mating strategies offer different advantages. A strategy can directly affect the **number of mates**, which tends to help **males** as their reproduction is limited by **access to fertile partners**. **Females** are most likely to benefit from strategies which provide access to key **resources** or **high-quality mates**, because their reproduction is limited by egg supply and ability to care for the young.

- The four mating strategies are **monogamy** (1 male:1 female), **polygyny** (1 male:many females), **polyandry** (many males:1 female) and **promiscuity** (many males:many females).
- Monogamy provides help from the male to assist the female in care of the young, raising the fitness of both parents. The pair may bond for life (**perennial monogamy**), as swans do, or may court an new partner each year (**annual monogamy**), as seen in robins.
- In monogamous relationships, males risk **cuckoldry** (caring for the offspring of other males) and females risk male **desertion**. **Paternity certainty** is raised by **mate guarding** or **territoriality**. Desertion is reduced by **synchronous breeding** and **extensive courtship**.
- **Polygamous** strategies, involving multiple mates, include polygyny, polyandry and promiscuity. In polygyny there may be separate meetings between a single male and a series of different females (**serial polygyny**) or relatively permanent groups of females may stay with a male (**simultaneous polygyny**).
- In **resource defence polygyny**, males compete to control scarce resources which will attract females, as seen in impala. In **female defence polygyny**, males (such as red deer stags) defend a **harem** of females, denying access to other males.
- **Male dominance polygyny** arises when males fight for **dominant** status, as seen in birds such as turkeys and ruffs. Males may indicate dominance at a **lek** by defending symbolic **territories** (which contain no useful resources). Females choose to mate with high-ranking males.
- In **scramble competition polygyny**, males do not compete for resources or defend territories, they simply fight over females directly.
- Polygyny is good for some males because they have **access to more mates**. Other males may defer to allow kin (brothers) to breed (gaining an increase in inclusive fitness), or because they are subordinate and have no choice. Even subordinates may gain from the females other males have attracted if they can **sneak opportunities to copulate**.
- Females gain access to mates with superior genes

(sexy son hypothesis) or resources. The **polygyny threshold model** suggests that females can gain from monogamous males which offer assistance, but may gain more by sharing a polygynous male in a better territory.

- Polyandry is rare because females generally make larger initial contributions to each offspring so should be reluctant to leave them. Advantages may arise in habitats where nestling mortality is high, so abundant egg laying could counteract losses due to environmental hazards or predation. This accounts for polyandry in birds such as the jacana.
- Promiscuity is beneficial to males because their reproduction is limited by opportunity, not by gamete supply. Disadvantages to females include costs of time, energy, risk of injury and vulnerability, but gains may arise through **sperm competition** or **variability of offspring**.
- Monogamous pairs are formed and maintained by courtship. A mate may be selected from solitary or social individuals and **pairs** may be dispersed or may stay within a group (e.g. a **colony**). Great crested grebes and herring gulls illustrate these two arrangements respectively.
- Polygyny and polyandry often result in temporary clusters during courtship – for instance, polygynous harems and leks. In both of these groups, **dominant** males mate most, and subordinates may sneak copulations.
- Associated with polygyny, other groupings may occur. Unpaired males may form **bachelor herds** and mothers with young may congregate into **nursery herds**. These individuals gain foraging and defence advantages by grouping.
- **Parental care** patterns show a close relationship to mating strategy. Monogamy tends to result in **biparental care**, polygyny in **maternal care**, polyandry in **paternal care** and promiscuity in no care or maternal care only.
- **Humans**, biologically, show gamete and phylogenetic specialisations from which predictions about mating strategies can be made. Males, producing lots of low-investment sperm, would benefit most from polygyny. For females, with few eggs, long gestation and suckling, reproduction is limited by mate quality and resources. They should seek monogamous mates, who will assist in care, or wealthy ones, who can provide resources. Some evidence supports these predictions.
- Monogamy is the social norm in Western societies, although statistics suggest that many of these relationship are neither permanent nor exclusive.

Many marriages fail and children are not always conceived within the monogamous partnership.

- Some human societies are polygynous.

Historically, wealthy males in many cultures have kept harems, and today polygyny is still practised, both legally and illegally, across the world.

PARENT–OFFSPRING CONFLICT

Introduction and overview

Issues addressed in Chapters 4, 5 and 6 suggest that sexual reproduction is as much about conflict as co-operation. However, the conflicts discussed have been predominantly between *adult* members of a species. This chapter examines evolutionary explanations for *parent–offspring* conflict and represents the final part of the 'Reproductive Strategies' section of this book.

While there are many common and overlapping interests between parents and offspring, there are also some important points of divergence. The conflict has been analysed from the point of view of the interests of adults and the young. The most common conflict arises when the offspring, in trying to maximise its own interests, attempts to manipulate the feeding parent into providing extra resources. In extreme cases this may lead to siblicide (killing one's brothers and sisters) or, after parental care has ceased, the killing and eating of a parent. Conversely, if a parent inherits young that are not his (or her) own, the existence of the offspring may be counter to the future reproductive interests of the parent, and infanticide (the killing of children) may result. This may also occur in the case of direct offspring, where numbers are 'fine tuned' to match available resources.

In this chapter, an attempt is made to explain the genetic basis of the tension which exists between the demands of offspring and the future reproductive success of parents.

Background to the conflict

According to Trivers (1974), the basis of parent–offspring conflict is genetic asymmetry. A parent is equally related (50%) to each of its offspring, but an offspring is twice as related to itself (100%) as to its siblings (50%). The conflict is due to the mother having other potential offspring to raise. She will view all her offspring as roughly equal and will best further her reproductive success by producing more and sharing her time and energy between them. The infant, however, is more self-centred. It will have some interest in the welfare of its siblings, but will be far more concerned with itself. Offspring therefore tend to favour a longer period of parental investment than the parent is selected to give, and conflict results. This dispute can be seen most clearly in weaning conflict.

Weaning conflict

Weaning conflict occurs in mammals when a lactating mother tries to wean her offspring off milk, while they attempt to prolong the period of suckling (Grier & Burk, 1992). Studies have shown that the period of lactation is enormously demanding physiologically on the female, and she cannot begin setting aside body reserves for the next litter until she has weaned the current one (Clutton-Brock et al., 1989).

Figure 7.1 shows parent–offspring conflict with changes in the ratio of cost to parent/benefit to offspring, as proposed by Trivers (1974). When the offspring is very young, the benefits of parental care are so large relative to the costs that the parent gains more by feeding the offspring than by ignoring it. As the offspring grows, the *cost–benefit* (C/B) *ratio* increases and it will eventually reach a point where it can do as well on its own as it can by receiving parental help. At this point (where the C/B ratio = 1), the parent will have been selected to avoid any further investment in the offspring, since such investment would decrease the total number of offspring surviving. However, because of the genetic asymmetry mentioned above, it is advantageous for the current offspring to become independent only when the C/B ratio has risen to 2. We should not expect any conflict beyond this point as each of the offspring has some genetic investment in its brothers or sisters. Independence becomes desirable for the offspring because its inclusive fitness (gene transmission

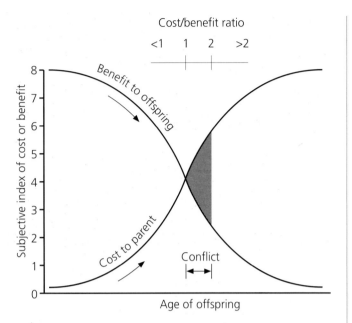

Figure 7.1   **Changes in the ratio of cost to parent/benefit to offspring as the age of the offspring increases (Trivers, 1974). Parent–offspring conflict occurs during the time represented by the shaded area, when the parent is expected to attempt weaning and the offspring is expected to resist**

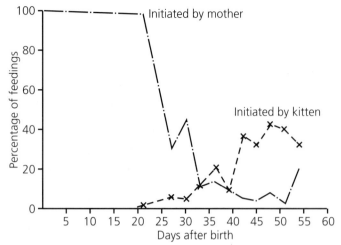

Figure 7.2   **Weaning conflict in cats (*Felis catus*) as illustrated by changes in mother-young interactions during the post-natal period. There is a distinctive shift from parent to offspring in who initiates care (Schneirla et al., 1963)**

by the individual and by relatives carrying the same genes) is best served by the mother's production of new siblings. During the time represented by the shaded area on Figure 7.1, the parent is expected to attempt weaning and the offspring is expected to resist.

The changing C/B ratio of parental care can be seen in the interactions between cats (*Felis catus*) and their kittens (Figure 7.2). Female cats initiate almost all nursing bouts from the time their kittens are born until the young are approximately twenty days old (Schneirla et al., 1963). Between twenty and thirty days after birth, kittens and mothers initiate feedings with equal frequencies. However, soon after day 30, suckling is initiated almost entirely by the kittens, and mothers begin to avoid and actively discourage nursing by their offspring (Goodenough et al., 1993). A similar situation has been observed in rhesus monkeys (Hinde, 1977).

In species in which most siblings are half-siblings, parent–offspring conflict would be expected to last longer (until the C/B ratio equals 4). This may be the reason for the particularly intense parent–offspring conflict in langur monkeys (*Presbytis entellus*), for which male takeovers are frequent (Trivers, 1985).

Who wins the conflict?

On theoretical grounds, there is no expected winner of parent–offspring conflict, although arguments have been advanced in favour of both parents (see Box 7.1) and young. In their attempts to manipulate each other, we would expect adaptation and counteradaptation to occur, as described for predator–prey arms races in Chapter 3. However, in the case of parent–offspring conflict, the competition would be expected to be less severe because they share genes.

OFFSPRING MANIPULATION OF PARENTS

Parents are physically superior to offspring, more experienced, and they control the resources at issue. Offspring therefore usually employ *psychological* tactics and attempt to *induce* more investment than the parent is selected to give. Trivers (1974) argued that selection should favour parental attentiveness to signals from offspring because the offspring are best at evaluating their own needs. As adults become increasingly proficient at assessing the needs of their young, Trivers predicted that successive offspring would have to employ more convincing tactics to elicit additional care from their experienced parents.

Offspring typically become less helpless and vulnerable with age, so parents will have been strongly selected to respond negatively to signals emitted by the offspring the older it gets. During parent–offspring conflict,

Box 7.1 Parental manipulation of offspring

Richard Alexander (1974) disagreed with Trivers' description of conflict between parents and offspring, claiming that parents are heavily favoured to win the contest. His argument was based on the fact that most offspring eventually become parents. An offspring that successfully manipulated its parents when young would lose out when it became a parent because its offspring would inherit the ability to manipulate. Over the long run, therefore, the most successful reproducers would be parents which did not get manipulated. However, it is possible that genes exist for the superior tactic of being successfully manipulative offspring when young and successfully manipulative parents when old.

Richard Dawkins (1989) has pointed out that Alexander's argument is flawed because it rests on the assumption of a genetic asymmetry which is not really there. There is no fundamental *genetic* asymmetry between parents and offspring, the relatedness being 50% whichever way round we look at it. Dawkins claims that the argument could just as easily be made with the parent and offspring actions reversed and then the opposite conclusion would be reached. Alexander's prediction of routine parental victory has also not stood up to examination with mathematical models (Parker, 1985). Therefore, it appears that the most likely outcome is a level of investment intermediate between the best situation for parents and offspring.

Figure 7.3   Psychological manipulation of a parent by its offspring, as shown by the begging behaviour of a young herring gull (*Larus argentatus*). By stooping and withdrawing its head, the gull gives the impression of smaller size. This act of regression fools the parent into thinking that the offspring is younger and more vulnerable than it really is, thus inducing the parent to continue feeding

biting their own wings. This may convince the parents that withholding food will have dire consequences for the health of the chick (Trivers, 1985). Similar temper tantrums have been observed in chimpanzees (*Pan troglodytes*).

Generally, adaptations in offspring would be expected to include faking symptoms of hunger/need and suppressing signals indicating satiety. This deception should, in turn, be counteracted by parental evolution of discriminatory powers to detect the *true* state of the offspring. Either or neither participant may achieve outright success.

therefore, the offspring may be selected to revert to the gestures and actions of an earlier stage of development in order to induce parental care. In short, it may be tempted to *regress* when under stress (Trivers, 1985). Young herring gulls (*Larus argentatus*), for example, although virtually fully grown by about three months, still manage to obtain food from their parents by concealing their size. Begging behaviour involves the young gull stooping and withdrawing its head to give the impression of smaller size (Figure 7.3), inducing the parent to continue feeding (Cartwright, 1996).

Temper tantrums may be used by youngsters to threaten the parent by suggesting that the offspring may actually harm itself. Young pelicans (*Pelecanus erythrorhyncus*), for example, sometimes indulge in convulsions, throwing themselves on the ground and

Timing of the conflict

The nature and extent of parent–offspring conflict are influenced by the age of the parent and that of the offspring. In general, the older a parent, the less will be its future reproductive success and the lower will be the cost of current investment, measured in terms of future offspring (Trivers, 1985). This should result in a longer period of parental investment and reduced conflict with offspring. In Californian gulls (*Larus californicus*), for example, rates of nest attendance, territorial defence and feeding the chicks all increase with parental age (Figure 7.4).

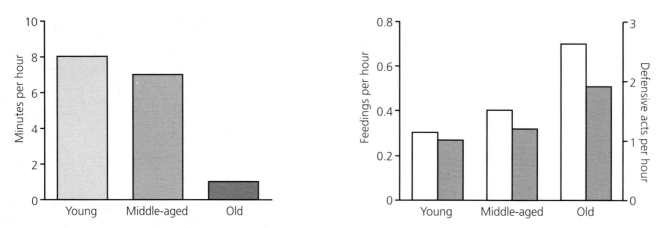

Figure 7.4   Parental investment as a function of age in the Californian gull (*Larus californicus*). (a) The average minutes per hour in which neither parent attended the nest as a function of age. Young are 3–5 years old, middle-aged are 7–9 years and old are 12–18 years. (b) The average number of times per hour in which the parents fed chicks (unshaded bars) or engaged in territorial defence (shaded bars). All three measures show increasing parental investment with increasing parental age. Based on Trivers (1985)

PRENATAL CONFLICT

During pregnancy, the mother has to share her bodily resources with the fetus and her best interests are served by providing adequate, though not excessive, resources. The mother must consider her own state of health, as well as her future reproductive potential, and retain some resources to safeguard her well-being (Trevathan, 1987). The fetus's interests are also in not damaging the mother's state of health during the pregnancy (or subsequent parental feeding period), but it may still attempt to demand more resources than the mother will be adapted to supply.

It has been suggested that 'morning sickness' and food cravings in pregnant women may be due to the fetus attempting to avoid certain food-based toxins and demand certain essential minerals respectively (Profet, 1992). High blood pressure in expectant mothers may also be caused by the fetus in its attempts to garner more blood-borne resources for the placental supply. This is shown in Box 7.2. It has even been suggested that pregnancy-related diabetes is induced by the unborn child in order to receive more glucose (blood concentrations of which are raised as a result of the condition). This extra glucose is probably used to lay down fat as food reserves, increasing the chances of survival after birth.

EARLY CHILDHOOD CONFLICT

As previously mentioned, the infant's strategy in parent–offspring conflict is predominantly psychologi-

cal. Crying is a typical example of an honest signal to parents (of hunger, cold or other distress) which is also used deviously to gain extra food, warmth or attention. This may also be true of other childish behaviour, which is the basis of regression. Smiling and temper tantrums are further examples of such attention-seeking strategies aimed at eliciting additional parental care.

> **Box 7.2   High blood pressure in pregnancy as a result of parent–offspring conflict**
>
> High blood pressure is a common problem in pregnant women. Occasionally, it may be severe enough to result in kidney damage, a condition known as pre-eclampsia. One explanation of this condition is that it occurs as a result of conflict between the fetus and the mother.
>
> In the early stages of pregnancy, fetal cells destroy the nerves and muscles that adjust blood flow to the placenta. When the fetus perceives that it is receiving inadequate nutrition, it releases substances into the mother's circulation which constrict arteries throughout her body (except in the placenta). This causes her blood pressure to increase and more blood is delivered to the fetus via the placenta. Data on thousands of pregnancies show that moderate increases in maternal blood pressure are associated with lower fetal mortality and that women with pre-existing high blood pressure have larger babies (Nesse & Williams, 1996).

If faced with the choice of saving the life of one child or saving the life of another, the mother should prefer the older one because she has more invested in him. However, if the dilemma is less serious, such as the provision of a particular morsel of food, she should prefer the younger one. This is because the older child is more capable of finding his own food unaided, and is the basis of weaning in mammals (Dawkins, 1989).

ADOLESCENT CONFLICT

Several of the examples mentioned above may also be used as strategies to induce additional care during adolescence. However, this is also the time when offspring become independent from their parents, and weaning occurs. Parental avoidance of offspring in cats, for example, encourages the young to wean and to become independent (Goodenough et al., 1993).

Infanticide: cases of extreme conflict

Baby-killing is commonplace in nature. Fathers, mothers, siblings, close relatives and parents' new mates have all been known to destroy infants or eggs under certain circumstances. For example, infanticide by male house mice (*Mus musculus*) is described in Box 7.3. When a female poison-arrow frog (*Rana pipiens*) comes across a male brooding a nest for another female, she crushes the eggs and then mates with him. In black eagles (*Haliaetus albicilla*), the first-hatched (larger) chick harasses its sibling and monopolises the food, causing the second chick to starve to death.

Some of the most detailed studies on infanticide have been conducted on lions (*Panthera leo*) in the Serengeti region of Tanzania (Halliday, 1980). When new males (or groups of males) take over a pride, they often kill the cubs already present (Figure 7.5). From a species point of view, this act seems wasteful and purposeless, but from the point of view of the male lions, it makes good genetic sense. Killing the cubs fathered by previous males brings the females into reproductive condition again much sooner (nine months as opposed to twenty-five months if the cubs are left alive) and so hastens the day that the takeover males can father their own offspring. Such infanticide also removes competition for the new offspring. Typically, a male's repro-

---

Box 7.3   Infanticide by male house mice

Immediately after copulation, male house mice become highly aggressive towards mouse pups and attempt to kill them. The males remain prone to commit infanticide for about three weeks, but then gradually switch into paternal behaviour. They then protect and care for the young pups attentively until about fifty days have passed since intercourse. At this point, they regain their infanticidal tendencies.

This behaviour has obvious adaptive value. Female mice usually give birth three weeks after copulation. Attacks on pups during this period are almost definitely directed towards a rival male's offspring, reducing competition for the newborn young of the infanticidal male. After three weeks, a male that switches to paternal behaviour will almost invariably direct his caregiving to his own offspring. After fifty days, his weaned pups will have dispersed, so that once again infanticide can be practised advantageously (Alcock, 1993).

---

ductive life in the pride is short (on average, two years), so any individual that practises infanticide when he takes over a pride will father more of his own offspring and therefore the tendency to commit infanticide will spread by natural selection (Krebs & Davies, 1993). Similar patterns of infanticidal behaviour have also been observed in primates (Sugiyama, 1984).

Figure 7.5   Infanticide in lions (*Panthera leo*) is an extreme example of parent–offspring conflict. Here, a male lion has killed the cub of a rival male

Infanticide is not exclusively a male trait. Female jacanas (*Jacana spinosa*) have been known to kill other females' chicks in order to gain access to extra males, an observation which has been supported by experimental evidence (Emlen et al., 1989). By committing infanticide, the females gain caretakers for their future clutches of eggs sooner than if they waited for the males to finish rearing their current broods.

It is interesting to note that the process of infanticide described for lions *decreases* the reproductive success of the females (and of the species as a whole), and it is surprising that females do not appear to have evolved counteradaptations. They could, for example, eat their own young once they have been killed in order to minimise their losses. Female adaptations to counter infanticide are discussed in Box 7.4.

Infanticide by males may help to explain the Bruce effect in mice. Bruce (1960) showed that urine from a strange male (the presence of which may indicate a takeover) caused pregnant mice to reabsorb their embryos. If the infants would have been killed, reabsorption may represent a reduction of losses by the female. The materials of the current embryos could be recycled and used for the next litter, sired by the new male. A similar situation appears to occur in horses, where mating with a strange male causes spontaneous abortion by the female (Berger, 1983).

Box 7.4   Female strategies to avoid infanticide

Certain female behaviours may represent strategies to attempt to avoid infanticide by males. For example, post-fertilisation copulation may dupe males into thinking that they are the father of the offspring subsequently produced. This could make infanticide less likely because the males would not be sure that the youngsters were not their own. In addition, the risk of infanticide in lions may be one of the reasons for the existence of coalitions of lionesses (which are usually related to one another). By sticking together, females have some chance of protecting their cubs from males intent on a takeover of the pride and destruction of the young cubs present. When infanticidal males encounter a single female parent, her cubs have almost no chance of survival, whereas groups of two or more females occasionally succeed in preventing males from destroying all their cubs (Alcock, 1993).

Surprisingly, infanticide is also observed with direct offspring (that is, those that are genetically related to *both* parents). Female acorn woodpeckers (*Melanerpes formicivorus*), for example, smash eggs laid by close relatives. The evolutionary basis of such 'kin-directed infanticide' appears to be unknown and is the opposite to what would have been expected. It has been suggested, however, that kin are more likely to be direct competitors for resources, as they will be very similar to each other. Therefore, the woodpeckers may be attempting to reduce such competition for their own offspring. Alternatively, this behaviour may represent a mechanism to avoid inbreeding. Sometimes parents will kill their own offspring in order to 'fine tune' numbers to available resources and ensure that the remaining young have the maximum opportunity to survive and reproduce. In other words, a small number of 'superior' offspring may be more desirable than many 'average' ones. This may be the basis for the killing and eating of *runts* (weak or undersized offspring) by both parents and siblings in a variety of species.

A runt bears just as many of its mother's genes as its litter mates, but its life expectation is less. Depending on the circumstances, it may pay a mother to refuse to feed a runt, and allocate all of its share of her parental investment to its siblings. She may feed it to its brothers and sisters, or eat it herself and use it to make milk. Indeed, Dawkins (1989) has argued that if a runt is so small and weak that its life expectancy is reduced to the point at which benefit to it from parental investment is less than half the benefit that the same investment could confer on its siblings, the runt should die 'gracefully and willingly'!

Sometimes it is not the adult members of a species which are responsible for infanticide, but the siblings of the victim. The concept of siblicide is considered in Box 7.5. In several species of spiders, the young eat their mother at the end of the brood care period (Seibt & Wickler, 1987). This would appear to represent the mother's final act of parental care as she sends her offspring into the world on a full stomach and therefore enhances their chances of survival. This would be a particularly effective strategy if she could not produce another brood.

If infanticide appears to make such sound genetic sense, why is it not more common? There are probably two main reasons for this. First, in many species females are larger than males and may be able to

Box 7.5   Siblicide

Examples of siblicide appear to be relatively common in certain species of birds (Stinson, 1979). The advantage to the offspring is clear, in that it will receive a larger proportion of parental investment. However, it is not immediately obvious why the parents appear to tolerate such siblicidal aggression. It appears that the basis of such parental behaviour is *insurance*. The production of a second or subsequent chick is parental insurance against the failure of the first chick (or chicks) to survive. This tactic may also exist to maximise reproductive success. Survival of the chicks depends upon the amount of food available. In poor years, the later-hatching chicks often starve, but the parents have not wasted much food or effort on these failures and can salvage part of that effort by feeding the carcass to the surviving young. In good years, however, there will usually be enough food to raise all the chicks successfully. Therefore, producing more offspring than can usually survive represents an opportunistic strategy by the parents, keeping their options open in case it happens to be a particularly good year.

physically prevent infanticide. Second, the advantage of infanticide depends on a high frequency of takeovers and a relatively long lactational delay of ovulation (during the period when the mother is providing milk for the offspring, she is incapable of ovulating and so cannot be fertilised by the new male). Where neither of these conditions applies, males gain less by being infanticidal, but they may still incur costs such as risk of injury from protecting females (Grier & Burk, 1992).

Parent–offspring conflict in humans

Many of the evolutionary explanations of parent–offspring conflict outlined above are probably also relevant to humans and need not be repeated here. Even infanticide is committed by humans, although this is invariably sex selective and usually for socio-economic reasons. The Chinese, deprived of the chance to have more than one child, killed more than 250,000 girls after birth between 1979 and 1984 (Ridley, 1993).

In one recent study of clinics in Bombay, of 8000 abortions, 7997 were of female fetuses (Hrdy, 1990).

Parent–offspring conflict has also been used as an explanation for the existence of Freud's anal stage of psychosexual development. According to Badcock (1994), retention of urine and faeces may represent a psychological ploy by young children to suggest that insufficient food has been provided and therefore solicit additional care. Similar arguments have been advanced by Badcock for other stages of development, although these are not always totally convincing.

Problems with investigating parent–offspring conflict

In practice, models of parent–offspring conflict are difficult to test (Clutton–Brock, 1991). It is often difficult to assess just what the best level of investment is for parents and for offspring. Also, measures of overt behaviour – for example, rates of begging by nesting birds or tantrums in young mammals that are not permitted to nurse – may not accurately represent the intensity of the conflict. Other ways of establishing potential conflict may be required (Goodenough et al., 1993).

Conclusions

In sexually reproducing species, parents and offspring are expected to be in conflict over the amount of parental investment the offspring receives. This is because the offspring are selected to attempt to gain more resources than the parents are selected to give. The conflict is expected to increase during the period of parental investment, which is characterised by a shift, from parents to offspring, in who initiates care. Parents are physically superior to offspring, more experienced and they control the resources at issue. Offspring are therefore selected to use psychological manipulation in order to induce greater investment. Overall, there is no expected outright winner of the conflict.

SUMMARY

- **Parent–offspring conflict** has been analysed from the point of view of the interests of adults and the young. The most common conflict arises when offspring, trying to maximise their own interests, attempt to manipulate feeding parents into providing extra resources. In extreme cases this may lead to **siblicide** or **infanticide**.

- The basis of parent–offspring conflict appears to be **genetic asymmetry**. A parent is equally related to each of its offspring, but an individual offspring is twice as related to itself as to its siblings. Parents will attempt to divide time and energy equally between their offspring, but individual youngsters are selected to want more than their fair share. Therefore, offspring tend to favour a longer period of parental investment than the parent is selected to give, resulting in conflict.

- When offspring are very young, the benefits of parental care are so large, relative to the costs, that the parent gains more by feeding the offspring than by ignoring it. However, the point will eventually arise when an individual youngster can do as well on its own as it can by receiving parental help. At this point, the parent is selected to cease feeding, but the offspring is selected to continue to demand food. This is seen during **weaning conflict** in mammals. The conflict is expected to cease when the cost of investment by parents is exactly twice that of the benefit received by an individual offspring. Independence then becomes desirable for the offspring because its **inclusive fitness** is best served by the mother's production of new siblings.

- On theoretical grounds, there is no expected winner of parent–offspring conflict, although arguments have been advanced in favour of both parents and young. In their attempts to manipulate each other, we would expect **adaptation** and **counteradaptation** to occur, although the competition would not be expected to be too severe, because they share genes.

- Parents are physically superior to offspring and more experienced, and they control the resources at issue. Therefore, offspring usually employ **psychological** tactics and attempt to **induce** more investment than the parent is selected to give. These tactics include **regression** (reverting to infantile behaviour) and **temper tantrums**, as seen in pelicans and chimpanzees.

- It has been suggested that the parents are heavily favoured to win the conflict. However, this argument does not stand up to examination by both theoretical arguments and mathematical models. The most likely outcome is a level of investment intermediate between the best situation for parents and offspring.

- The nature and extent of parent–offspring conflict are influenced by the age of parents. The older a parent, the less will be its future reproductive success and the lower will be the cost of current investment, measured in terms of future offspring. Therefore, older parents usually provide a longer period of investment, resulting in reduced conflict with offspring.

- **Infanticide** is commonplace in nature. Individuals that practise infanticide will often increase their reproductive success, and the tendency to commit the act spreads by natural selection. However, infanticide is advantageous for males only when there is a **high frequency of takeovers** and a relatively **long lactational delay of ovulation**. If this does not apply, or if females are the larger and more powerful sex, infanticide is unlikely to occur.

- Infanticide by males **decreases** the reproductive success of females, and certain female behaviours may represent strategies to attempt to avoid the death of their offspring. These strategies include the formation of **female coalitions** to protect the infants and **post-fertilisation copulation**.

- Infanticide is also observed with **direct** offspring, who are genetically related to **both** parents. It is generally thought that this is done to 'fine tune' numbers to available resources and ensure that the remaining young have the maximum opportunity to survive and reproduce. This may be the basis for the **killing and eating of runts** by both parents and siblings in a variety of species.

- Sometimes it is not the adult members of a species which are responsible for infanticide, but the **siblings** of the victim. The siblicidal infant gains a greater proportion of parental investment, but the parents suffer a decrease in reproductive success. However, siblicide is tolerated as it usually occurs in species in which parents produce extra offspring as **insurance** against losses.

- Many of the evolutionary explanations of parent–offspring conflict in non-human animals are probably also relevant to humans. Even infanticide is committed by humans, although this is invariably **sex selective** and usually for **socio-economic reasons**. Some psychologists have suggested that parent–offspring conflict may explain Freud's psychosexual stages of development.

PART 3
Kinship and social behaviour

APPARENT ALTRUISM

Introduction and overview

Chapter 1 showed how natural selection can shape behaviour in animals to maximise their survival and reproduction. One behaviour in which an animal might engage, that may increase fitness, is social behaviour. The rules of natural selection would lead us to believe that in those species in which social behaviour is seen, it has arisen because it confers a selective advantage upon those who engage in it.

This chapter focuses on perhaps the most 'social' of the behaviours considered in Part 3, *altruism*. This is the performance of a behaviour which benefits the recipient and carries a cost for the performer. For example, a bird which sees a cat should selfishly hide. However, through its altruistic alarm call, which potentially helps others to escape, the bird risks being caught by the predator. Three genetic explanations of altruism are described: Wynne-Edwards' (1962) *group selection* theory, Maynard Smith's (1964) *kin selection* theory and Trivers' (1971) theory of *reciprocal altruism*. This chapter also evaluates these theories, and discusses the extent to which they 'explain away' altruism, leaving us with the concept of *apparent altruism* (acts which *appear* to be altruistic, but which may be best explained by another route, such as individual selection).

What is altruism?

An altruistic act can be defined as one which is performed at cost to the altruist with corresponding benefits for a recipient. Benefits could include receiving food, protection from predators, or preferential access to a mate. Costs might include reduced survival (by sharing food or increased exposure to predation), or a reduction in reproductive potential (by forgoing opportunities to mate). Parental investment, as discussed in Chapter 5, appears to be altruistic, because parents feed and protect their offspring at cost to themselves. Care of one's own young, however, does not constitute an altruistic act, as defined above, since it benefits the parent (via an increase in fitness). Altruism could therefore be better defined in terms of losses and gains to fitness. An altruistic act would thus be one which enhances the fitness of the recipient whilst lowering the fitness of the altruist. Do animals perform such behaviours? Both casual observation of wild animals and documented examples suggest that they do. Two such examples are described in Box 8.1.

Apparent altruism

If animals were really to perform behaviours that were selfless, surely they would rapidly lose the evolutionary race against those that were not? Selfish recipients would gain without cost, altruists would encounter costs without gains, and the selfish individuals would win hands down. At least that is what natural selection would predict in a competitive world. The question of how altruism could arise perplexed Darwin, and now presents a central problem for evolutionary biologists. Several attempts have been made to explain how altruistic behaviours are preserved in populations. These theories suggest that for the altruist there *is* an inherent gain – that is, that the altruism is only *apparent*. The

Box 8.1   Two examples of altruism

A blackbird (*Xanthocephalus xanthocephalus*) will give an alarm call if it detects a potential predator. This benefits individuals nearby, as they are alerted to the risk and so can hide or flee. The altruistic caller suffers not only the very small energetic cost of sounding the alarm but, potentially, a very large cost, having made its whereabouts known to the predator.

Lions (*Panthera leo*) behave altruistically towards all the young in their pride, rather than just showing parental investment in their own offspring. Males give cubs preferential access to the kill, and a lioness will allow any cub to suckle from her. These acts carry energetic costs and they provide nutrition for youngsters which are in competition with their own offspring. The recipients of this altruism are the other members of the pride and their offspring (Figure 8.1).

Figure 8.1   A lioness (*Panthera leo*) will altruistically suckle all the cubs in a pride

theories are distinguished by the nature of the benefit to the altruist, and how the altruistic trait evolves. Three different genetic explanations for apparent altruism are discussed below: group selection, kin selection and reciprocal altruism.

Group selection theory

Wynne-Edwards (1962) proposed the theory of *group selection*, which suggests that co-operative groups are better adapted than non-altruistic ones. This, Wynne-Edwards believes, is possible because selection pressures act via the differential survival of groups. A group which includes altruists will benefit from their behaviour, and be better able to compete against non-altruistic (entirely selfish) groups.

EVIDENCE FOR GROUP SELECTION AS AN EXPLANATION OF ALTRUISM

What could an altruistic individual do to enhance the survival of its group? Wynne-Edwards identifies the avoidance of overpopulation as a role altruists might play. Altruists could regulate population size by observing numbers and employing restraint in breeding, so ensuring the survival of the group in lean years. To do this, they must first demonstrate an ability to estimate population density. For this, Wynne-Edwards proposes *epideictic displays* – that is, communal parades of the whole population. A gathering such as the evening chorus of roosting birds could allow individuals to estimate population density and deduce the need to control population growth. Secondly, altruists must act on information about population density to avoid overpopulation. In other words, some fertile, but altruistic, individuals must forgo the opportunity to mate. This should occur when the population threatens to exceed the *carrying capacity* (maximum population size) of the environment, that is, if vital resources such as food or space become scarce. The presence of non-mating, sexually mature adults can be seen in many species, such as turkeys (*Meleagris gallopavo*), sea-lions (*Zalophus californianus*) and red deer (*Cervus elaphus*) (see Chapter 6). Altruists in other species may be regulating population size when adults commit infanticide, as seen in lions (see Chapter 7, page 67).

Kalela (1957) suggested that group selection could account for reproductive restraint in subarctic voles. Whilst food shortage would ultimately control populations, Kalela thought that 'altruistic self-control' in times of plenty would prevent starvation during food shortages. The evolution of successful 'self-regulating' groups could only occur if those groups which were not operating altruistically were periodically destroyed as a direct consequence of their lack of restraint.

EVIDENCE AGAINST GROUP SELECTION AS AN EXPLANATION OF ALTRUISM

Group selection, like many other areas of comparative psychology, can be supported by examples of behaviour from a wide variety of carefully selected species. However, this does not mean that the theory has widespread or well-founded application (see the limitations of the evolutionary approach, Chapter 1, page 10). Examples of epideictic displays and evidence of mating restraint cannot, for instance, be found in the same species, even though the group selection theory predicts that one is dependent on the other. Wilson (1975) suggests that epideictic displays and altruistic breeding restraint are unlikely to play a significant role in population control.

It is true that animal groups tend not to overpopulate, but this is largely the consequence of ecological factors. A large group is harder to feed, easier for a predator to locate, and will suffer rapidly spreading disease (see Chapter 9). Group size is self-limiting because ecological pressures increase as the population grows. Examples of 'altruistic restraint' in mating may also be more simply explained. A dominant gorilla (*Gorilla gorilla*) mates the most because he can prevent others from doing so. Subordinate individuals are not altruistically refraining from mating, but simply have no choice. Similarly, the killing of offspring can be explained without recourse to group selection. A mother rat (*Rattus rattus*) will eat her pups if their survival chances are low (due to lack of food) as this will ensure that she survives to breed again. In lions, new pride males will kill young cubs to bring the lionesses into season (see Chapter 7, page 67). These examples of infanticide are selfish rather than altruistic behaviours.

A second criticism of the use of group selection theory to explain altruistic traits lies in the logic of natural selection. 'Survival of the fittest' demands that those best adapted leave more offspring than their competitors. If individuals could either altruistically refrain from mating or selfishly mate, which kinds of individuals would be in the majority in subsequent generations? Altruists, it seems, would cease to exist. Imagine a group of mice (*Mus musculus*) with some altruistic (sexually restrained) individuals and some selfish ones. Whilst there is sufficient food, both will reproduce at the same rate, maintaining the balance of altruistic and selfish members of the population. If food becomes scarce, the altruists will refrain from mating but the selfish individuals will not. In subsequent generations there will be fewer altruists, since they will have fewer offspring. The increasing proportion of selfish individuals will continue to mate, so the population will con-

tinue to rise and the remaining altruists will still refrain from breeding. Eventually the population will consist entirely of selfish mice whose breeding is unrestrained. The 'altruistic genes' will have been lost.

Kin selection theory

Hamilton (1964) and Maynard-Smith (1964) proposed an explanation which could account for altruism between *kin* (related individuals). *Kin selection theory* suggests that traits which directed an individual's altruism towards its relatives, but not to non-relatives, would evolve. Only those sharing genes would benefit, thus promoting the survival of related individuals which are also likely to be genetically predisposed to be altruistic. The altruist thus gains via 'inclusive fitness' (see Chapter 1, page 5).

As kin selection relies on altruists helping related individuals, greater altruistic sacrifices would be expected for closer relatives. The relatedness of two individuals can be expressed as the *coefficient of relationship* (r). This is the proportion of genes they share. An offspring shares 50% of its genes with each parent ($r = 0.5$). Full siblings will, on average, share 50% of their genes with each other as each has inherited some in common from each parent (but not necessarily the same genes). Box 8.2 shows the proportion of genes shared by different relatives. We would expect altruism to be more likely when the value of r is large.

EVIDENCE FOR KIN SELECTION AS AN EXPLANATION OF ALTRUISM

Bertram (1976) used his own studies of lions and those

Box 8.2   Degree of kinship (relatedness) between different individuals

Relationship	Expected proportion of shared genes (coefficient of relationship, r)
Identical twins	1
Parent/offspring	0.5
Full sibling [brother or sister]	0.5
Grandparent/grandchild	0.25
Aunt, uncle/niece, nephew	0.25
Cousin	0.125
Non-relative	0

of Schaller (1972) to generate data about a 'typical pride', consisting of four 'resident' females and two 'pride' males. The females may have different mothers and fathers, but tend to remain with the same pride, and the males are typically brothers, which have taken over a new pride together. Bertram used evidence from observations of copulations, and the movements of animals between prides, to establish the relationships between individuals. From many examples of different prides, he calculated average coefficients of relationship for each of the adults in a pride, concluding that females were related on average by $r = 0.15$ and males by $r = 0.22$. Using these figures, Bertram was able to explain the altruistic behaviours he had seen in the prides. These included the males' tolerance towards cubs fathered by either male, and the lack of competition between pride males for oestrus (fertile) females. These are discussed in more detail in Box 8.3

Box 8.3   Altruism in lions

Bertram (1976) found that adult male lions were more tolerant of cubs feeding on a recent kill, such as a zebra, than were females. Bertram proposed that this was because the males were more closely related to the cubs, on average, than were the females. A male is related to his own cub by 0.5 and to the other male's cubs by $(0.5 \times 0.22) = 0.11$. His coefficient of relationship to all cubs is therefore $(0.5 + 0.11)/2 = 0.31$. A female is related to her own cub by 0.5, but to the other three females' cubs by $(0.5 \times 0.15) = 0.075$. Her coefficient of relationship to all cubs is therefore $(0.5 + 3 \times 0.075)/4 = 0.18$. Since 0.31 is larger than 0.18, males gain a greater increase to inclusive fitness by being altruistic to the cubs than do females.

Bertram also observed that pride males do not compete for oestrus females (those in breeding condition) as fiercely as one would expect. One male may mate more often than the other. Their genetic similarity causes the less active male's genes to have a greater representation in subsequent generations than would be predicted on the basis of his mating frequency alone. As lions could easily harm each other, the benefits to inclusive fitness of co-operation must exceed the risks associated with fighting for sole access to the females.

Box 8.4   When will altruism evolve? (Hamilton 1964)

We would expect altruism to occur if the cost (**c**) of the behaviour to the altruist is low (c is small) and the benefit (**b**) to the recipient is great (b is large). The ratio of benefits to costs (**K**) can be expressed as **b/c** and we would expect this figure to be large where altruism occurs – that is, for the benefits to exceed the costs. If **K = b/c**, then the higher the value of K, the greater the probability of altruism occurring. If the costs are too high, altruists are unlikely to survive to be altruistic, and if the gains are too small, the behaviour may not have a significant effect on the recipient. Of course, the degree of kinship (**r**) matters too. Altruism should only occur when **K > 1/r**. This will only be fulfilled when either the cost/benefit ratio is very favourable, or when the degree of relatedness is very high (so 1/r is very small). This makes sense: individuals will risk more for close kin as they stand to gain more in terms of inclusive fitness.

Horrocks and Hunte (1983) studied altruism in vervet monkeys (*Cercopithecus aethiops*). They found that females only helped one another in conflicts if they were related. Even assisting in conflicts can carry costs, so the females were behaving in accordance with the predictions of kin selection. Box 8.4 describes Hamilton's (1964) prediction of when such altruism will evolve. In this case, because the risks associated with fighting (*c*) are high, *K* will be small. Females are only altruistic if they are related to the recipient (when *r* is large), so that *K* > 1/*r*. The females only take risks to help when the gains in terms of inclusive fitness are high.

EUSOCIALITY: A SPECIAL CASE OF KIN SELECTION?

Naked mole rats (*Heterocephalus glaber*) are *eusocial* animals – that is, they have a social system characterised by overlapping generations, specialised reproductive individuals and co-operative care of the young. Mole rats are unusual because few species, other than insects, show eusociality. Mole rats live in underground colonies of 70–300 individuals, and their social system demonstrates division of labour and altruism similar to that of bees (see page 76).

Figure 8.2   A queen naked mole rat (*Heterocephalus glaber*) and her young. The surrounding workers keep them clean and bring them food

Young 'workers' collect food and nesting, and clear the burrows. As they get older, they dig burrows, and finally become 'soldiers' which defend the burrow system from predators and intruders (Figure 8.2). Only one female, the queen, breeds and nurses young. The other females engage only in the altruistic care of the queen's offspring. If the queen dies, her successors fight it out for the position. All of the females are capable of breeding, they simply do not. The active queen prevents ovulation of female workers by suppressing their ability to produce a hormone called progesterone. She achieves this by releasing a *pheromone*, an airborne chemical which affects the physiology of the other females (see Chapter 11, page 108). In non-breeding males, the sperm count is low and those sperm produced are inactive. However, this reproductive suppression is reversible: in the absence of the queen's influence, individuals of both sexes regain their sexual effectiveness (Sherman et al., 1992).

A mole rat, away from the suppression of the queen, could mate for itself and enhance its own fitness, rather than being altruistic. What stops individuals making a break for it? Ecological constraints on colony establishment limit the success of this strategy. The patchiness of food means that one selfish individual alone might have to travel for so long without finding food that it would be too exhausted to continue. With many altruistic individuals searching, one forager is likely to find a sufficiently large patch to feed the whole colony.

Genetic fingerprinting has shown that members of a colony are much more closely related than would be expected, being almost identical from one individual to the next (C. Faulkes, quoted in Young, 1990). A single queen, and up to three breeding males, should only produce siblings and half siblings, but the coefficients of relationships (as indicated by DNA testing) are much closer than this. The high degree of kinship can be explained by the inbreeding which results from genetic isolation. Patchy distribution of food makes contact between colonies rare, and makes dispersal of the young impossible, so they stay within the group. Such high kinship accounts for the apparently altruistic breeding restraint shown by the majority of the colony. Investment in the offspring of closely related brothers and sisters represents a genetically successful strategy. The proportion of shared genes is high, the benefits of caring are great, so the effect of altruism on inclusive fitness is significant. Helping is a more effective way to pass copies of shared genes into the next generation than risking survival by starting a new colony.

Eusocial insects such as bees, wasps and ants, show peculiarly high relatedness as a result of their genetics. These species are *haplodiploid*; the females are *diploid* (have two sets of chromosomes), whereas the males are *haploid* (have only one set of chromosomes). This arises because females are formed from a *zygote* (fusion of a sperm and egg), but males develop from unfertilised eggs so have no paternal chromosomes (from the father). Males produce many identical sperm and, therefore, highly related daughters. It is this closeness of kinship between sisters which accounts for much of the unusual behaviour of eusocial insects. Females can make a greater contribution to the genes of the next generation by helping sisters than they can via their own offspring. This is described in Box 8.5.

EVIDENCE AGAINST KIN SELECTION AS AN EXPLANATION OF ALTRUISM

The high degree of kinship between male lions in a pride has been used to explain their altruistic behaviour (see page 74). Bertram (1976) traced the relationships between lion pride members to establish average coefficients of relationship. He found that males, related on average by $r = 0.22$, would be more likely to show altruism than lionesses, whose coefficient of relationship is lower ($r = 0.15$). However, lionesses also demonstrate altruism. For example, when nursing, lionesses will allow the cubs of other females in the

Box 8.5 Eusocial insects: why do bees sting?

In eusocial insects, all the workers are sterile females. However, female sterility, when it arose, would not have led to a reduction in fitness. The workers are related to one another by $r = 0.75$, so they can contribute to the next generation most effectively not by producing daughters (to whom they would be related by only $r = 0.5$), but by making more sisters. Consequently, they can best enhance their inclusive fitness by protecting and feeding the queen's broods. Workers belong to specialised classes. In the honey bee (*Apis mellifera*), their roles include foraging, nursing larvae and defending the hive. These bees will surrender their lives by stinging in order to save the nest. Such absolute altruism can be understood when we consider the number of copies of identical genes to the altruist which lie in the hive. The cost of sacrificing one set of genes is likely to be outweighed by the gain from preserving thousands of 75% similar sets.

Whilst the logic of this argument is compelling, there may be other reasons for the high degree of altruism. Trivers and Hare (1976) provided empirical evidence for haplodiploidy, but this has been criticised (Alexander & Sherman, 1977). Certainly genetic similarity does not seem to guarantee altruism. Animals that reproduce by *polyembryony*, such as the armadillo (*Dasypus* sp.), split their embryos to produce many identical offspring (Craig et al., 1997). If the principles of kin selection (as applied to haplodiploid insects) are extended to polyembryonic species, these ought to be even more altruistic. However, this does not appear to be the case. The relatively minor importance of haplodiploidy to altruistic behaviour of insects is further defended by the absence of eusociality from many haplodiploid species (Stubblefield & Charnov, 1986).

pride to suckle from them. This is altruistic for the female as it bears the cost of making milk which is then unavailable to her own offspring. The behaviour of the lionesses is surprising because they are not so closely related to one another as are males (nor so closely related to all the cubs in the pride), so they stand to gain less via increased inclusive fitness. A process which is *not* dependent on kinship must be responsible for the females' altruistic behaviour.

Hoogland (1983) compared the altruistic alarm calling of male and female prairie dogs (*Cynomys ludovicianus*). In this species, females are more closely related than males because the latter disperse at maturity. It would therefore be expected that females would show more altruistic behaviour than males. In fact it appeared that males made the most alarm calls, opposing the predictions of kin selection.

Reciprocal altruism theory

Kin selection can only explain altruism when the helper and recipient are related, but in many cases they are not. For example, Packer and Pusey (1983) found that Tanzanian lions forming co-operative groups for hunting included large numbers of non-relatives. Furthermore, Faaberg and Patterson (1981) observed that unrelated groups of male Galapagos hawks (*Buteo galapageonis*) often share a mate, and copulate equally often. Trivers (1971) proposed that in these instances *reciprocal altruism* may be operating. This is where one individual (the altruist) helps another, and is later 'repaid' by assistance from that unrelated recipient. The initial altruist suffers a short-term reduction in individual fitness, but both individuals eventually achieve a gain in fitness.

Reciprocal altruism is a better explanation for the nursing behaviour of lionesses described on page 72. Each cub benefits from a variety of females' milk as they each provide different antibodies, therefore increasing the cub's resistance to disease. Each female is being altruistic by allowing other cubs to suckle, but gains reciprocal benefit for her own cub. Packer (1977) provided evidence for reciprocal altruism from observations of olive baboons (*Papio anubis*). Competition for oestrus females is fierce and competitors will attempt to steal the female away from the *consort male* (the male defending a female who is ready to mate). Take-overs are more likely to be successful if intruding males form an alliance. A male seeking to depose a consort male will enlist the help of an altruist. If he is successful, these two threaten the consort male, causing him to desert his female. He is replaced by the soliciting male, whilst the altruist is potentially left to fight with the ex-consort male. However, the altruist ultimately benefits because he is more likely to receive reciprocal assistance if he subsequently solicits help (Figure 8.3). This system could be open to cheats, individuals who solicit help but do not reciprocate. To avoid this, males are

Figure 8.3   Reciprocal altruism in olive baboons (*Papio anubis*). The males on the right have formed an alliance to compete with the consort male on the left. The altruist will gain later when his ally reciprocates

Figure 8.4   A vampire now, an altruist later. Vampire bats will regurgitate blood for hungry roost mates if they are familiar and likely to reciprocate

able to recognise one another, and remember which individuals assisted them. As a consequence, a cheating strategy is usually ineffective.

One of the most impressive examples of reciprocal altruism is illustrated by vampire bats (*Desmodus rotundus*). Wilkinson (1984) studied kinship relationships between bats at a roost site. He found that bats were only altruistic to one another if they were either close relatives or unrelated individuals who were regular roost mates. A vampire bat without food will only survive for about two days. If it has been unsuccessful in finding a host from which to suck blood, it returns to the roost and solicits food from a neighbour who regurgitates blood for it. When the altruist and recipient are related, this can be explained by kin selection. Reciprocal altruism can explain regurgitation between unrelated individuals. The bats are aware of which individuals they help and receive help from, assistance being restricted to those who reciprocate. This would not be the case if the only force at work were kin selection (Figure 8.4).

For reciprocal altruism to evolve, the benefit from reciprocation must outweigh the cost of donation – that is, the altruist must end up better off in the long run (after the good turn has been repaid). For vampire bats, a small amount of blood given by a well-fed individual represents a very small cost, but is of significant benefit to a starving individual. The altruist's meal may enable the recipient to survive, in order to forage again the next night (and maybe return the favour). The necessity for reciprocity in the examples of baboons and bats is clear: an individual which failed to reciprocate would not be helped again. Cheating would only

be an effective strategy in a population of altruists with poor memories. Reciprocal altruism will only be maintained if the majority of individuals reciprocate. This is explained further in Box 8.6.

Individual selection

To what extent can 'altruistic acts' be explained by individual selection alone? Are they in fact altruistic at all? Take, for example, the 'altruism' of lionesses in allowing communal suckling. It may be in a female's own interests to assist the development of all cubs. Her offspring will have a greater chance of survival if the pride is maintained, thus her own reproductive success depends on the survival of other cubs which may be smaller or more needy than her own. The costs are small, but the potential benefits may be great. Similarly, she is more likely to survive in a larger pride which could sustain her if, for instance, she was injured. There is no suggestion that females need to 'reason' this behaviour, simply that females who allowed communal suckling would, in the past, have enhanced pride survival. This appears to be a group selectionist argument, but in fact simply relies on raising individual fitness.

Infanticide is seen when new males take over a pride (see Chapter 7, page 67). This is unlikely to be of genetic benefit to the species or pride, as group selection theory would predict, since it occurs when

Box 8.6   The prisoner's dilemma: a model for reciprocal altruism

The prisoner's dilemma is a game which allows us to model the behaviour of two individuals who could co-operate or defect (Axelrod & Hamilton, 1981). The pay-off from each strategy, co-operation or defection, depends on the strategy employed by the opponent, as illustrated below (from the point of view of player X.)

		Player Y	
		Co-operate	Defect
Player X	Co-operate	Mutual co-operation (investment pays off)	Sucker (exploited)
	Defect	Cheat (best net result)	Mutual defection (no pains, no gains)

Because the biggest pay-off results from defection when the opponent co-operates, cheating can pay. Always defecting avoids being exploited and might lead to a big net gain, but if both players defect they profit less than if they had both co-operated. Encountering cheats is costly, so individuals should operate strategies which avoid exploitation and maximise mutual co-operation. Axelrod (1984) investigated many different strategies, of varying complexity, pitting them against one another in computerised games. The winning strategy was the simplest one, 'tit for tat', which co-operated on the first move and from then on copied the opponent's previous move. By using the strategy of retaliation in response to defection, the opponent is discouraged from cheating. By forgiving as soon as co-operation is resumed, mutual co-operation is encouraged, and this is the most rewarding option for both players.

numbers are small. It is, however, of genetic value to the incoming males since it causes the females to come into oestrus much more quickly than they would if they continued to suckle. A new male must inseminate the females quickly as the reign of a pride male is short, so by killing the existing cubs he ensures he will pass on his genes. He is acting in a selfish way.

The actions of animals which give alarm calls could be altruistic, or they may be acting selfishly. By raising the alarm, the caller may cause other individuals to move towards the predator whose whereabouts are unknown, especially if the 'altruist' has retreated before calling. Even without recourse to devious behaviour, callers themselves may gain, as a predator which has been spotted is less likely to attack. If the hunter has been unsuccessful (because others have responded to the alarm), it is also less likely to return (Hoogland, 1983). Therefore, by alerting others to the risk, the caller enhances its own survival.

Conclusions

Three genetic explanations of altruism (group selection, kin selection and reciprocal altruism) have been described and evaluated in this chapter. Only in group selection is there any real sacrifice by the altruist, and this is the most difficult theory to defend. It would appear that, in most cases, altruistic behaviour is only *apparent* (because there are gains to individual or inclusive fitness). It may also be the case that, in some instances, individual selection is sufficient to explain behaviours that at first appear to be altruistic.

SUMMARY

- **Altruism** is taking place when an individual performs a behaviour, at **cost** to itself, that **benefits** another individual. For example, the alarm calls of birds are altruistic: the caller risks being caught by the predator, the recipient, who hears the call, benefits by being able to escape.
- It is difficult to explain how truly altruistic behaviours could evolve, since they would disadvantage their performers. Since altruism is preserved in populations, there must be a hidden advantage to

the performer, hence we refer to **apparent altruism**.
- **Group selection theory** (Wynne-Edwards) suggests that altruistic groups are better adapted to survive as they can avoid overpopulation. Altruistic individuals could measure population size during **epideictic displays** and refrain from mating. Having fewer offspring would be altruistic in that it would be of benefit if population growth would result in the group exceeding the

carrying capacity of the environment. Alternatively, altruists could engage in **infanticide** to shed excess offspring.

- Group selection as an explanation of altruism is not well supported. Epideictic displays and consequent breeding restraint are difficult to demonstrate and, although some evidence can be found, these observations may be interpreted in other ways. The **dominance** of breeding animals over others may explain why only some individuals within a group mate, and infanticide is best explained by **individual selection**.

- If altruists in a group did refrain from mating, they would leave no altruistic offspring. **Cheating** (being selfish in an altruistic group) would be a more successful strategy. Selfish cheats would prosper, whilst altruistic celibates would be lost from the population.

- **Kin selection theory** (Maynard Smith) proposes that altruists perform helpful behaviours for **close relatives** in order to reap benefits from the additional shared genes, which are passed into the next generation as a consequence. This increases the **inclusive fitness** of the altruist.

- Animals such as lions and vervet monkeys preferentially help **closely related** individuals. Altruism would be expected between close relatives when the costs were low and the gains high. This is **Hamilton's rule**.

- Altruism between **eusocial** animals such as insects and mole rats can be readily explained by their high **degree of relatedness (kinship)**. They help to feed and protect one another at cost to themselves and altruistically care for the offspring of the queen, rather than investing in their own progeny. Being highly related, however, does not guarantee altruism or eusociality.

- The vicarious genetic success explained by kin selection only accounts for altruism between **kin** (relatives), not between unrelated individuals. Kin selection cannot explain why lionesses (which are not closely related to all the cubs in a pride) let cubs suckle communally.

- Helping behaviours between **non-related individuals** can be explained by **reciprocal altruism** (Trivers). This 'you scratch my back, I'll scratch yours' theory relies on animals being able to **recognise** and **remember** one another. They are then able to selectively assist those individuals which have been helpful in the past.

- Reciprocal altruism provides an immediate benefit for the recipient and a delayed increase in individual fitness for the altruist when help is received in return. Packer describes reciprocal altruism in unrelated male baboons which help each other to fight for a female. Wilkinson showed that vampire bats remembered their roost mates so that reciprocal regurgitation of blood could occur.

- The **prisoner's dilemma** model has shown that **tit-for-tat** is the best strategy to employ when two individuals could either co-operate or cheat. In tit-for-tat, cheating does not pay because the opponent retaliates by cheating. Co-operation is responded to in kind, so mutual co-operation can be sustained.

- Many apparently altruistic behaviours may in fact be **selfish**. Actions such as **alarm calling** and **breeding restraint** may have advantages for the performers themselves which directly enhance their individual fitness.

SOCIALITY IN NON-HUMAN ANIMALS

Introduction and overview

There are very few animals whose entire life is spent without the contact of *conspecifics* (members of the same species). Most species meet to mate, some gather for short time periods to care for their young, and others spend part (or all) of their year in social groups. This chapter considers the nature and functions of *sociality* (the tendency of individuals to form social links). The variety of social groupings which exist among non-human animals are described, and the costs and benefits of membership of such groups are evaluated. For *prey* species (those which get eaten), social co-operation can provide a means of defence. *Predators* (animals which hunt prey) may co-operate to attack. The role of sociality in such predator–prey relationships is discussed. (See Chapter 3 for a more detailed examination of predator–prey relationships).

Social organisation

Some animals remain alone throughout their lives, such as the palalo (a marine worm), which does not even meet to mate. The adult worms live on rocks in the sea and shed their sperm and eggs into the water, an event which occurs once every lunar month (28 days). Other animals, such as spiders, meet conspecifics only to mate. Species like the palalo and spider, which spend all, or most, of their lives alone, are defined as *solitary*.

Other species form social links to rear young after mating, but do not remain together for the rest of the year. Some of these, such as robins (*Erithacus rubecula*), raise their offspring in a *pair*, isolated from other members of their species, Others, such as the herring gull (*Larus argentatus*), form larger groups, or *colonies*, consisting of many pairs living in close proximity, but raising their young independently. Finally, some animals spend most or all of their lives in social groups which show attraction, or co-operation, between individuals. Lions (*Panthera leo*), for instance, may be solitary for part of their lives, but also live in relatively permanent prides which display some social activities such as hunting and suckling. However, other behaviours, such as sleeping, are solitary. Honey bees (*Apis mellifera*) live in lasting, stable groups in which all activities are communal and organised. The variety of groupings seen in different animals can be distinguished according to the extent and function of social behaviours exhibited.

An *aggregation*, as distinct from a social group, is an unstructured group formed by individuals being independently attracted to an environmental feature. Birds on a bird table, or reptiles warming themselves on a rock in the sun, would be such aggregations (Figure 9.1). Freeman and Grossman (1992) studied the dynamics of groups of minnows (*Clinostomus funduloides*) at a food source. The fish appeared to form aggregations rather than structured schools because

Figure 9.1   An aggregation. These birds show none of the characteristics of a flock; they did not arrive together, do not maintain fixed distances between each other, and will not depart together

individuals arrived and left independently. Group size did not affect their arrival or departure, so attraction between individuals seemed weak.

Natural selection operates on social behaviour, as on any other. It would be expected, therefore, that in social animals the presence of others, or their activities, would enhance fitness. For social animals, survival, reproduction, or both, must be better for individuals within the group than it would be for each one alone.

SCHOOLS AND FLOCKS

Fish school and birds flock. In both cases there is a social attraction between individuals in the group. Individuals form mixed sex groups, which maintain proximity by swimming or flying together. They show cohesive movements when schooling or flocking, often with fixed inter-individual distances and matched orientation and speed (Figure 9.2). There may, however, be constant reorganisation within, and interchange between, groups. This suggests that these groups lack *social order* – that is, individuals do not occupy fixed social positions relative to one another.

Flying birds, such as ducks and geese, show patterned movement similar to that of fish. Other birds demonstrate greater degrees of sociality. Rooks or gulls, for instance, roost communally and nest in colonies. Other bird groups have a relatively rigid social organisation, such as the peck order of chickens (Schjelderup-Ebbe, 1935). These are dominance hierarchies, fought out between individuals. Once established, these hier-

Figure 9.2   A school of fish showing fixed inter-individual distances and matched orientation

Box 9.1   Structured groups formed by mammals during the breeding season

Group type	Example	Group members	Function
Polygynous group	Red deer (*Cervus elaphus*)	One stag (male) and several hinds (females)	Defence of harem (group of females) against other males
Nursery herd	Wildebeest (*Connochaetes taurinus*)	Cows and calves	Defence of young against predators
Bachelor herd	Red deer	Immature males	Foraging (eating) and predatory defence

archies provide preferential access to resources for high-ranking individuals (see Chapter 2, page 14). Highly structured, but temporary, social groups can arise during the breeding season. This is illustrated at the leks (display sites) of ruffs discussed in Chapter 6 (page 56).

HERDS

Herds of mammals, like schools or flocks, may show little structure. In general, herds of prey species, such as zebra (*Equus zebra*), are large and unstable. However, structured herds are sometimes seen during the breeding season, as shown in Box 9.1. Herding species benefit from co-operation in food finding and predatory defence, often doing so simply by remaining close together. They may also show simple co-operative behaviours, such as mutual grooming, which help to reduce parasites. Hart and Hart (1992) observed *allogrooming*, where partners alternately groom each other's head and neck, in impala (*Aepyceros melampus*), a species of African gazelle. They found that grooming occurred between related and unrelated pairs, and was reciprocated. This was described as *co-operation* (both individuals gain immediately from participation in the activity), rather than *reciprocal altruism* (benefit for the individual who helps first is delayed until the favour is returned) because both individuals benefited simultaneously. (See Chapter 8 for a more detailed discussion of altruism.) Social groupings of predatory mammals may be more complex than those of prey because these species require integrated behaviour to hunt. This is seen in chimpanzees (see page 84) and lions (see Chapter 3, page 25).

EUSOCIAL GROUPS

Eusocial animals were discussed in Chapter 8 (page 74) with regard to genetic explanations of their altruistic behaviour. Eusocial groups are typified by overlapping generations, specialisation of some individuals for reproduction, and co-operative rearing of the young. In insects such as bees, wasps and ants, some castes of workers are anatomically adapted for different jobs in the colony. In bees, the role each individual plays changes with age. *Foragers* collect pollen in baskets on their legs (see Chapter 13, page 125), *nurses* feed developing larvae, and *soldiers* will sting in order to defend the colony against intruders. These roles are outlined in Box 9.2. With such complex organisation and dependence on the colony, eusocial species represent an extreme example of sociality.

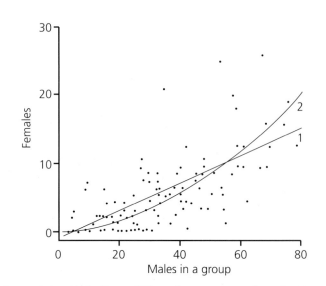

Figure 9.3   Male frogs (*Physalaemus pustulosus*) attract females by singing. The curved line of best fit above suggests that males in larger groups are more successful. The number of females per male increases as the group size increases

Box 9.2	The life of a honey bee

The role of a worker honey bee within a colony is dictated by her age. Typical changes in activity are shown below.

Age (in days)	Role in the hive
0–2	Cleaning brood cells
3–6	*Nurse* (feeds older larvae)
7–13	Attends to younger grubs and the queen
14–17	Cleans and builds the hive, produces wax
18–20	*Soldier* (defends the hive against intruders)
21–40	*Forager* (flies out of the hive to collect pollen and nectar)

Advantages of sociality

Social co-operation can enhance fitness in a variety of ways, affecting both reproduction and survival. Success in reproduction depends upon finding a mate and caring for the young. These tasks may be easier, or more effective, in a group. In addition, searching for food, hunting for prey, and avoiding predators may all be improved by the presence of other individuals.

SOCIAL CO-OPERATION FOR REPRODUCTIVE SUCCESS

Forming social groups, temporary or permanent, helps in finding a mate. For example, Ryan et al. (1981) investigated the relationship between group size of singing male frogs (*Physalaemus pustulosus*) and the number of females they attracted. Larger numbers of males attracted disproportionately more females. In other words, there were more females per male in big groups than in small ones (Figure 9.3).

Social groups may also be safer, or more effective, places to rear young. In Chapter 6 (page 54), the Darling effect was described (Darling, 1938). Observing other pairs courting stimulates the courtship of nearby birds in a colony, so the birds' sexual cycles become synchronised. This results in almost simultaneous laying and hatching of eggs throughout the colony. As an individual predator can only consume a finite number of eggs or chicks, this protects each individual by *dilution* (see Chapter 3, page 26). In a bigger group, each individual has a smaller chance of being the one that gets eaten. This conclusion is supported by Lack (1968), who observed that the dilution effect in colonies of terns (*Sterna hirundo*) and black-headed gulls (*Larus ridibundus*) is greatest in midseason. At this time, there are many eggs in the colony, so any particular nest is less likely to suffer predation, and more chicks are reared per pair. Sexual synchronisation is also essential in herd animals which give birth during migration, such as the wildebeest. All of the females need to be inseminated within a few days and their offspring born within a similar limited period. This timing enables the males of the herd to offer maximum

Figure 9.4   Elephants (*Loxodonta africana*) will surround their calves to protect them

protection against predators and the herd to alter its pace as the young increase in size and strength. Groups are also more effective at protecting their young. Adult elephants (*Loxodonta africana*) and zebra will surround their calves to protect them from predators (Figure 9.4). Even lion cubs are at risk from nomadic male lions and leopards (*Panthera pardus*). They are safer in the care of a pride than being protected by a solitary lioness.

Pairs and groups of birds are better at rearing chicks than solitary individuals are. They can provide better defence and more food. This can be studied in species in which different mating strategies are employed, such as monogamy (pairs), or polygyny, where the female rears the brood alone (see Chapter 6). Askenmo (1984) found that pairs of pied flycatchers (*Ficedula hypoleuca*) raised more young per nest than single parents, and Woolfenden (1975) described the increased reproductive success in Florida scrub jays (*Aphelocomo coerulescens*) where there were helpers at the nest (see Chapter 1, page 6).

Within an organised social group there may be division of labour for care of the young. Eusocial insects illustrate this well, with a caste of workers specialised to nurse the offspring. In other species, this task may be shared. Adult and immature female primates may be seen '*auntying*' (sharing the role of care for the young). They provide stimulation, food and security for the youngster, whilst learning about how to raise offspring.

Meerkat (*Suricata suricatta*) adults 'tutor' juveniles in foraging techniques in a similar way. Chapter 8 discussed the benefits to lionesses and their cubs which arise from communal suckling. The cubs not only have milk available from more sources, but they gain from the diversity of antibodies that different females provide, so are healthier. This behaviour has also been seen in other species, such as fallow deer (*Dana dana*) (Bigersson et al., 1991).

SOCIAL CO-OPERATION IN FOOD FINDING

Foraging (finding food) in groups is often more successful than searching alone, especially if the food is patchy rather than evenly distributed in the environment. A single individual which is foraging might fail to find any food before it starved, but a dispersed group is more likely to hit upon a clump of food, which would be sufficient to feed them all. Crook (1964) compared the behaviour of different bird species. Those eating patchy food (such as seeds in grassland) fed in flocks, whereas similar species feeding on evenly dispersed food (such as insects) fed alone. The success of a co-operative strategy depends on communication between the successful forager and the rest of the group. This is highly developed in eusocial species, such as honey bees, whose complex dances indicate the location of food to others (see Chapter 14, page 133).

Communication of foraging success is also observable in other, less social, species. For example, foraging in carrion crows (*Corvus corone corone*) is described in Box 9.3. Elgar (1986) describes the behaviour of sparrows

---

Box 9.3   Foraging in carrion crows

Carrion crows appear to use their communal roost to learn about food sources. This would support the *information centre hypothesis* (Weatherhead, 1983), which suggests that unsuccessful foragers learn where new food sources are located by sharing information with others. Successful foragers also gain from the system, because their predation risk is decreased by the presence of other birds. Richner and Marclay (1991) tested this hypothesis experimentally using wild crows. They found, however, that more birds learned the location of the new food patch by themselves than via the roost, contradicting the information centre hypothesis.

which will 'chirrup' to call the flock if the food they have found, such as bread crumbs, is divisible.

However, members of a group do not necessarily have to engage in deliberate information sharing. Simply observing the behaviour of others may provide sufficient information to locate a new food source. De Groot (1980) demonstrated that weaver-birds (*Ploceus cucullatus*) could follow another bird which had found food or water to the correct location.

Some species may learn how, rather than where, to feed from others. Chapter 1 we described blue-tits opening milk bottles to drink (Sherry & Galef, 1984). More recently, Sherry and Galef (1990) have demonstrated experimentally that not only does the opportunity to observe another individual opening a food source accelerate learning, but its mere presence has a similar effect. This may be because conspecifics reduce fear, reduce the need for *vigilance* (watchfulness), or encourage foraging behaviour.

Social co-operation in predator–prey relationships

Predator–prey relationships represent an evolutionary arms race (see Chapter 3, page 27), with each evolving to be more effective at killing, or avoiding being killed. One way to improve one's chances in such a race is to gang up, and both predators and prey use social grouping to their advantage.

SOCIAL CO-OPERATION IN ATTACK

Predatory species gain from co-operation as a strategy to counter group defence by their prey. Hyaena (*Crocuta crocuta*), for instance, can take bigger prey when they are in larger packs (Kruuk, 1972), and predatory fish hunting in schools capture more prey per individual than solitary animals (Major, 1978). Lions demonstrate particularly sophisticated co-operative hunting behaviour. They surround their prey, as well as simply using multiple individuals to chase, tire and fell their quarry. Scheel and Packer (1991) found considerable variation of individual participation on communal hunts. Male lions tended to participate in hunts less often than females, and to show more 'non-conforming', in which the behaviour of the active participants within a hunting group varied. There were also differ-

ences relating to the prey being pursued. More individuals refrained from participation in pursuit of small prey, such as warthogs (*Phacochoerus aethiopicus*), than they did when large prey, such as zebra, were being chased.

The value of co-operation also depends on the hunting strategy employed by the species. Different species of fish, for instance, hunt in different ways. Pike (*Esox lucius*) employ a 'sit and wait' policy, whilst perch (*Perca fluviatilis*) actively search for their prey. Eklov (1992) found that, at higher predator densities, perch were more successful than pike. The perch benefited from each other's presence because larger numbers of predators could more easily split schools of prey. If an isolated individual evaded capture by one perch, it was often caught by another. Pike, by contrast, found ambushing their prey more difficult at higher predator densities. They suffered interference from other predators (see Chapter 2, page 14). Furthermore, prey animals were more likely to approach the pike when the predator density was low. As the pike strategy relies on the prey being near, an increase in predator density reduced the frequency of opportunities to strike. Even within one species, different strategies may be employed according to circumstances (Box 9.4).

SOCIAL CO-OPERATION IN DEFENCE: AVOIDING BEING EATEN

Sociality is important for prey as well as for their predators. In fish, schooling is most frequent amongst the

---

Box 9.4   Co-operative hunting in chimpanzees

Ecological factors can affect the success of different hunting strategies. Boesch (1995) studied the relationship between social grouping and environment in chimpanzees. He studied chimps hunting for colobus monkeys (*Colobus geureza*) in two environments, which differed in the height of the vegetation. Where the trees were tall, the chimps hunted successfully in groups, whereas in the environment with lower vegetation they hunted alone. Boesch concluded that co-operation was the only effective strategy when the prey could readily escape (sideways, and up or downwards) in tall trees. In lower vegetation, where prey were easier to catch, the chimps did not co-operate and shared kills less often.

small species, which are 'easy prey'. Even within one species, such as tuna (*Thunnus albacares*), small individuals school, whereas larger ones are solitary. These observations suggest that those individuals most likely to be eaten derive the greatest benefit from schooling.

In a large group, each individual runs a smaller risk of being killed by a predator than if it was solitary. This is the effect of *dilution*. In addition, individuals can improve their own chances of survival (at a cost to others) by 'hiding' in the centre of the group. Hamilton's (1971) notion of the *selfish herd* suggests that prey animals should attempt to take up central positions in their group so that they are 'sheltered' by other group members (see Chapter 3, page 26). Patterson (1965) has shown that birds occupying marginal nests (on the edges of colonies) are at the greatest risk from predators, raising fewer young per nest.

Black et al. (1992) studied the dynamics of goose (*Branta leucopsis*) flocks. Comparison of the energetic costs of feeding and vigilance of birds in the centre and on the periphery revealed no difference. In the middle, geese gained in terms of reduced vigilance because they were protected, but only had access to poor-quality food. The birds on the edge of the flock (dominant individuals) had to spend longer being vigilant, and expended energy fighting with neighbours, but by so doing gained access to ungrazed areas to feed. Selfish individuals, therefore, may not always seek out the centre of the herd.

Prey species can also gain by grouping together because individuals may alert each other, intentionally or otherwise, to the presence of a predator. Alatalo and Helle (1990) observed that willow tits (*Parus montanus*) were more likely to give an alarm call if the predator was 40 m away than they were if it was only 10 m away. The birds' caution suggests that there are risks involved in alarm calling. Bertram (1980) found that in larger groups of ostriches (*Struthio camelus*), each individual spent less time with its head up, looking for predators. This has the advantage of enabling the birds to feed more easily without any increase in risk (Figure 9.5).

From the total increase in vigilance in larger groups of prey animals, we would expect them to detect predators more quickly. This was demonstrated by Kenward (1978), who found that pigeons (*Columba palumbus*) were less likely to be killed by goshawks (*Accipter gentilis*) when the pigeons were in groups. The pigeons

Figure 9.5   Many ostriches (*Struthio camelus*) with their heads up are more likely to spot a predator

were safer in groups because they took flight at greater distances (Figure 9.6). Sociality may also be an advantage when confronting predators, as described in Box 9.5.

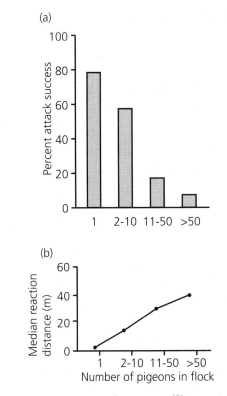

Figure 9.6   Goshawks (*Accipter gentilis*) are less likely to kill a pigeon (*Columba livia*) when the prey are in larger groups. This is because bigger groups detect the predator at a greater distance (Kenward, 1978)

Box 9.5 Confronting predators

Mobbing is an activity in which groups of birds of prey species, such as starlings (*Sturnus vulgaris*), chase and swoop at predatory birds, such as magpies (*Pica pica*) and kestrels (*Falco tinnunculus*) (see Chapter 3, page 26). Pursuit by the prey demonstrates to the predator that it has been seen, so an attack would be futile. Mobbing of kestrels causes them to vacate the area immediately (Pettifor, 1990), and black-headed gulls (*Larus ribibindus*) use mobbing effectively to protect their eggs (Kruuk, 1964).

Thrush-like birds called fieldfares (*Turdus pilaris*) have a spectacular form of predatory defence (Andersson & Wicklund, 1978). Groups of fieldfares fly upwards, simultaneously defecating on the predator, which, disabled by somewhat sticky flight feathers, beats a hasty retreat! The fieldfares' defence would appear to be effective because colony-nesting fieldfares have greater reproductive success than solitary ones (Haas, 1985).

Neill and Cullen (1974) have suggested an explanation for how mobbing-like behaviour by prey species of fish could protect them from predation. They observed predatory fish (such as pike) and cephalopod hunters (octopus and squid) in response to prey behaviour. Their findings suggested that large numbers of moving prey confused the predator, so the prey avoided getting caught.

which have been unlucky, but for the successful ones, sharing is disadvantageous. By drawing attention to their find, they will certainly reduce their own share. The ideal strategy would be to eat their fill on finding a source of food and then call the rest of the group if there is any left over. This ensures that they reap the greatest selfish benefit from their find, but by sharing can expect to benefit from later reciprocity. This seems to be the strategy employed by sparrows (*Passer domesticus*). The results of Elgar's (1986) study, described on page 83, showed that individuals would call if the food was divisible. If, however, the food was indivisible, such as a slice of bread, the sparrow stayed quiet. To call others might risk losing the food altogether. One way to gain would be to cheat, taking advantage of more productive members of the group. The most obvious manifestation of this is stealing food (Figure 9.7). For example, some of the lions observed by Scheel and Packer (1991) (see page 84) refrained from participation in hunts. These lions may have been 'cheating' by exploiting the hunting behaviour of their companions.

INTERFERENCE

Neighbours may threaten the success of foraging by scaring away prey. For example, the feeding habits of redshanks (*Triinga totanus*) on coastal mud flats were studied by Goss-Custard (1976). In daylight, redshanks feed on shrimps which they can see sticking out of the mud. However, the shrimps can retreat quickly in response to the birds' footsteps. As a consequence, the birds tend to space out to maximise feeding rate (as

Disadvantages of sociality

Not all species are social, so for some the benefits of group living must be outweighed by the costs. What are these costs?

INCREASED PREDATION

A high density of individuals may make prey more conspicuous. Andersson and Wicklund's (1978) study of fieldfares used artificial nests which were either solitary or arranged in colonies. The colonies attracted more predators than the solitary nests, and more predatory attempts were made.

REDUCED RESOURCES AND CHEATING

Sharing food is clearly an advantage for those foragers

Figure 9.7 Group living means having to share. These two marabou storks are fighting over food

neighbours are a disadvantage). At night, however, the birds cluster as they search by touch for slow-moving snails which are undisturbed by the patter of feet. This change in strategy seems to represent the payoff between interference by group members by day and benefits (perhaps anti-predatory ones) from clustering at night.

AGGRESSION AND INFANTICIDE

Whilst social animals are somewhat protected from the dangers of external predators, aggression may be greater in larger groups. As population density increases, so does competition for resources (see Chapter 2). The fighting which may result carries the risk of physical injury. Social animals may even have to contend with the threat posed by cannibalistic neighbours. Sherman (1981) found that Belding's ground squirrels (*Spermophilus beldingi*) with small territories were more likely to lose their young to conspecifics than those with larger territories. This infanticide, unlike that by male lions (see Chapter 7, page 67), cannot be explained by attempts to bring females into breeding condition (oestrus), as ground squirrel reproduction is not controlled in the same way.

DISEASE

The close proximity of individuals in a group can also pose a threat to health. In large colonies of prairie dogs (*Cynomys ludovicianus*), Hoogland (1979) found more parasites per burrow than in small colonies. The effects of the increase in risk of the spread of disease can be seen in the recent success of relatively solitary, ground-living rabbits over those inhabiting warrens. Myxomatosis, a disease introduced to control rabbit populations, is passed between individuals by the rabbit flea. Rabbits in burrows are at greater risk of contracting the disease, so those individuals with a tendency to live alone have been more likely to survive.

THE EFFECTS OF OVERCROWDING

The physiological effects of high population density also adversely affect health. Overcrowding causes stress, and the body responds with hormonal changes which are damaging and eventually fatal. Green et al. (1939) described the effect of overpopulation in wild snowshoe hares (*Lepus americanus*). The hares showed a hormonal change to the stress of crowding. The effects of this were irreversible, even if the hares were removed into favourable laboratory conditions. Their reproductive function was depressed, their growth and sexual maturity were inhibited, they suffered reduced resistance to disease, and deficient lactation impaired the growth of their young.

It appears that physiological responses to crowding are not the only mechanisms causing reduced fertility. When the number of pigeons in a population increases, males interfere with each other's attempts to copulate, reducing their reproductive effectiveness. The presence of others can also detrimentally affect care of the young. Calhoun (1962) observed nest building in rats and found that, in crowded situations, the females failed to build complete nests. As a result, the pups left prematurely, causing high infant mortality.

Conclusions

This chapter has looked at the diversity of social organisation in animals. It shows that there are advantages to sociality which enhance fitness (for instance, in terms of parental care and foraging), which have also been encountered in other chapters. Two key advantages are co-operation for predatory defence and for hunting. The disadvantages of living in a social group have also been considered. For social animals, these problems must be outweighed by the benefits of group living.

SUMMARY

- **Sociality** is the tendency of individuals to form social links. Sociality is demonstrated between **conspecifics** (members of the same species). Most species meet to mate, some gather to care for their young, and others spend part (or all) of their lives in social groups.
- Social groups show a range of organisation.

Solitary animals live alone, or meet only to mate. **Pairs** (e.g. robins) often form just for the breeding season. Pairs may also unite into unstructured groups or **colonies** (e.g. gulls). **Social** animals may live in a group temporarily or permanently. **Aggregations** are not true groups; they show no cohesiveness or social structure.

- **Schools** (e.g. of tuna), **flocks** (e.g. of starlings) and **herds** (e.g. of zebra) show **cohesive movements**, **orientation** and **fixed interindividual distances**. Herds of prey species are generally **large** and **unstable**. They may be mixed, or consist of a male and his harem (**polygynous**), mothers and their offspring (**nursery herd**), or may be all non-breeding males (**bachelor herd**).
- Structured groups, such as **leks** (e.g. in ruffs) and the **hierarchies** of chickens, have dominant and subordinate individuals. Hierarchy status dictates access to resources such as food or mates. **Predatory species** often form small stable groups, such as prides of lions, and some highly integrated behaviours are seen (e.g. hunting). **Eusocial** animals, such as **bees** and **mole rats**, live in highly organised colonies with **division of labour** and **co-operative care of the young**. The role of a **worker** honey bee changes with age, from nurse to hive builder, then to soldier, and finally to forager.
- The **advantages** of sociality arise because each individual is benefiting selfishly from the presence or activity of others, for instance in **mutual grooming**.
- Finding a **mate** and **caring for offspring** (e.g. **communal suckling** in lions and **auntying** in primates) are easier in groups. For example, bigger groups of singing male frogs attract more mates; the number of females per male rises with group size. In addition, the young in the middle of a group in space or time are safer from predators. Offspring may be protected by the **dilution effect** or **guarding** by groups of adults.
- **Sharing food**, and **information** about its location, ensures an individual within a group obtains food. Grouping also improves **foraging** (e.g. for patchy food), so it has energy and nutritional benefits. The success of a co-operative strategy depends on communication between the successful forager and the rest of the group.
- **Predators** benefit from more efficient hunting (**co-operative attack**) in groups. Hyaena kill larger prey when in bigger groups, predatory fish in schools take more prey than solitary ones, and chimpanzees hunt in groups when the environment allows for easier escape of their prey.
- **Prey** species achieve effective **co-operative predatory defence** in groups. 'Safety in numbers' means each individual is less likely to get eaten (**dilution**). **Hamilton** described the **selfish herd**, suggesting that each individual should aim to stay in the centre of the group to be safest. However, animals on the edge of the group may gain access to extra food. Selfish individuals, therefore, may not always seek out the centre of the herd.
- Prey groups benefit from having more 'heads up' looking for danger at any time (**vigilance**) and as a consequence are **faster to respond** to threats. **Kenward** found that goshawks kill fewer pigeons when the prey are in bigger groups because the pigeons take flight earlier.
- Groups of prey may **confuse** the predator. **Neill and Cullen** found that many moving, coloured prey made hunting more difficult for fish, squid and octopus. Defence by **mobbing** helps to protect prey and to **deter** unsuccessful predators. Andersson and Wicklund described the success of fieldfare mobbing in which the predator is the target for communal defecation.
- The **disadvantages** of sociality arise from the fact that a group is more **conspicuous** than individuals alone, from the limitations that larger numbers place on **resources**, and from the detrimental effects of living in close confines with others.
- For **prey** species, being in a social group may make them easier to detect and more attractive to predators. For hunters, other individuals may scare prey away.
- Other drawbacks of sociality include having to **share food** or **information** about food sources, and increased risk of **cheats** stealing food.
- Whilst social animals are somewhat protected from the dangers of external predators, **aggression** may be greater in larger groups. As population density increases, so does competition for resources. The fighting which may result carries the risk of physical injury. Social animals may also have to contend with the threat posed by **cannibalistic** neighbours and increased risks of infectious **disease**.
- High population densities have detrimental effects on **health**, leading to **reduced reproductive success** and sometimes even **death**. Some of the effects are mediated by **hormones** in response to **stress**. Others act directly: for example, crowded rats build poor nests and thus suffer increased **infant mortality**.
- For social animals, natural selection has ensured that the advantages of sociality outweigh the disadvantages. The reverse is true for solitary animals.

IMPRINTING AND BONDING

Introduction and overview

The first social relationship in which most animals need to engage is an attachment to an adult which will provide care. For most non-human animals, this is the mother (exceptions have been discussed in Chapter 6). The nature of this attachment is determined by the degree of care the offspring requires. *Precocial* young, which enter the world fairly well developed and independent, such as ducklings, require relatively little care and tend to *imprint* on the mother. *Altricial* young, which are less well developed and helpless at birth, such as monkeys, need extensive care. These species form a reciprocal attachment – that is, the offspring and mother *bond* to one another. This chapter discusses the nature and consequences of imprinting and bonding in a range of non-human animals.

Imprinting

Konrad Lorenz (1935) conducted systematic studies on the effects of isolation on geese, ducks, jackdaws (*Corvus monedula*) and other bird species. He was particularly interested in the early behaviour of precocial species. Lorenz artificially incubated eggs and observed the reactions of the hatchlings. As he was easily seen by the newly hatched chicks, he became a focus for their attention. Rather than demonstrating interest in an adult of their own species, Lorenz found that the chicks followed him (Figure 10.1). He concluded that the young of precocial species demonstrate *imprinting*. This is a highly constrained type of learning in which offspring form a rapid and permanent attachment to the first moving object they see. Under normal circumstances, when this is their mother, it would be an adaptive behaviour. Such a response would ensure they were fed and protected, and would provide a model from which to learn the appearance of an adult of their species (to guide later courtship). The features which

Figure 10.1   Imprinted goslings (*Anser anser*) following Lorenz

Lorenz believed were characteristic of imprinting are listed in Box 10.1.

FILIAL AND SEXUAL IMPRINTING

The type of imprinting refered to above is known as *filial imprinting* (by offspring onto a parent). This often

---

Box 10.1   Features of imprinting (Lorenz, 1935)

Lorenz suggested the following features were characteristic of the imprinting process.

- Only precocial species imprint
- Imprinting must occur during a critical period
- The effects of imprinting are irreversible
- Imprinting governs filial (parent–offspring) behaviour
- Imprinting governs sexual behaviour
- Sexual imprinting is complete before the appropriate responses are needed
- Imprinting is directed towards the first moving thing which is seen
- Imprinting is different from other forms of learning

---

takes place during a specific time period in early development, know as the *sensitive period*, and is difficult to change with subsequent experience. Many animals imprint on particular characteristics of their mother, so that they approach only her rather than other adults which may attack them. Filial imprinting therefore has adaptive value in terms of survival.

In *sexual imprinting*, young animals learn the characteristics of members of the opposite sex within their own species, such as colouration or plumage. This is very important if later courtship and mating are to be successful. Sexual imprinting occurs most readily to members of an animal's own species, less readily to members of a related species, and least readily to members of an unrelated species. It is more likely to be achieved if conspecifics of the opposite sex are easy to distinguish from other species, such as by their bright plumage. Some birds which have been hand-reared by humans do sometimes imprint upon them (see page 92), and as the effects of sexual imprinting are long lasting, this may cause severe problems for mating with their own species at a later date. Effective sexual imprinting therefore has adaptive value in terms of reproductive success.

An evaluation of the imprinting concept as envisaged by Lorenz

IMPRINTING IN PRECOCIAL SPECIES

Imprinting has been observed in many species, including domestic chickens, ducks, geese, jackdaws and finches. These are, without exception, precocial. Therefore, in this respect, it would appear that Lorenz is correct. Imprinting *is* a characteristic of precocial species, although it may not be exclusive to them. Some relatively altricial species also show aspects of imprinting such as rapid attachments and following behaviour (see page 94). It must be noted, however, that there are precocial species which do *not* imprint, nor indeed show any kind of attachment, such as newly hatched fish.

CRITICAL PERIODS VERSUS SENSITIVE PHASES

Lorenz believed imprinting to be unique because it could occur only during a brief *critical period* early in life. Failure to expose the newborn to a suitable stimulus within this genetically governed time limit would result in failure to imprint. Certainly, there appears to be plenty of evidence to support the early occurrence of imprinting. Different techniques, however, generate very different estimates of effective time spans for imprinting within the same species (see Ramsay and Hess (1954) and Boyd and Fabricius (1965)).

The time span may be less crucial than Lorenz supposed because the period during which imprinting occurs can be extended. Such observations support the idea of a *sensitive phase*, a period when imprinting occurs most readily but beyond which it is still possible. The distinction between a critical period and a sensitive phase depends on one's definition of imprinting. If the definition 'follows a moving object at first exposure' is used, the time during which imprinting can occur would be quite long, like a sensitive phase. If a tighter definition such as 'the formation of a lasting attachment following a single exposure to an object' is used, the critical period would be correspondingly shorter (Manning, 1979).

Filial behaviour, such as following, is a key identifier of imprinting. This appears to be governed by a sensitive phase separate to that of sexual imprinting. Vidal (1976) studied cockerels (*Gallus domesticus*), isolating them for up to 150 days, to investigate the effects upon following behaviour and mate choice. The results showed that filial imprinting occurs first, between one and thirty days, whilst sexual imprinting occurs later, between thirty-one and forty-five days.

FILIAL IMPRINTING

Reversibility

The irreversibility of filial imprinting demonstrated by Lorenz is not well supported by experimental studies. Salzen and Meyer (1967) exposed chicks to a coloured ball for three days, to which the chicks initially imprinted. This was immediately followed by another three days' exposure to a different coloured ball, which the chicks subsequently preferred. In a similar experiment, Cherfas and Scott (1981) confirmed that filial imprinting could be reversed, but discovered that the chicks' preferences reverted to the original stimulus after a three-day isolation period. In both Salzen and Meyer's, and Cherfas and Scott's experiments, chicks showed reversibility. This contrasts with Lorenz's prediction that the process was irreversible. However, the reversion of the chicks' preference in Cherfas and Scott's experiment casts some doubt on this conclusion, and could support the view held by Hess (1972), that irreversibility is a product of the natural environment, to which laboratory experiments have only limited resemblance.

Colour, shape and generalisation

The disinclination of chicks to imprint on yellow objects has been demonstrated by Salzen and Meyer (1968), and by van Kampen and de Vos (1991). Bolhuis and Bateson (1990) also suggested that this effect occurred in their own experiment described in Box 10.2 because the stimuli differed only in colour. However, when chicks were tested with objects which differed in colour, shape and pattern, their response to yellow objects did not differ from that to any other colour. Nevertheless, chicks may have an innate preference for some stimuli. If a chick is going to follow its mother (who can provide for it) rather than another chick (which might get into trouble), 'avoiding yellow' might be a good strategy.

The tendency of hatchling chicks to prefer some stimuli over others was investigated by Impekoven (1969). The preferences of naive, incubator-hatched, black-headed gull chicks (*Larus ridibundus*) for different coloured models of parent birds were tested. Hungry chicks approached and pecked at bills of models painted red or blue. Cold chicks, which had been placed outside the heated incubator, additionally approached black models. Startled chicks, which had heard recordings of alarm calls, preferred black models to any other. Impekoven concluded that colour preference was dependent on motivational state. It would appear that these preferences corresponded to a chick's normal experience. Red is the colour which attracts hungry chicks to the parent's bill to be fed. Cold or frightened chicks do not approach the parent's bill, but snuggle under its body where it is dark. As the chicks used in the studies were incubator reared and naive, their choices must have been innate. Such inborn discriminations may account for the oddities in the findings of Bolhuis and Bateson (1990) (see Box 10.2.).

Van Kampen and de Vos (1991) investigated the effect of manipulating the shape and colour of imprinting models on the behaviour of jungle fowl chicks (*Gallus gallus spadiceus*). They found that, when models were red, the chicks discriminated, exhibiting distress (by calling) in the presence of an unfamiliar shape of the

---

Box 10.2   The competitive exclusion model

The competitive exclusion model (Bateson, 1987) suggests that exposure to a stimulus during imprinting creates links between a *recognition system* (which interacts with the environment) and an *executive system* (for storage). Information in either system fades with disuse, so initially a new stimulus will be preferred to an older one because it can be more readily recalled. An older item, having been seen first, occupies a larger part of the executive system, so is subsequently preferred. In terms of chicks' (*Larus ridibundus*) behaviour, this means that in tests immediately following exposure to two novel objects, the second should be preferred, but the memory for this will fade and the stronger preference, for the first stimulus, will resurface. This is exactly what was found by Cherfas and Scott (1981).

Bolhuis and Bateson (1990) supported the competitive exclusion model by exposing chicks to one coloured cylinder (blue or yellow) for three days, and then to one of the other colour. The chicks' original preference for the first colour changed to the second, unless they were isolated following exposure or were subsequently exposed to both objects simultaneously. In these two situations, preference for the first cylinder was re-established, but only when it was blue. The executive system helped the chicks to remember their first exposure, and the recognition system enabled them to select which stimulus was most recent. The systems compete and the recognition system wins most of the time. However, if the animal is isolated, or exposed to the first (blue) object as well as the second, the strength of the earlier preference (now stored in the executive system) becomes apparent.

---

familiar colour. If their original model had been yellow, however, the chicks were content with a change in shape. Van Kampen and de Vos suggest that chicks pay more attention to attractive (not yellow) shapes, therefore learn more about them. Bolhuis and Horn (1992) conducted a similar experiment with domestic chickens (*Gallus gallus domesticus*). The chicks were incubator reared and exposed to imprinting models, which varied systematically in shape and colour. The results suggested that chicks generalised their imprinting experience to objects of the same shape but a different colour. This is surprising because the colours used were red and blue. Van Kampen and de Vos' results would suggest that these chicks should have discriminated between the shapes, as both red and blue are 'attractive' colours to chicks. However, in line with this expectation, the generalised imprinting response seen in Bolhuis and Horn's experiment was in fact weaker than the original response. This supports the view that chicks imprint on both shape and colour aspects of the stimulus.

It should be noted that the results of Bolhuis and Horn's (1992) experiment further contradict Lorenz's original view of imprinting. Their findings contradict the notion that imprinting is a special form of learning. The existence of a degree of generalisation is a property shared with other learning processes such as operant and classical conditioning (see Chapter 12).

SEXUAL IMPRINTING

There is some evidence that sexual imprinting, unlike filial imprinting, is highly resistant to reversal. Immelmann (1969) showed that finches are very inflexible once they have imprinted upon a model of a mate. He cross-fostered Bengalese (*Lonchura striata*) and zebra finches (*Taenopygia guttata*). Males preferred to court their foster species, and even when compelled to mate with their own species, he found they still preferred their foster species afterwards. This illustration also serves to support Lorenz's notion that imprinting governs sexual behaviour. Lorenz himself described a similar response in jackdaws (*Corrus monedula*), as described in Box 10.3.

Box 10.3   Sexual imprinting in a jackdaw (Lorenz, 1952)

A jackdaw that had imprinted on Lorenz demonstrated the full extent of this learning when it reached sexual maturity. In addition to filial imprinting, Lorenz had become the focus of sexual imprinting. Unfortunately for Lorenz, jackdaw courtship involves the male providing the female with food, so the imprinted jackdaw persistently attempted to feed Lorenz. If Lorenz failed to oblige by opening his mouth, the jackdaw did not give up, but attempted to drive beakfulls of worm pulp into his ears.

Immelmann's evidence for the irreversibility of sexual imprinting has been replicated successfully, but it does not seem to be as robust as was first thought. Like filial imprinting, there appears to be a degree of flexibility. As with Immelman's study, Kruijt and Meeuwissen (1991) found that a male zebra finch reared by a Bengalese finch would prefer to mate with a female of the species he has imprinted on (Bengalese). Birds in this study were additionally given breeding, or non-tactile, experience of a conspecific (separated from them only by wire). Either of these latter experiences shifted the preference in favour of a zebra finch mate. In a second part of their experiment, Kruijt and Meeuwissen showed that cross-fostered zebra finches which had been given a choice test between a mate of their own or their foster species behaved differently. This further experience of the 'wrong' (foster) species consolidated their imprinted image, so they were less affected by subsequent breeding or non-tactile experience with a conspecific. Nevertheless, their preferences were still somewhat swayed by the later experimental experience.

Kruijt and Meeuwissen's findings bring two further characteristics of imprinting into question. Lorenz suggested that sexual imprinting was complete long before the appropriate responses (that is, courtship and song) had developed. This would appear, however, to be inaccurate. It would seem that mating opportunities, and non-tactile experience of conspecifics in adulthood, are sufficient to modify mate preference of cross-fostered males. It would appear that sexual imprinting may be affected by reinforcement, and can be modified during adulthood. In this sense, imprinting resembles other forms of learning (see Chapter 12).

IMPRINTING AND MOVEMENT

Guiton (1959) demonstrated that chicks would imprint upon, and follow, coloured boxes which they had seen move. The importance of the movement of the imprinting stimulus was also illustrated by Hess' (1958) studies. Hess showed that ducks which have to try the hardest to follow the model, such as jumping hurdles or following up an inclined plane, demonstrate the strongest imprinting. Subsequent studies have shown, however, that movement is not an essential property for the model.

Auditory and olfactory imprinting

Lorenz observed only visual imprinting, but other senses can provide a medium for such attachments. In species such as wood ducks (*Anas strepera*), whose eggs are hatched in darkness, ducklings imprint on the mother before they are able to see her. Klopfer (1959) demonstrated that naive wood ducks approach an intermittent sound in the absence of visual stimuli, suggesting their following behaviour is initiated by auditory (sound) stimuli.

Miller and Atema (1990) experimentally tested the development of ducklings' (*Anas platyrhynchos*) freezing response to the mother's alarm call. This is an adaptive response to the threat of predation. Miller and Atema found that the probability of an appropriate response to the call of the imprinted model (the mother) was affected by both the presence of other ducklings and whether the ducklings were able to hear themselves. Ducklings which had been devocalised (were unable to make sounds), or which were reared or tested in isolation, were less likely to respond correctly. Therefore, imprinting is important in the development of simple fear responses, but it is not the only factor. The presence of siblings (see Box 10.4), and feedback of an individual's own sounds, are also important in learning to respond appropriately to the imprinting model.

Whilst imprinting was a phenomenon that Lorenz demonstrated in birds, it has been observed in a variety of other species. Zippelius (1972) reported the formation of caravans of shrews (*Sorex araneus*) on the basis

Figure 10.2 Olfactory imprinting in shrews. Young shrews learn the smell of the mother so that she can lead them by formation of a caravan

of olfactory (smell) imprinting (Figure 10.2). Like birds, the shrews have a critical period during which to imprint. Until they are seven days old, they will clutch the back of any substitute mother, such as a piece of cloth, to form a 'caravan'. Between days 8 and 14 they become imprinted upon the smell of the mother, and only she can then initiate the formation of a caravan. If shrews are exposed to a substitute olfactory stimulus during this critical period, they will not subsequently follow their natural mother.

The biological significance of imprinting

From an evolutionary viewpoint, it is often important that mating should only occur between members of the same species and that parents should care only for their own offspring. Imprinting tends to occur in species in which attachment to parents, to the family group, or to a member of the opposite sex is an important aspect of social organisation (McFarland, 1996). For example, the sensitive period for sexual imprinting in ducks, geese and finches corresponds closely to the period of parental care. The sensitive period usually ends before the juvenile is likely to mix with birds other than its immediate kin. Sexual imprinting may be more important for kin recognition than for species recognition. Bateson (1979) suggests that sexual imprinting enables an animal to choose a mate that appears slightly different, but not too different, from its parents and siblings. This may enable the animal to strike a balance between the advantages of inbreeding and outbreeding.

Some researchers have suggested that humans tend to choose mates that are socially, psychologically and

---

Box 10.4   Social ducklings are more flexible

Gottlieb (1991) found that social rearing of ducklings made their imprinting more flexible. He demonstrated that pre- and post-hatching exposure to a chicken call overrides the innate preference of a duckling to mallard (duck) calls. This only occurred, however, if they were reared in social conditions. Isolated ducklings preserved their species-specific preference, despite exposure to chicken calls. Gottlieb suggested this may have occurred because social ducklings called less and so did not buffer themselves against the alien (chicken) sounds.

physically similar to themselves (Lewis, 1975). However, there is also evidence that satisfactory marriages are not formed between people who spend their early childhood together (Wolf, 1970). Although human relationships are complicated by cultural factors, the evidence for some biologically based negative imprinting is considerable.

Imprinting: some conclusions

In conclusion, many of Lorenz's original beliefs about imprinting have been criticised. However, it remains evident that imprinting is a vital response for young precocial animals. Imprinting provides them with information about when, where and how to feed (with protection), and with an image for a future mate. It is sufficiently flexible to be adaptive if the situation changes, but is pre-programmed in order to occur rapidly to provide immediate security.

Bonding in precocial and altricial species

Bonding is a mutual process in which an attachment is formed between two individuals, the mother and infant, and in which both actively participate and benefit. This is in contrast to imprinting, in which the model providing a stimulus for the process does not have to 'respond' (although this distinction is not always clear-cut, as described in Box 10.5). Whilst precocial species do receive care, such as being fed, directed to food or protected by the adult, this may be incidental to their following behaviour. Altricial species, by contrast, need active and sometimes continual care. Here it is important that the mother and offspring can recognise one another. Altricial young need to know from which adults to attempt to gain help. They will not survive without care from their parents, so must be adept at recognising them and eliciting assistance. The parents need to ensure that their efforts are directed only at their own young, not the offspring of others. This error would reduce their fitness, not only by lowering the chances of their offspring surviv-

ing, but also by enhancing the survival of competitors. (The investment of parents in their offspring and the role of parental care is discussed more fully in Chapter 5.)

Box 10.5   Burrowing bee-eaters: what do adults imprint to?

Lessells et al. (1991) demonstrated the ability of adult bee-eaters (*Merops apiaster*) to recognise their own nestlings using auditory cues. Like wood ducks, bee-eaters do not nest in the open; instead, they use burrows underground. Playback experiments used recordings of a pair's own, or different, young. This enabled Lessells et al. to test whether adults recognised their own nestlings' calls. Recognition was measured by timing how long adults hovered outside an artificial burrow from which recorded sound could be heard. The adults responded positively to calls from their own chicks (but not from others) at four weeks. It would seem that acoustic recognition is important to parents as well as to offspring. This property of a two-way interaction blurs the distinction between imprinting and bonding.

Bonding in mammals: a two-way process

THE ROLE OF THE MOTHER

In a synthesis of factors affecting maternal motivation in mammals, Pryce (1992) identifies two classes of infant-based effects on the bonding process, passive and active ones. *Passive factors* (non-behavioural ones), comprise thermal, olfactory, gustatory (taste), and some visual processes. *Active factors* include changing visual stimuli, such as characteristic patterns of locomotion, tactile (touch) stimulation, such as suckling, and auditory signals.

Goats and sheep will readily attach to humans if hand reared. This resembles the olfactory imprinting described in shrews (see page 93). Klopfer et al. (1964) demonstrated that a mother goat (*Capra hircus*) is only sensitive to the smell of her kid for a brief period immediately after birth. Unless she has access to the kid within an hour, it will be rejected, but just five minutes' contact is sufficient to prevent rejection up to three hours later. This appears to be the cue for the onset of lactation (production of milk). The strength of these attachments has proved useful for fostering calves and lambs which have been orphaned at birth. A surviving ewe, for instance, can be persuaded to adopt a 'new' lamb by swaddling it in the skin of her dead offspring. The smell of her own young is sufficient to signal the formation of a bond. This attachment is then lasting.

THE ROLE OF THE INFANT

A mother of altricial young develops selective maternal care. She learns to recognise the key features of her offspring. This increases fitness, as she can selectively feed her own young and avoid assisting their competitors. Altricial young could attempt to elicit extra care from alien parents, but this would be unsuccessful as adults of most species recognise, and selectively avoid, the young of others. The young animals should, therefore, also develop a preferential relationship. This discrimination could be based on sound, smell, appearance or behaviour.

Most research has focused on the mother's role in the bonding process. Nowak (1991), however, considered which factors influence attachment formation for the offspring. Nowak selectively deprived newborn lambs (*Ovis aries*) of different senses. None of the treatments was surgical, and all were reversible. Olfaction was impaired using an anaesthetic spray into each nostril, vision by placing the lambs behind a screen, and hearing by using earplugs and earmuffs. The effectiveness of these treatments was tested by the absence of a startle response. Recognition of the mother by the lambs was measured as time spent with its own, or an alien, mother. Surprisingly, Nowak found that, in contrast to the ewes, lambs do not rely on olfaction to discriminate between individuals. (Olfactory cues may, however, be necessary stimuli for suckling.) Twenty-four-hour-old lambs used auditory and visual cues to identify their mothers at close quarters. The auditory cues might be a quality of the particular mother's bleats, or a feature dependent on whether she recognises the lamb as her own or not, such as increased bleating by alien mothers. The visual cues might similarly be properties of the mother, or her activities. Alien mothers may have been more restless. Three-day-old lambs also use visual and auditory cues, but are less impaired than younger lambs by visual deprivation. We can conclude

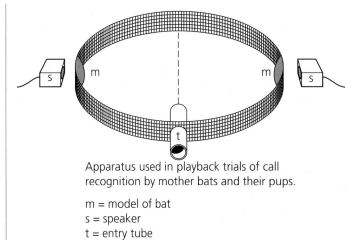

Apparatus used in playback trials of call recognition by mother bats and their pups.

m = model of bat
s = speaker
t = entry tube

Figure 10.3   Apparatus used in playback experiments to test recognition by mother and infant bats (Balcombe, 1990; Balcombe & McCracken, 1992)

that lambs learn to recognise their mothers by sight and sound within three days.

EVIDENCE FOR RECIPROCAL BONDING

The bond formed by mammals is not simply one of offspring to adult, as in imprinting. Both individuals are participants in the bonding process. Studies of a rather different mammal, the bat (*Tardardia brasiliensis mexicana*), have revealed a mutual recognition processes. Balcombe (1990) used the apparatus shown in Figure 10.3 to test vocal recognition by mother bats. Bat mothers and pups were caught in their cave roost, tested in a laboratory, and returned to exactly the same site in the roost within twenty-four hours. Recordings were made of each pup's vocalisations. These were used to test the ability of each mother to recognise her own or a 'foreign' pup's call. The mothers were put into the auditory arena through the tube. When they emerged, the playback recording was started and lasted five minutes. The observer scored the number of occasions the females approached bat models in front of the speaker and the amount of time the female spent near, or with, each bat model. (The models were necessary to give the females a 'target'.)

As can be seen from the graphs shown in Figure 10.4, the mothers preferred their own pup on every measure. The differences for time spent in contact, and for number of contacts, were significant. We can conclude from these results that mother bats can recognise their young using auditory cues. Balcombe and McCracken (1992) looked for a reciprocal ability in bat pups, using an

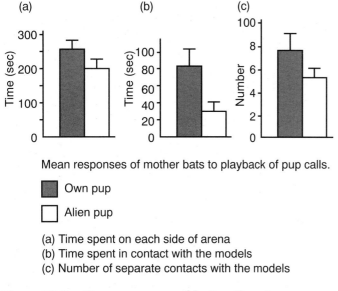

Mean responses of mother bats to playback of pup calls.

■ Own pup

□ Alien pup

(a) Time spent on each side of arena
(b) Time spent in contact with the models
(c) Number of separate contacts with the models

Figure 10.4   Mean responses of bat mothers to playbacks of pup recognition calls

identical technique to Balcombe's (1990). They concluded that young bats could recognise their mother by her call. The maternal calls are sufficiently loud to be heard above the substantial background noise in the roost.

We can conclude from the findings of the preceding studies that the bond between mother bats and their young is reciprocal. The importance of this bond becomes apparent when the conditions in a roost are considered. The caves are dark and crowded. Pups roost separately from mothers, in creches which may contain millions of individuals, at densities of 5000 per square metre. Pups are mobile from their day of birth, so whilst females return with accuracy to within a metre of where they left their pups, the pups may have moved. Both pups and mothers can use olfactory cues for recognition, but these are probably unhelpful except at close quarters. It is important for a female to locate her own pup to feed it, as bat milk is high in fat and costly to produce. For the pup, recognising the mother is essential, as feeding is non-random (mothers usually nurse only their own pups) (McCracken & Gustin, 1987). If the mother and pup do not reunite, the pup will starve, so both parties have a vested interest in effective recognition.

FUNCTIONS OF BONDING

Attachments such as those formed between lambs and

ewes, and bat mothers and pups, serve to keep the young animal safe and well nourished. When the offspring is old enough to fend for itself, we would expect this bond to be severed (see Chapter 7, page 63). It appears that this is not always the case. Some breeds of sheep, such as the Scottish blackface (*Ovis aries*), show mother–daughter bonds which persist well beyond weaning, sometimes for up to two years (Rowell, 1991). This is not, however, typical of all breeds. Such lasting bonds, when seen in carnivores and primates, may form the basis of a dominance hierarchy.

Dogs (*Canis familiaris*), as anyone who has owned a puppy will know, readily form attachments to both dogs and people. Scott and Fuller (1965) found that for puppies there was a sensitive period from about three to ten weeks after birth. During this time they were able to form filial and sexual attachments with the minimum of exposure. Isolation beyond fourteen weeks, however, produced abnormal behaviour. This deviance resulting from failure to bond may be typical of many mammals. Bonds, therefore, seem to provide more than just a guide to follow to food, or a search image for a mate. In altricial animals, the attachment figure seems to provide a model for a wider variety of social behaviours.

The mother–infant bond is particularly significant in some species because maternal status bestows rank to her offspring. A *matrilinial* society is one which is led by a dominant female, and in which hierarchy position is passed down from mother to daughter. Males tend to leave the group at maturity. This type of organisation is typical of primates, but is seen in some other species, such as elephants (*Loxodonta africana*). Female Japanese macaques (*Macaca fuscata*), a kind of monkey, 'inherit' their mother's hierarchy position. In dominance conflicts, daughters of dominant females simply 'pull rank', if necessary calling for assistance from their mothers. The same privilege is not, however, extended to the sons of dominant females which, like other juveniles, emigrate from the group (S. Kawamura, quoted in Altmann, 1965).

ATTACHMENTS IN HIGHER PRIMATES

Rhesus monkeys (*Macaca mulatta*) cling to, or are held against, the mother's body immediately after birth. This does not, however, lead automatically to feeding as contact would for a newborn foal. A baby rhesus monkey may not feed for up to nine hours after birth, and even upon latching on to the nipple, the infant will not suckle continuously. Close body contact between the mother and infant is maintained for one to two weeks, after which the offspring begins to move away – not out of reach initially, but over the next two years, contact is progressively reduced until it is negligible. During this time the infant benefits from the protection of the mother, but is also exposed to opportunities to learn about feeding, nesting, predators and the social structure of the group. The importance of such a bond to the normal development of young monkeys was illustrated by the deprivation experiments of Harlow (1965), as described in Box 10.6.

Box 10.6   Harlow's monkeys

Harlow (1965) conducted a series of experiments to investigate the effect of rearing baby rhesus monkeys without their mothers. In the simplest experiment, infant monkeys were placed in individual cages which contained a pair of model 'mothers'. One surrogate provided nourishment; it was made of wire and had a teat supplying milk. The other provided comfort; it was covered with soft cloth.

The infant monkeys spent most of their time clinging to the soft surrogate (Figure 10.5). If the infants were frightened (for instance by a novel object placed in the cage), they ran to the soft surrogate. They also used this model as a secure base from which to explore, running back between bouts of exploration. In the absence of the soft surrogate, the monkeys either froze or ran around the cage displaying intense fear.

The contact comfort gained by the monkey seemed to be important to the formation of a strong bond between the infant and the soft surrogate. The provision of food by the wire surrogate did *not* result in the formation of a bond. In adulthood, these deprived monkeys were socially disturbed. They were readily dominated by other monkeys, often failed to mate, and were poor mothers. These consequences, however, cannot be attributed without question to the deprivation of bonding. Subsequent studies showed that the behavioural abnormalities could be avoided by housing maternally deprived monkeys with a peer group. This suggests that at least some of the effects were mediated by a general lack of contact, rather than a specific deprivation of a maternal bond.

Figure 10.5   Deprivation of the maternal bond. The young monkey, deprived of its mother, clings to the soft model for comfort

---

Chimpanzees (*Pan troglodytes*), orang-utans (*Pongo pygmaeus*) and gorillas (*Gorilla gorilla*) are much slower to develop than rhesus monkeys (Figure 10.6). They spend up to four months in continuous contact with and many months in the immediate vicinity of, the mother. She will gather her infant up if it strays too far, and the infant will, for several years, run to her side in the face of danger. Goodall (1965) suggests that adolescence in chimpanzees lasts until about seven years, and that they are not fully mature until 10 or 11. She believes that the mother–infant bond persists into adult life and across generations, forming the only stable social unit within larger, changing, social groupings.

ATTACHMENTS IN HUMANS

The formation of attachments in humans is not the focus of this chapter, and the topic is covered in detail in *Developmental Psychology* (McIlveen & Gross, 1997). However, as humans are highly altricial primates, we would expect a high degree of bonding between parent and offspring. There are interesting parallels between bonding in higher non-human primates and in ourselves – for instance, in our use of smell (see Box 10.7)

– and the need for the bond between an infant and its mother to be reciprocal.

Bowlby (1971) observes a continuum in attachment formation between the lower and higher primates. In the least advanced primates, such as lemurs and marmosets, the baby must do all the clinging (it receives no support from its mother). In more advanced primates, such as the rhesus monkey, the mother provides some support for the baby, until it is strong enough to cling tightly while she moves around. In the most advanced primates, such as gorillas and humans, the infant will cling but is only kept in close proximity to the mother by her own actions. Where the initiative to cling comes from the baby, it is more important that it can distinguish one adult from another. Where the responsibility lies with the mother, she must be able to identify her offspring. This evolutionary shift, from the baby to the mother taking the initiative for maintaining contact, has a consequence for studying attachment. It makes reliable comparison between species more difficult.

Figure 10.6   Higher primates, such as the orang-utan, form strong bonds between mother and infant

> **Box 10.7   Smell matters to mothers and babies**
>
> Cherfas (1985) reported an experimental investigation into the effects of the mother's smell on babies. Gauze pads were worn next to the mother's skin and later presented to babies aged two to ten days. Babies preferred their own mother's smell, regardless of whether it was the smell of her neck or breast. The effect of the smell was to calm the babies down ('foreign' or clean pads caused increased activity and distress). The mothers were then asked to identify, by smell, T-shirts worn by their babies. In a sample of forty mothers choosing from a selection of three T-shirts, most could do the task, although some mothers were better than others. Out of a large range of factors, such as cosmetics, washing, and previous children, only one, birth practices, was found to be important. Mothers who had skin contact with the baby, and breast fed immediately, were the best at subsequent identification. Greatly reduced contact (for instance following anaesthesia) reduced the mother's ability to recognise her baby's smell. Nevertheless, this ability is highly resistant. Even a mother whose baby had been born by Caesarean section, and who had experienced only 2.5 hours contact with her baby prior to the test, could still identify by smell alone.

Conclusions

This chapter has reviewed the evidence for the characteristics of imprinting as proposed by Lorenz. Our consideration would seem to suggest that whilst imprinting occurs, it is not so constrained, or as special, as Lorenz believed. The formation of mutual bonds in non-human animals, between mothers and their infants, has also been discussed. Comparisons have been made with humans, but such generalisations may not be valid.

SUMMARY

- **Precocial** animals are born well developed, become independent quickly, and require relatively little care. **Altricial** animals are relatively

less well developed, and dependent at birth. They need extensive care.

- **Lorenz** suggested that precocial species formed

an attachment by **imprinting**. He described this process in **precocial** birds. He believed that imprinting occurred during a **critical period**, was **irreversible**, was responsible for directing both **filial** (family) behaviour and **sexual** behaviour, was directed towards the **first moving object they saw**, and that this attachment was **different from other forms of learning**.

- Subsequent research has shown that imprinting is widespread among precocial species, occurring in many birds but also in mammals.
- Imprinting occurs most readily **early** in development, but beyond this it is still possible. This time, which extends beyond the critical period, is called a **sensitive phase**.
- The effects of imprinting may sometimes be **reversible**. A chick can become imprinted upon a model, but exposure to a second stimulus will alter its preference. If a period without a model follows its exposure to the two different models, chicks revert to their initial imprinting preference.
- **Bateson** proposed a **competitive exclusion model** to account for such findings. **Attractiveness** (e.g. colour) and **isolation**, as well as order of presentation, determine which model will be imprinted upon.
- Chicks show innate preferences for imprinting on some types of model. In particular, they imprint more strongly to **colours** other than yellow. **Impekoven** suggested that colour preferences in gulls may be a function of **motivational state**: cold and frightened birds prefer black because they would hide under the parent's body where it is dark.
- Chicks are also able both to **discriminate** and to **generalise** between **shapes** of models. These properties are shared with other forms of learning, suggesting that imprinting is not a special case.
- There is some evidence to suggest that sexual imprinting is irreversible, but this too has been criticised. **Kruijt and Meeuwissen** successfully reversed the sexual imprinting of zebra finches that had been cross-fostered to Bengalese finches. Both mating experience and non-tactile contact (being separated only by wire) could return mate preference to a conspecific (member of the same species) following imprinting on the foster species. These findings may be the result of the reinforcing effect of the breeding experience, or of conspecific contact. If so, this further refutes the idea that imprinting is a special form of learning which is not dependent on **reinforcement**.

- Chicks will imprint on moving objects, but **movement** is not an essential property for imprinting to occur.
- Imprinting can arise from **auditory** or **olfactory** stimulation as well as **visual cues**. Ducklings become imprinted on their mother's call, although this process is affected by the presence of other ducklings and the ability of the ducklings to hear themselves. Therefore, **social contact** affects imprinting.
- Species which nest in the dark (e.g. underground) cannot use vision. **Shrews** show **olfactory imprinting**, assembling in a caravan behind the mother, recognising her by her **smell**.
- The **function** of imprinting in precocial animals is to provide them with information about when, where and how to **feed**, with **protection** and with an **image for a future mate**.
- **Altricial** animals form a relatively lasting **bond** with the mother. This ensures their survival whilst they are unable to fend for themselves, and provides an opportunity for maturation, learning, and the acquisition of status.
- Bonding in altricial species is dependent upon the participation of the **mother** and the **infant**. Both have a vested interest in each other. Parents should evolve not to waste effort on young which are not their own. Infants should evolve to selectively solicit assistance from those most likely to provide it.
- **Ewes** and nanny **goats** learn to recognise their offspring by **smell**. Mother **bats** recognise their pups by their **calls**. **Lambs** learn to recognise their mothers using **visual** and **auditory** cues. Bat pups, like their mothers, use **auditory** cues. Many species of mammal use olfactory cues at close range as a cue to **suckling**.
- Bonding serves several functions. It keeps the mother and young in contact, so the young can be **protected** and **fed**. The formation of a bond is necessary for the **normal development of behaviour**. For some primates, such as the Japanese macaque, females gain their **position in the hierarchy** from the bond with their mother.
- Bonds in **primates** last longer than in other species. Young primates cling to the mother as soon as they are born, although in the higher primates they are assisted because they cannot initially support themselves. They remain in contact even when they are not feeding.
- **Harlow** demonstrated the essential nature of the bond for normal development in **rhesus monkeys**. Maternal deprivation led to **fear, inability**

to integrate into a social group and **failure to breed spontaneously or rear young**.

- In primates such as the **chimpanzee**, mother–infant bonds may persist for life.
- **Humans**, like other primates, rely on **smell** as a cue to bonding at close quarters. **Mothers** can recognise their own babies using olfactory cues. **Babies**, too, use olfactory cues and are calmed by their own mother's smell. These attachments form very quickly, very early in the baby's life. **Bowlby** suggests that the rapid formation of such bonds is essential for highly altricial species because the infant is so helpless. Mothers must be able to recognise their own young reliably because the infant cannot cling to or follow them. Such differences between species make reliable comparisons difficult, even between humans and higher primates.

SIGNALLING SYSTEMS IN NON-HUMAN ANIMALS

Introduction and overview

This final chapter of Part 3 aims to explore how animals communicate. The behaviours discussed so far in this section have been social acts, which require interaction between individuals. Co-ordinating and executing these actions rely upon individuals being able to signal their knowledge or intentions to one another. The nature and function of communication are, like any behaviour, subject to selection pressures. Signals which enhance fitness should evolve. We would therefore expect to find evidence to suggest that communication plays an essential role in the survival and reproduction of animals. Signals about food, finding a mate, or danger have clear implications for the fitness of both the sender and the receiver. This chapter uses some of the examples of social behaviours already discussed to consider the types of messages which are passed between individuals. It also examines the function of these messages.

What is a signal?

What is a message, and how do we know when one has been communicated? We all know that sending messages is not the same as communicating. We can talk without being listened to, and send e-mails that 'bounce' (fail to reach their target). So what are the essential criteria for communication? It is a two-way process, where a message is conveyed from a sender to one, or more, recipients. Its reception is denoted by a change in the recipient. For example, Tinbergen and Perdeck (1950) studied the begging behaviour of herring gull chicks (*Larus argentatus*) (Figure 11.1). The chick communicates its need for food to the adult using a signal: it pecks a red spot on the parent bird's bill. The reception of this signal is indicated by the par-

ent's response: it feeds the chick. Note the difference between this *active* communication by the chick, and the *passive* sign (a sign stimulus) of the red spot on the parent's bill.

The effects of signals on behaviour are the easiest consequences to detect, but changes in physiology, motivation or cognition (thought processes) could also arise from a communication. Behaviour that causes a change in others is not always equivalent to communication. For example, tripping someone up causes his or her behaviour to change, but not as a result of any message. Communication, therefore, requires a *deliberate* attempt on the part of the sender to impart information to others.

Signals provide information of benefit to the recipient. In the case of the herring gull, the parent is informed about when to feed its young to maximise growth and minimise wasted effort. The sender also benefits selfishly: the chick gets fed. Other benefits could include

Figure 11.1   A chick communicates its need for food with a pecking signal

gaining a mate through courtship signals (increasing individual fitness), or assisting kin by giving an alarm call (raising inclusive fitness). For communication to be effective, the sender and recipient must attach the same meaning to the signal. Without this correspondence, the mutual benefits are lost. So a *signal* is a deliberate message, sent to one or more recipients. Decoding the message results in behavioural or other changes in the recipient, and consequent benefits to both parties.

Guilford and Dawkins (1991) propose that there are two aspects of an effective signal: *strategic design*, whether it contains the necessary information, and *efficacy*, whether it gets that information across to the receiver. They suggest that the importance of efficacy has been relatively neglected in psychological research. When studying efficacy, three aspects of receiver psychology are important: whether the signal is easy to detect, easy to discriminate and easy to remember.

Communication can only evolve if it is of benefit to both signaller and recipient. If it is not, the tendency to expend effort, in sending messages or responding to them, will be eliminated by selection. Once established, however, communication signals can be exploited, as shown in Box 11.1.

Eavesdropping and deceitful signalling

Unintended recipients may benefit from the content of the message, or simply by deducing the location of the sender. For example, the scent released by a female

bark beetle to attract a mate also attracts competing females to the signaller's egg-laying site. These *eavesdropping* females gain because they avoid spending time and energy searching for a suitable tree. The signalling female loses because her offspring must compete with those of the cheats (Raffa & Berryman, 1983). Similarly, predators may be the unintended recipients of calls or displays which provide them with a meal, whilst the signaller suffers the ultimate cost of its life.

Hoverflies (*Helophilus pendulus*) send a *deceitful message* to potential predators. They mimic wasps, signalling that they are dangerous, without incurring the costs associated with generating a sting and venom. The duped predator loses the chance of a palatable meal. (Mimicry is discussed in detail in Chapter 3, page 22.) Male cricket frogs (*Acris crepitans blanchardi*) use auditory signals to display their strength to their competitors, lower tones indicating a stronger male. Wagner (1992) reports that males may be deceitful by lowering the tone of their call during a signalling session, suggesting that they are larger than they really are. To counter this, other males can judge whether or not to fight using just the initial tone produced, which is usually a reliable indicator of size.

The function of communication is to serve senders and recipients, but it can only do so if it is effective and reliable. To avoid errors, signals are consistent and situation specific. Species differ in their capacity to communicate, and in the media available within their habitat. Therefore they use different *signalling systems*. *Visual*, *auditory* (sound), *olfactory* (smell), *touch* and *taste* senses are used. Many animals exploit combinations of signals, or use different systems for different functions. In the following sections, examples are used to show how different species send accurate signals to their intended receivers.

Visual signalling systems

Visual signalling systems are one of the easiest to study. Psychologists, as illegitimate receivers (eavesdroppers), can readily observe both the signals sent and the response of target individuals. The visual signalling system is a flexible one, as the nature of the message can be varied in three ways: *position*, *movement* and *colour*. Animals can adopt static positions or *postures* which convey particular meaning to others. These may be exaggerated by physical structures. For example, the

Box 11.1	**Signal legitimacy and effects on fitness**		
Effect on fitness		*Term used*	*Description*
Signaller	Receiver		
+	+	Communication	Legitimate signaller and receiver
−	+	Eavesdropping	Legitimate signaller, illegitimate receiver
+	−	Deceitful signalling	Illegitimate signaller, legitimate receiver

+ represents an increase in fitness; − represents a decrease in fitness.

threatening stance of a robin (*Erithacus rubecula*) is enhanced by fluffing up the breast feathers. It is better able to defend its territory by looking larger and more aggressive to potential competitors. Postures may form part of a sequence of movements or *gestures*, such as the courtship dances performed by great crested grebes (*Podiceps cristatus*) (Figure 11.2).

The use of colour in signalling is clearly seen in the display of peacocks (*Pavo cristatus*) discussed in Chapter 4 (page 36). Colour is also fundamental to the responses of robins. A robin will attack as little as a few red feathers nailed to a stake in its territory, but will ignore a whole stuffed robin that has been painted brown (Lack, 1943). The coloured feathers of a dominant male ruff (*Philomachus pugnax*, a wading bird) indicate his status to females during courtship. Subordinate (inferior) males have white ruffs and get fewer mates (see Chapter 6, page 55).

When we see a visual signal, and the response of a receiver to it, we can infer the meaning of the signal. On some occasions the mechanism by which the signal has arisen is obvious, often because there is some functional significance to the signalling behaviour itself. In the courtship of the common tern (*Sterna hirundo*, a sea bird), the male provides the female with fish to eat. This is a signal for mating to proceed, and implies that the male is a good forager and will provide well for his mate and their young (Nisbet, 1977). The wedding gift of the male balloon fly (*Hilara sartor*) to his bride is a little harder to explain: it is a hollow silken ball. Why does he offer it, and why must the female receive this apparently bizarre signal as a prerequisite to mating? A possible answer is described in Box 11.2.

Behaviours such as those of the balloon fly and grebe are described as being *ritualised*; evolution has operated to make the signal more effective. Ritualisation makes signals *conspicuous* (improving detection by the receiver), and *stereotyped* (reducing the likelihood of a misunderstanding). These characteristics of signals are aspects of the 'strategic design' described by Guilford and Dawkins (1991).

When considering the evolution of behaviours, we must remember the explanations given in Chapter 1. Signals, like any other actions, evolve because they are adaptive. They enhance the fitness of the signaller. The evolution of communication seems complex because it appears to require a simultaneous change in the behav-

Figure 11.2   Courtship of the great crested grebe (*Podiceps cristatus*) (Huxley, 1914). On inland waters, from mid-winter onwards, the great crested grebe can be seen performing its elaborate courtship dance. The male and female may play different roles, as in assuming the cat position (where their partner stands upright in the 'ghost position'), or during invitations to mate. Sometimes the male and female mirror each other's behaviour, such as during the head-shaking ceremony and in the 'weed', or 'penguin' dance. This is where the birds, each with a beakful of weed, rise up in the water to perform an exaggerated version of the head-shaking ceremony. (a) Cat position, (b) invitation, (c) approach, (d) clicking calls accompany swaying of the heads; (c) and (d) are stages in the head-shaking ceremony

Box 11.2   The evolution of a worthless visual courtship signal (Kessel, 1955)

The comparative method in animal behaviour offers a way to answer questions about how behaviours may have evolved. It provides a means to deduce hypothetical evolutionary sequences, by identifying a plausible series of changes based on the behaviour of present-day species. The suggestion is not that these are ancestral forms, but that they represent possible behaviours of earlier forms. There are several thousand species of empid fly (from the same family as *Hilara sartor*) which show diverse courtship patterns. The flow-chart below offers a possible evolutionary pathway which could have led to the balloon fly signal. The starting point is a simple, understandable, behaviour. This transforms, through the course of evolution, to one which is apparently worthless and consequently incomprehensible in isolation.

Carnivorous flies which hunt for smaller insects such as midges. The females are courted in isolation.

↓

Carnivorous flies as above. The males capture prey then seek a female. She takes the prey prior to copulation and consumes it to provide herself with energy.

↓

Prey capture and courtship as above, but males with prey form groups to attract females.

↓

As above but the male restrains the prey with strands of silk.

↓

As above but the prey is entirely wrapped in silk

↓

As above, but before wrapping, the male removes juices from the prey, so the female receives a non-nutritious husk.

↓

Nectar-feeding species find an insect fragment around which to construct a silk balloon. This is presented to the female before copulation.

↓

Hilara sartor omits the insect fragment, constructing only a silken ball to present to the female.

appears. Novel signals are simply new behaviours to which others respond in advantageous ways. The key element is the effect of the action on other individuals; the nature of the signal is less important. It can be similar to existing behaviours, such as variations of aggression, preening or parental care, but does not have to be. Signals may be unrelated to the message conveyed, but still be effective. If, however, new behaviours were to arise which were effective signals, but carried large costs (e.g. attracted predators), they would probably be eliminated by natural selection.

ADVANTAGES AND DISADVANTAGES OF THE VISUAL SIGNALLING SYSTEM

Why are visual signals used in so many contexts? The variables of colour, position and movement offer an enormous variety of messages. Their complexity is one way to ensure that they are understood. If the signal differs greatly from any other, it is less likely to be misinterpreted. Some visual signals, such as colours, are enduring and have few costs (they use little energy to maintain). Their permanence ensures that when a potential recipient is encountered, it is unable to avoid the message. Signalling and reception are guaranteed.

One disadvantage of visual signalling is that the certainty of reception relies on encountering conspecifics (members of the same species), and this cannot be assured. Furthermore, postures and gestures are transient (lasting only a short time) and energetic, and are more costly than colour signals. A vigorously moving animal uses energy and runs the risk of attracting predators. Visual signalling is not as effective over a long range as other media; the recipient has to be nearby and within a line of sight. Finally, visual signals are useless in the dark, unless, of course, the organism is bioluminescent (generates its own light), such as fire flies (*Photinus consimilus*).

Auditory signalling system

Auditory communication, like visual signalling, is highly flexible. Messages can vary in terms of *pitch, volume* or *sequence*. In toads, the pitch of the male's croak indicates his size to females, which prefer deep croaks, as these imply bigger, fitter males. The sequence of notes produced by crickets (*Gryllus integer*), using their legs, informs potential mates of the sender's species. In many forms of auditory communication, all three vari-

iour of both signaller and recipient. There can be no value in a signal, no matter how elaborate, unless it is understood and acted upon by the intended recipient. This problem is, however, not as complex as it first

ables are changed, producing a huge array of potential signals. Human language provides an example of communication which exploits this variability to the full, and is discussed briefly in Chapter 14 (page 140).

Female red deer (*Cervus elaphus*), like toads, judge their mates by the sounds they make. McComb (1991) used recordings of red deer stags to identify the characteristics of their roar which females preferred. The females showed no preference for different pitches, but were attracted by high roaring rates, and by males which started to roar first. In terms of Guilford and Dawkins' criteria, this signal is strategic in its design, as it conveys information about the male's status. High roaring rates were positively associated with reproductive success and fighting ability. The signal is also effective because the females can easily detect, and discriminate between, roars.

As discovered in Chapter 9, one of the advantages of sociality is a reduction in risk from predators. In animals such as ground squirrels (*Spermophilus beldingi*),

this is achieved by the communication of impending threats between group members. For vervet monkeys (*Cercopithecus aethiops*), the nature of the hazard dictates the most appropriate response. (There is no point in going up a tree to avoid a martial eagle!) For signals to be helpful to the recipients, the message must indicate the appropriate response. Seyfarth et al. (1980) studied vervet alarm calls through observations and field experiments. By using recordings of different calls, they could be sure that it was the auditory message, not some other feature of the situation, which was informing the vervets about appropriate evasive behaviour. They described three distinct alarms for different predators, which produce different responses (Figure 11.3).

ADVANTAGES AND DISADVANTAGES OF THE AUDITORY SIGNALLING SYSTEM

Sound is a highly effective medium for communication. It is both penetrating and flexible. Van Bushkirk

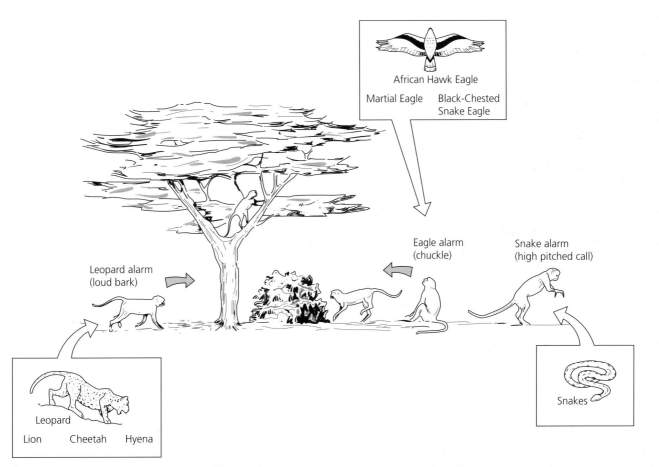

Figure 11.3   Vervet monkey (*Cercopithecus aethiops*) alarm calls. Different signals elicit appropriate predator-avoidance behaviours

(1997) discovered that similar species of bird living in different habitats exploit the auditory medium to their best advantage. For example, birds living in deciduous forests need penetrating calls to travel long distances. They use lower frequency calls than their 'open country' cousins. A similar phenomenon is seen in dolphin communication (see below).

Complex and variable messages can be created with sound, as illustrated by the diversity of bird song. Even when similar species of bird inhabit the same area, they can be distinguished by their song. This is a bonus for bird watchers, but essential for their potential mates. To ensure that a young bird acquires a song that others will recognise, it learns the fine details by listening to adults singing. It knows which adults to copy because it has an innate 'blue print' on to which to map the correct 'full song' (see Chapter 1, page 7).

If you happen to be looking the wrong way, it is possible to 'miss' a visual signal. It is much more difficult to avoid receiving an auditory message if you are within earshot (cantankerous aunts are an exception to this rule). On land, sound will permeate some structures and bounce off others, so travels 'around corners', which visual signals cannot do. This capacity of sound to penetrate is exploited by sea animals (see below).

The same features which make sound such a good medium for sending and receiving legitimate messages also make errors more likely, and make it easy to cheat. Vervet alarm calls, for instance, are learned. During infancy, vervets make errors in their calls and responses, with potentially fatal consequences. The sounds intended for conspecifics could be abused by others. Predators, for instance, can use messages intended for legitimate receivers to locate prey. It is interesting to note that alarm calls are similar across many species. This is an attempt to counter their illegitimate reception, as the frequencies used make the source hard to locate.

Illegitimate senders can also be found. Male great tits (*Parus major*) pronounce ownership of their territory using between two and seven different songs. They tend to change song each time they change perch (Krebs, 1977). This behaviour could deceitfully indicate to prospecting males that there were more occupied territories in the area than really existed. Yasukawa (1981) observes, however, that this may not be the reason that intruders are deterred. They may be aware that all the calls emanate from the same male, but his scope for song may be (correctly) interpreted as an indicator

of age or strength. Therefore, the appropriate judgement would be to depart.

Communication in marine mammals: a special case of auditory signalling?

Many of the sounds produced by marine mammals, such as dolphins and whales, are audible to the human ear. This, coupled with their eerie tone, has attracted the interest of humans for centuries. It is only within the last few decades, however, with the aid of underwater microphones (hydrophones) and sophisticated recording equipment, that we have been able to gain insight into their communication. Understanding the function of any signal requires that we can observe its effect on the recipient. This is problematic in wild marine animals. Researchers can readily identify the signaller by its call. However, locating the recipient, when it may be deep underwater or many miles away, is more difficult. One way this can be overcome is by studying marine mammals in captivity.

DOLPHINS

Dolphins produce a huge variety of noises, which can be divided into two classes, pulsed and unpulsed sounds. The pulsed sounds include clicks and bursts. Unpulsed sounds, which may last several seconds, include whistles and squeaks of pure tones. Whistles were believed to be the dolphin's main form of communication, but this misassumption has arisen simply because they are readily audible to the human ear. The pulsed clicks are too high for us to hear, although they can be detected and amplified.

Those species of dolphin forming smaller groups (of three to twenty individuals) use only pulsed sounds. The high-frequency clicks travel only relatively short distances in the water, so are suitable for use by small groups. Bottlenosed dolphins (*Tursiops truncatus*), and other highly gregarious (sociable) species, produce high-pitched whistles, which are unpulsed. They form schools of hundreds of animals which forage together. The lower frequency whistles carry well through the water so are better for larger, more dispersed groups. The function of dolphin calls has been explored experimentally, as described in Box 11.3.

Box 11.3 Dolphin clicks

An individual dolphin (*Stenella attenuata*) has its own *click* signature, a sequence of clicks which is unique. This may help to identify it in the group and to allow other individuals to locate it. Bright (1984) describes an experiment which investigated the role of dolphin calls. A recording was made when a dolphin was removed from its school and taken into captivity. Its persistent bouts of whistling appeared to be alarm or distress calls. When played back to its own school, they fled instantly. The same recording played to another school elicited curiosity rather than flight. The difference in response suggests that the individual's own group was able to detect danger from some aspect of the familiar call, indicating that it did indeed act as an alarm. Click signatures are also produced by sperm whales (*Physeter catodon*) which, like dolphins, are gregarious. These click signatures are again likely to be important to the social structure of their group.

Box 11.4 A whale of a party

The role of social calls in humpback whales was demonstrated experimentally by Tyack (1983), using a tape recording of an active whale group. When broadcast at sufficient volume, with the aid of a gigantic US Navy loudspeaker, singing whales stopped and headed towards the source of the sound. They approached the boat at speeds of up to 12 km per hour, submerged and circled the boat. They seemed to be looking for the group of whales apparently making the sounds. If songs were played, rather than social calls, the whales moved away from the boat. Furthermore, whales singing within range of the broadcast responded to recorded songs by ceasing to sing and moving away. Therefore social calls and singing appear to have different signalling functions in this species.

In an experiment to explore the capacity of dolphin communication, a pair of captive bottlenosed dolphins were isolated from each other by sight, but not by sound (Bastion, 1967). The female was taught to push a particular paddle to obtain a reward. The male's pool contained an identical set of paddles but he received no training. He did, however, learn to push the correct paddle. This was seen as evidence that the female had communicated the solution to him acoustically. Throughout the tests, both dolphins emitted whistles, squeaks and clicks, but none of this can be identified as deliberate communication. At the very least, any increase in signalling may have been caused by the isolation, or by raised arousal due to the novelty of the test situation.

HUMPBACK WHALES

Humpback whales (*Megaptera novaeangliae*) produce both social calls, as described in Box 11.4, and songs. They sing after their migration south to the warm sheltered regions of the Atlantic and Pacific oceans, off the African and American coasts, where the females give birth. Their songs are built up from small units which are repeated and combined into phrases. Groups of similar phrases make up a theme. A song is composed

of between four and ten themes repeated without a pause (Figure 11.4). Analysis of songs in this manner shows that all humpbacks in a particular area sing the same song – that is, they have a dialect. Geographical differences in song probably arise because there is no contact between Atlantic and Pacific populations because their migration routes are unlikely to cross.

The function of whale song is still unclear. One proposal is that it acts as a courtship signal. Songs could be used to proclaim the species, age, sex, location or

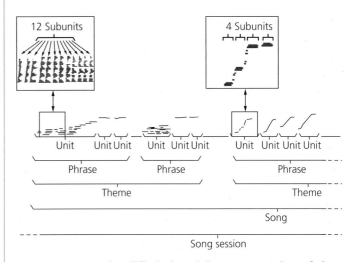

Figure 11.4   A simplified pictorial representation of the song of the humpback whale (*Megaptera novaeangliae*) song. The insets illustrate the pattern of sound in a unit if they are slowed down

willingness of a prospective mate. They could also serve a role in competition for mates, somewhat like birds displaying at a lek (see Chapter 6, page 56).

During courtship, singing males may approach a cow and her calf. Non-receptive cows will swim away from a singing male, but if he catches up he will stop singing and become an escort to the cow. The pair will later dive for up to fifteen minutes, during which mating may be taking place, but this has not been observed under water. If a singing male approaches a group of whales, he falls silent, but aggressive activity, with thrashing of flukes (tails) and ramming, ensues. This is accompanied by an, as yet, indecipherable array of grunts, trumpets and elements of songs. These social calls attract other singing whales, any of which may displace an existing escort male.

Olfactory signalling systems

Olfaction is the process of detecting and identifying smells. Many of these smells may be *pheromones*, which are volatile chemicals released by animals which have an effect on the physiology or behaviour of con-specifics. *Releaser pheromones* have a short-term effect, initiating the performance of a behaviour in the recipient. *Primer pheromones* have longer term effects, often operating by changing the recipient's physiology (for instance, by altering hormone activity).

Territories of many animals are marked by scent. This can be an enduring message that does not require the signaller's continual activity. Pheromones left in urine, or anal scent deposits, clearly indicate the presence of a resident. For example, house mice (*Mus domesticus*) use odours in urine to mark out their territories (Hurst, 1990). Similarly, many other species, including badgers (*Meles meles*), otters (*Lutra lutra*), dogs (*Canis familiaris*) and cats (*Felis catus*) (both domestic and wild) mark out their territories using scent.

In some species, the status of an individual can be deduced from its scent marking. Rozenfeld and Rasmont (1991) investigated odour recognition in bank voles (*Clethrionomys glareolus*). Dominant voles deposited their own urine and faeces over that of other rodents, 'over marking' it. Further results suggested that the voles could additionally deduce the sex and status of individuals from their olfactory signals.

Figure 11.5   The antennae of a male moth. Some are so sensitive that they can detect a female over a mile away

Sexual behaviour is highly sensitive to olfactory cues. For example, male moths are attracted to sexually active females by their scent. This is an example of a releaser pheromone. In order to detect females effectively, males have large fluffy antennae (Figure 11.5), and are capable of detecting just a few molecules of the pheromone the females release. Each antenna of a male silk worm moth (*Bombix mori*) is covered with about 10,000 sensory hairs. A single molecule of the female's pheromone, *bombykol*, is sufficient to activate a sensory hair cell (Schneider, 1969).

Pheromones can serve another function in sexual behaviour, namely the avoidance of inbreeding (being able to select an unrelated mate increases fitness). Simmons (1990) demonstrated that female crickets (*Gryllus bimaculatus*) were sensitive to scent cues as well as auditory ones. The females were able to differentiate between olfactory signals from individuals with various degrees of kinship. They preferred the odour of males which were unrelated.

After the birth of offspring, pheromones are important in the formation of attachments between the mother and offspring. These were discussed in Chapter 10 (page 94). The maintenance of paternal care may also

Box 11.5   Signalling systems compared

Criterion	Effectiveness of system		
	Vision	Audition	Olfaction
Operates in darkness	✗	✓	✓
Difficult to obstruct	✗	✓	✓
Can reach moving target	✗ & ✓	✓	✓
Operates in windy weather	✓	✓	✗
Unaffected by pollution	✓	✓	✗
Variable messages possible	✓	✓	✗
Lasting message	✗ & ✓	✗	✓
Little risk of attracting predators	✗	✗	✓
Effective without attention of recipient	✗	✓	✓

✓ signalling system fulfils criterion; ✗ signalling system does not fulfil criterion.

be under pheromonal control. Male California mice (*Peromyscus californicus*) respond with parental behaviour to odours present in their mate's excreta, licking the pups and huddling over them (Gubernick, 1990).

ADVANTAGES AND DISADVANTAGES OF THE OLFACTORY SIGNALLING SYSTEM

Communicating by smell combines some of the advantages of both vision and audition. Like sounds, olfactory signals can cover long distances, relatively uninterrupted by obstacles, which they pass around. They can reach recipients which are moving or not paying attention. They can also travel in darkness. Like colours, pheromonal signals are lasting, requiring little 'maintenance' to perpetuate. However, olfaction as a medium has some disadvantages. For example, pheromonal signals can be interrupted by poor weather, they may be obliterated by rain, or blown in the wind (with the result of sending an intended recipient off course).

Box 11.5 provides a comparison between the advantages and disadvantages of the three major systems.

Conclusions

Signalling systems, operating through the senses, offer animals different ways to communicate. Some signals use a mixture of systems. This chapter has discussed the advantages and disadvantages relating to the systems of vision, audition and olfaction. Features of effective signalling have been discussed, as have some of the functions of signalling.

SUMMARY

- A **signal** is a deliberate message, sent to one or more recipients, causing behavioural or other changes. The communication benefits both sender and recipient, and it is essential to social animals to maintain the group and co-ordinate activities.
- Guilford and Dawkins identified two key features of an effective signal: **strategic design** (containing the necessary information), and **efficacy** (being easy for the receiver to detect, discriminate and remember so that the message is understood).
- **Cheats** might affect the fitness of communicators by **eavesdropping** or **deceitful signalling**. An illegitimate receiver, a predator or competitor, could eavesdrop on the signals of others to locate prey or nest sites. Illegitimate signallers, such as hoverflies, send a deceitful message. By mimicking wasps, they signal that they are dangerous when they are not.
- Signals may be sent through any sense. These represent the different signalling systems. **Visual, olfactory** and **auditory systems** are the most commonly used by animals.
- Visual signals include **colours**, **postures** (static signals) and **gestures** (movements). The courtship of the great crested grebe illustrates all of these. The courtship display functions to tell other birds about their potential partner's sex, species and willingness to mate.
- Sometimes there is an obvious functional relationship between the signal and its meaning. A male tern, which brings fish to the female during courtship, signals his suitability as a mate. A male balloon fly, which brings the female a silk ball,

also signals his suitability as a mate. In the first example, the value of the gesture is explicit (he will feed the young) and it is clear how this signal could evolve. The evolution of the courtship display of the balloon fly is harder to explain.

- The **visual signalling system** is capable of generating highly variable messages. Signals which are very different from any other are unlikely to be misinterpreted. Colours are low-cost, long-duration signals. When a conspecific is encountered, a coloured signal cannot be missed or ignored.
- Postures and gestures have greater energy costs and may attract predators. Visual signals can only be detected in the light, by receivers which are looking, so they need to be nearby already.
- **Auditory signals** can be varied in terms of **pitch**, **volume** or **sequence**. Female toads prefer deep-croaking males, female deer prefer frequently roaring stags.
- The alarm calls of vervet monkeys are predator specific, causing adaptive responses in the recipients. On hearing a leopard alarm, the vervets climb into trees; in response to an eagle alarm, they head for cover.
- The **auditory signalling system** is flexible and penetrating. Sequences of sound of different pitches can generate complex and variable signals. This **variability reduces errors**. Sound travels in the dark and around corners, even to receivers which were not paying attention. Low sounds (and whistles) travel well over long distances. These are used by forest birds and whales.
- Many complex auditory signals are **learned**. Young signallers and receivers may make **errors** in response to alarm calls and this may have high costs. Sounds can also attract unwanted receivers (predators and competitors). Male great tits act as deceitful senders, singing several different songs. This dupes receivers into leaving the area, as there appear to be more residents than there actually are.
- **Marine mammals** communicate with sounds spanning beyond our audible range. **Dolphins** use clicks and whistles as well as other sounds.

Pulsed clicks are used by species which live in small groups as these sounds do not travel well through the water. Species living in larger, more dispersed groups use lower frequency, unpulsed whistles.

- Each dolphin has a **click signature** which identifies it as an individual. These can be recognised by the other members of the group, which can use a familiar dolphin's call to detect danger.
- **Humpback whales** generate complex **songs**. These are built up from units into phrases and themes. They, too, have a dialect, but different groups still use the same song **rules**. The songs may be used as courtship signals, as singing is only demonstrated by the males. Singing males avoid one another, but approach females, and are attracted to social calls of an active group.
- The **olfactory signalling system** uses smell. **Pheromones** are airborne chemicals which affect the receiver's physiology and, therefore, behaviour. **Releaser pheromones** have short-term effects on behaviour, such as a female moth attracting a mate. **Primer pheromones** can produce long-term effects by altering hormone activity, as for a queen mole rat suppressing the sexual functioning of her colony.
- **Territories** of many species are marked with pheromonal signals in urine, faeces or from scent glands. **Mates** can be attracted, or avoided, on the basis of olfactory cues. The female silk worm moth produces a highly potent sexual attractant. Female crickets can recognise kin by smell, enabling them to avoid inbreeding. Smell is also important in the formation of **maternal bonds** and in maintaining **parental care** in the male (at least in California mice).
- The **olfactory signalling system**, like audition, can send messages over long distances, in the dark, around corners and can reach receivers which are not paying attention. Pheromones do not require constant maintenance, and are not especially costly in terms of energy. However, pheromones could be used by eavesdropping predators or competitors, and signals can be obscured by bad weather.

PART 4
Behaviour analysis

CLASSICAL AND OPERANT CONDITIONING

Introduction and overview

The previous three parts of this book have been primarily concerned with evolutionary explanations of behaviour. This section represents a departure from this approach, by examining environmental influences upon the behaviour of human and non-human animals.

Responses to the environment may be acute (short term) or chronic (long term). Acute responses to stimuli may include such behaviours as salivating at the sight of food, or a child learning a new word. Chronic responses would encompass differences in developed intelligence and the acquisition of language as a whole. The predominant approach in behaviour analysis is to concentrate on objective explanations of events. This scientific approach, based solely on evidence obtained by direct observation, is known as *behaviourism*.

Part 4 of this book (Chapters 12–15) considers the analysis of behaviour and examines classical and operant conditioning, foraging and homing behaviour, animal language and evolutionary explanations of human behaviour. This chapter describes the theories and procedures of classical and operant conditioning, beginning with an outline of the behaviourist approach to psychology.

Behaviourism

Behaviourism is an approach to the study of psychology founded by J.B. Watson (1913). It is based on the idea that only information which is observable and quantifiable is appropriate to use as evidence for psychological theories. The majority of studies conducted by behaviourists have used non-human animals, based on the assumption that we can generalise the results to humans. This is possible because all living organisms are related through the evolutionary process and differences between species are simply quantitative. Behaviourists believe that the basis of psychology is the stimulus–response (S–R) relationship and that the process of learning (changes in behaviour as the result of experience) is fundamental to the development of behaviour. It is a reductionist approach, maintaining that simple S–R relationships can be built up into complex behaviour through the processes of classical and operant conditioning.

In support of the behaviourist approach, there appears to be little doubt that conditioning does underlie some human behaviour. Furthermore, behaviourism has made successful contributions to both clinical and educational psychology. However, the approach is not without its critics, and the limitations of behaviourism are discussed at the end of this chapter.

Classical conditioning

BACKGROUND

Classical conditioning is also known as Pavlovian conditioning, after the Russian physiologist Ivan Pavlov, who is generally credited with discovering the process. Pavlov was investigating the salivatory reflex in dogs (*Canis familiaris*), a response which occurs automatically when food is placed on the animal's tongue. However, the animals did not just salivate in response to the presence of food, but also in response to other stimuli which regularly coincided with feeding. These included the presence of the food dish and the sight of the person who regularly fed them. Pavlov designed an experiment in which a bell was sounded each time a dog received its food. This was repeated for a number of trials and the quantity of saliva produced by the dog was measured each time. Pavlov then sounded the bell *without* giving the dog any food and the animal still salivated to the same extent (Pavlov, 1927). The dog had learned, through classical conditioning, to associate the sound of the bell with the arrival of food (stimulating salivation).

THE PROCESS OF CLASSICAL CONDITIONING

It is possible to generalise from Pavlov's experiments to other forms of classical conditioning. The food is referred to as an *unconditioned stimulus* (UCS), which is any stimulus that elicits an automatic or reflexive response. Salivation by the dogs in the presence of food represents an *unconditioned response* (UCR), which is produced automatically. Before conditioning, the bell is known as a *neutral stimulus* (NS), but afterwards it becomes a *conditioned stimulus* (CS). Finally, salivation in response to the bell is known as a *conditioned response* (CR). The interaction between these factors is summarised in Figure 12.1.

Before conditioning

Food (**UCS**) → Salivation (**UCR**) (Natural association)
Bell (**NS**) → No response

During conditioning
Bell (**CS**) + Food (**UCS**) → Salivation (UCR)

After conditioning
Bell (**CS**) → Salivation (**CR**) (Learned association)

Figure 12.1   The process of classical conditioning

Most classical conditioning experiments involve the pairing of a natural stimulus (one which normally triggers a particular reflex) with a neutral stimulus on a number of occasions. Eventually, the animal learns to associate the two stimuli and the previously neutral stimulus will elicit a reflexive response. The range of stimuli which can act as a CS appears to be very large.

It could be virtually anything that the experimental animal can detect through its senses.

FEATURES OF CLASSICAL CONDITIONING

Timing

The order in which the NS and the UCS are paired together is very important. For conditioning to be effective, the NS should occur just before the UCS (typically around 0.5 seconds). The NS should also remain 'on' while the UCS is presented and until the UCR appears. This is called *forward* conditioning. During classical conditioning, the NS (or CS, as it becomes) can be considered as a kind of signal to the animal, enabling it to predict the coming of the UCS. Learning becomes poorer as the time between the presentation of the NS and UCS increases, a situation known as *delayed* conditioning. In certain circumstances, the NS is presented and removed before the onset of the UCS. This is referred to as *trace* conditioning, as it leaves only a memory trace of the NS to be conditioned. In this case, the CR is usually weaker than in forward or delayed conditioning. Finally, conditioning may occur if the NS is given *after* the UCS. This is known as *backward* conditioning and it is generally ineffective.

Extinction

The CS–CR association is acquired, rather than innate (as for the UCS–UCR association). Therefore, it may be lost if the CS no longer predicts the coming of the UCS. If the bell is repeatedly presented without being followed by food, the CR disappears. This is known as *extinction*. The extinction process can be seen by measuring the extent of the CR over a number of experimental trials in which the CS is presented alone. The response gradually diminishes until it eventually seems to disappear (Figure 12.2).

Spontaneous recovery

A CR that has become extinct is always liable to reappear suddenly under the right conditions, a phenomenon known as *spontaneous recovery*. Any disruption of extinction training may bring back the CR (although not necessarily 100%). Furthermore, when the animal is retrained using the original CS–US pairings, the CR is quickly reinstated. The rapidity with which this reinstatement occurs implies that the CR had not disappeared but was simply inhibited.

Stimulus generalisation

If a stimulus is presented which is similar to the CS,

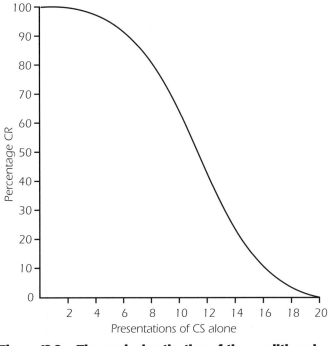

Figure 12.2   The gradual extinction of the conditioned response (CR) when the conditioned stimulus (CS) is presented alone

but not identical to it, the animal will often respond as it does to the CS. This is known as stimulus generalisation (the extension of the CR from the original stimulus to similar stimuli). The more similar the new stimulus is to the CS, the greater will be the response (Figure 12.3a). For example, if a dog is conditioned to a bell of a particular pitch, it will respond to bells of a similar pitch. As the bells become increasingly different from the original, the CR gradually decreases and eventually stops altogether. This is known as *stimulus discrimination* (see below). It has been suggested that stimulus generalisation is an adaptive feature of learning. The more alike two stimuli are, the more likely it is that the same response is appropriate.

Stimulus generalisation has important implications for many aspects of animal learning. For example, during extinction of a CR, omission of reinforcement changes the environment in which the conditioning was originally established. There is some evidence that the reduction in responsiveness seen during extinction is partly due to stimulus generalisation (McFarland, 1996). A similar situation is seen in the process of *habituation* (the cessation of a response to a meaningless or harmless stimulus). A response habituated to one stimulus will show generalisation to another similar stimulus. In other words, the animal generally treats the new stimulus as if it had been presented previously. Therefore, generalisation tends to counteract the effects of novel stimuli on habituated responses.

Stimulus discrimination

In addition to the spontaneous discrimination described above, it is also possible to train animals to discriminate such that the CR can only be evoked by the CS. During conditioning, the original bell is continually paired with food but similar-sounding bells are rung without food being presented. A dog can learn to discriminate between the various bells as long as it can distinguish the different sounds (Figure 12.3b). If discrimination training persists, such that the distinction between stimuli is very small, the dog may find it very difficult to detect the differences. In this case, a condition known as *experimental neurosis* may occur, characterised by whining, trembling, urinating and self-mutilation. It is as if the animal does not 'know' how to respond and demonstrates that excessive discrimination training has the potential for inflicting psychological distress on animals.

Pavlov (1927) believed that discriminations could be learned when some aspects of the CS are reinforced while other aspects are not reinforced. Most conditioned stimuli are composed of several factors, such as the frequency, intensity and duration of a bell (as well as other aspects of the animal's environment). An animal can be trained to discriminate between these factors and respond to only one, such as the frequency of the bell. Therefore, during the early stages of a classical conditioning experiment (before this discrimination has occurred), we might expect dogs to salivate during the intertrial intervals. Sheffield (1965) found that dogs did indeed salivate during the intervals, although, as expected, the extent of the salivation declined during training.

Higher order conditioning

If a dog has learned to salivate to a bell and then a flash of light is presented regularly before the bell is rung, the dog will eventually salivate to the light (although it does not usually salivate as much as it did to the bell). This is known as *second order conditioning* (or, more generally, *higher order conditioning*). Pavlov found that learning in dogs could not go beyond third or fourth order conditioning.

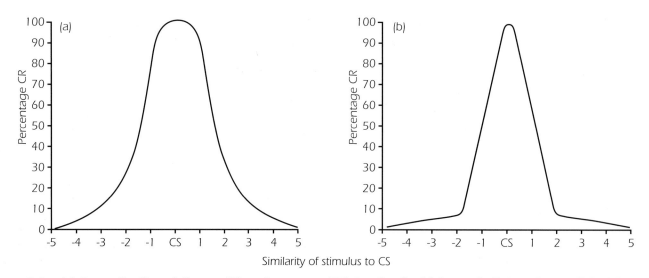

Figure 12.3 **(a) Generalisation of the conditioned response (CR) to stimuli which are similar to the conditioned stimulus (CS); (b) discrimination of the conditioned response (CR) to the conditioned stimulus (CS)**

CLASSICAL CONDITIONING IN HUMANS

Classical conditioning has been used to explain many aspects of human behaviour, such as the acquisition of phobias (anxiety disorders characterised by an excessive fear of a particular object or situation). In a classic study, Watson and Rayner (1920) conditioned a fear response in an 11-month-old boy, known as 'Little Albert'. This study is described in Box 12.1.

The case of Little Albert represents a deliberate inducement of a fear response. Can classical conditioning also help to explain how fears are acquired in everyday life? One example, suggested by Richard Gross (1996), relates to the development of a fear of dentists (Figure 12.4).

Before conditioning

Drill hitting a nerve (**UCS**) → Pain/fear (**UCR**)
Sound of the drill (**NS**) → No response

During conditioning

Sound of the drill (**CS**) + drill hitting nerve (**UCS**) → Pain/fear (**UCR**)

After conditioning

Sound of the drill (**CS**) → Fear (**CR**)

Figure 12.4 **A classical conditioning explanation for the development of a fear of dentists**

> **Box 12.1   The case of Little Albert**
>
> Little Albert was the son of a nurse who worked at the same children's hospital as J.B. Watson. At the age of 11 months, Albert became the subject of a classical conditioning experiment by Watson and Rayner (1920).
>
> While Albert was playing with a white rat (NS), Watson made a loud noise (UCS) behind the boy by banging a hammer on a steel bar. This elicited a fear response (UCR) and crying. After seven trials, over a period of seven weeks, Albert demonstrated a fear response (CR) to the rat (CS), even though its appearance was no longer accompanied by the loud noise. Albert's fear became generalised to objects similar to the rat, such as a fur coat, cotton wool and even a Santa Claus mask. The fear response was still evident a year later. It is not clear whether Watson and Rayner intended to remove the fear response (CR) because Albert's mother withdrew him from the experiment.
>
> Fear conditioning, as illustrated by the case of Little Albert, may take place after only *one* pairing of a neutral stimulus (NS) with an unconditioned stimulus (UCS). It is also highly resistant to extinction.

In addition to fear, other human reflexes have also been subjected to classical conditioning experiments. Menzies (1937) asked participants to place their hands in ice-cold water whenever a buzzer sounded. This caused vasoconstriction (constriction of the blood vessels) in the hands. Eventually, vasoconstriction occurred just in response to the sound of the buzzer.

APPLICATIONS OF CLASSICAL CONDITIONING

Two major ways in which classical conditioning has been put to practical use are behaviour therapy and advertising.

One of the earliest examples of behaviour therapy was reported by Jones (1924). Using *direct unconditioning* (now known as *systematic desensitisation*), Jones was able to remove a fear response in a 2-year-old boy known as 'Little Peter'. Peter had an extreme fear of rabbits, but was otherwise considered to be normal. Jones gradually exposed Peter to a rabbit while the boy ate his lunch. At first it was in a wire cage, at quite a distance from Peter. Then it was brought closer and closer, let free in the room and eventually sat next to the boy, who was able to stroke the animal. Another type of behaviour therapy, known as *flooding*, is discussed in Box 12.2.

Advertisements often make use of classical conditioning. Advertisers attempt to couple their products with a UCS that will produce pleasant emotions, such as happiness or sexual arousal. Classical conditioning may result in the product becoming associated with these positive feelings, encouraging people to part with their money. Coffee has been paired with romance, cornflakes with happy family life and ice-cream with sex.

Box 12.2   Flooding

Flooding is an example of behaviour therapy in which the individual is forced to confront the object or situation causing the fear response. For example, a patient with *arachnophobia* (a fear of spiders) might be taken into a room containing many spiders and physically prevented from leaving. By preventing avoidance of, or escape from, the spiders, the fear response is eventually extinguished.

Marks (1981) showed that flooding is generally more effective than systematic desensitisation. However, for some people, flooding leads to increased anxiety and the procedure is too traumatic. As a result, this form of behaviour therapy has to be used with considerable caution.

Operant conditioning

BACKGROUND

Operant conditioning (also known as *instrumental conditioning*) was first described by Thorndike in 1911. He devised a puzzle box in which animals were placed and had to solve the problem of how to escape. The more often they were placed in the box, the quicker their escape (rewarded by food). These studies led Thorndike to propose three laws of learning.

1 Law of trial and error: Learning does not depend on a sudden flash of inspiration, but is a gradual process (Figure 12.5).

2 Law of readiness: Maturation and previous learning determine whether a particular stimulus is a reward or a punishment.

3 Law of effect: A response that is followed by pleasant consequences is likely to be repeated, whereas a response followed by unpleasant consequences is not.

Skinner (1938) later expressed Thorndike's law of effect in slightly different terms. He said that behaviour which is reinforced tends to be repeated and behaviour

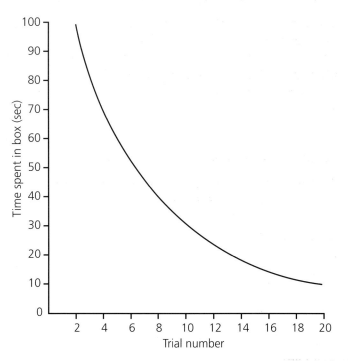

Figure 12.5   The learning curve for Thorndike's puzzle box

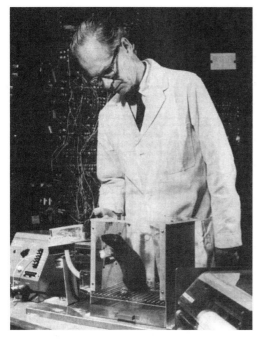

Figure 12.6   Burrhus Skinner (1904–1990), together with a rat (*Rattus rattus*) in a Skinner box

Box 12.3   The differences between classical and operant conditioning

Classical conditioning	*Operant conditioning*
Behaviour is reflexive	Behaviour is essentially voluntary
Mainly involves the autonomic nervous system	Mainly involves the central nervous system
Behaviour is elicited by the stimulus	Behaviour is emitted by the organism
Learner responds to the environment (passive)	Learner acts on the environment (active)
Conditions preceding a behaviour determine its expression	Consequences of behaviour determine its expression

which is not reinforced tends to be extinguished. In other words, behaviour is reinforced and maintained by its consequences.

THE PROCESS OF OPERANT CONDITIONING

Skinner conducted a large number of experiments into the process of operant conditioning using machines specially developed for the process, known as Skinner boxes (Figure 12.6). When placed in a Skinner box, an animal – usually a pigeon (*Columba livia*) or a rat – has to press a lever to obtain food (reinforcement). In the course of exploring the box, an animal will usually press the lever by accident and receive a quantity of food. This happens each time the lever is pressed, reinforcing the behaviour. Typically, an animal will exhibit a range of behaviours while in the box, but none of these is reinforced (except pressing the lever). These non-reinforced responses tend to decrease in frequency, whereas lever pressing becomes more frequent. When pressing the lever becomes a conditioned response, we can say that the operant conditioning process is completed.

FEATURES OF OPERANT CONDITIONING

Operant conditioning has several features in common with classical conditioning. Responses may become extinct if they cease to be reinforced, spontaneous recovery can occur (even in the absence of reinforcement) and stimulus generalisation has been observed. However, there are also crucial differences between the two types of learning, as shown in Box 12.3.

Reinforcement and punishment

Reinforcement is anything that increases the probability that a given behaviour will occur again. In other words, it strengthens a response. Positive reinforcers strengthen behaviours which result in their presentation, such as food. Negative reinforcers strengthen behaviours which result in their removal or avoidance, such as an electric shock.

Punishment is anything that decreases the probability that a given behaviour will be repeated. It has the opposite effect on behaviour to reinforcement, weakening the response. Positive punishers weaken behaviours which result in their presentation, such as smacking. Negative punishers weaken behaviours which result in their removal or avoidance. One example of negative punishment would be the withdrawal of pocket money from a naughty child.

One of the problems involved in operant conditioning is how to decide what constitutes a reinforcer and a punisher. One way around this problem is to define anything that strengthens a behaviour as a reinforcer and anything that weakens it as a punisher. However, this presents us with a circular argument. A partial solution may be to ensure that the animals are highly motivated to learn by depriving them of food for several hours in advance of the experiment. A final problem is that an intended punishment could turn out to be a positive reinforcement. This may occur in attention-seeking children. By misbehaving, they will receive punishment (such as shouting or smacking), but the children may actually prefer the punishment to being ignored and so it acts as positive reinforcement.

Skinner suggested that reinforcement is far more effective than punishment in regulating behaviour. One of the problems with punishment is that eradicating an undesirable behaviour does not imply that a desired one will arise in its place. It may also only suppress a behaviour while the punishing agent is present. In addition, punishment may have unpleasant emotional side-effects. For example, if an animal is continually punished in a certain situation, no matter what its actions, it soon gives up attempts to avoid the punishment. Furthermore, the animal also becomes less likely to learn an avoidance response in future situations in which punishment is avoidable. This condition is known as *learned helplessness* and has been used as an explanation for the onset of some forms of human depression (Beck, 1991).

Punishment can be effective in suppressing a behaviour if it immediately follows the undesirable action. The most effective way of changing behaviour is to use a combination of punishment for undesirable behaviour coupled with positive reinforcement for desired behaviour.

One final point to consider is that responses motivated by negative reinforcement should persist longer (take longer to extinguish) than those motivated by positive reinforcement. This is because avoidance learning prevents the animal from testing reality (it does not wait in a particular situation to see whether the unpleasant stimulus is still present). This idea has been supported by studies in humans (Solomon & Wynne, 1953) and may help to explain the persistence of certain phobias (Gross, 1996).

Primary and secondary reinforcers and punishers

Primary reinforcers satisfy biological needs and are naturally reinforcing in themselves, such as food, water and sex. Similarly, pain and extreme temperatures are naturally punishing and are known as primary punishers. *Secondary* reinforcers and punishers acquire their properties through association with their primary counterparts. We have to learn (through classical conditioning) to find them reinforcing or punishing. Money and praise are examples of secondary reinforcers, whereas

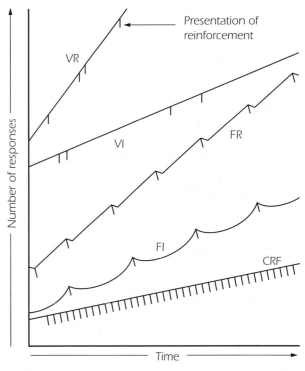

Figure 12.7   The pattern and rate of response for five schedules of reinforcement

criticism is a secondary punisher. Many secondary reinforcers or punishers are just as potent as primary ones.

Schedules of reinforcement

Instead of providing reinforcement after each response (*continuous* reinforcement), it is possible to reward only some of the responses. This is known as *partial* reinforcement. Skinner identified five major schedules of reinforcement, each of which is associated with a characteristic behaviour (Figure 12.7).

1 Continuous reinforcement (CRF): Every single response is reinforced, producing a low but steady response rate. Extinction occurs very quickly because the learner has been used to receiving a reward every time the response is made. Therefore, the learner gives up very quickly when no reward is received. An example of continuous reinforcement would be a waiter receiving a tip for every customer served.

2 Fixed interval (FI): A reinforcement is given after a certain period of time, provided that the response occurs at least once during that time. The response rate increases shortly before each reinforcement and decreases afterwards. The overall response rate is fairly low. In this case, extinction occurs quite quickly because reinforcement is being anticipated. If no reward is forthcoming, the response will soon cease. An example of fixed interval reinforcement would be receiving a monthly salary.

3 Variable interval (VI): Reinforcements are given after varying intervals (unpredictable), although the average time interval remains constant. This leads to a fairly high and stable response rate. Extinction occurs very slowly because the timing of the reward cannot be predicted. This leads to continued responses, in the hope of reinforcement in the near future. An example of variable interval reinforcement would be the irregular payments received by many small businesses.

4 Fixed ratio (FR): A reinforcement is given for a fixed number of responses, irrespective of the time taken. This produces a pause after each reinforcement and then a very high response rate leading up to the next reinforcement (the individual determines how quickly he/she will be rewarded). Extinction occurs fairly quickly, due to the predictability of the reward (see fixed interval). An example of fixed ratio reinforcement would be receiving commission on sales.

5 Variable ratio (VR): Reinforcements are given after varying numbers of responses (unpredictable), although the average number remains constant. This leads to a very high, stable response rate. Extinction is the slowest of all the schedules. This is because responses continue to be made in the hope of future reinforcement (the variability prevents any obvious response patterns from becoming established). In this way it is similar to the VI condition, except that the onus is on the respondent to elicit a reward through its own actions. In the VI situation, a reward is eventually given to the respondent after a certain time period (provided the response occurs at least once during that time). Under VR conditions, the reinforcement has to be 'earned' by making responses, meaning that extinction is less likely to occur. An example of VR reinforcement would be gambling. A slot machine, for example, averages a certain level of payoff, but the reward is unsystematic and variable.

Overall, CRF schedules produce rapid initial learning, a slower response rate and rapid extinction. Partial reinforcement schedules (FI, VI, FR and VR) produce slower initial learning, faster rates of responding and slower extinction (Gross, 1996).

OPERANT CONDITIONING IN HUMANS

Operant conditioning has been used to explain many aspects of human behaviour, such as the acquisition of language by shaping and superstitious learning.

Reinforcement can be used to build up relatively complex behaviours using a system called *shaping*. Shaping initially involves reinforcing any response which is even vaguely related to the behaviour in question. Subsequent reinforcement of closer and closer approximations to the required behaviour may result in its successful acquisition. Once an animal has been conditioned to perform a particular behaviour, it tends to generalise and use this as the basis of further behaviour. Skinner suggested that most skills in humans are learned in this manner, including the acquisition of language (Skinner, 1957).

Superstitious behaviour, such as avoiding walking under ladders, may arise through operant conditioning. The behaviour is strengthened, by chance, because it happens to precede a reinforcement. For example, a footballer may put his left boot on first when getting ready for a match and his team may subsequently win the game. He may then continue with this ritual because he believes that it brings him (or the team) good luck. (It should be remembered that the relationship between the behaviour and the reinforcer is accidental; the reinforcer would have occurred anyway.) It is possible, however, that if the footballer truly believes that his actions bring him luck, the consequent increase in confidence may actually help him to play better!

APPLICATIONS OF OPERANT CONDITIONING

Two major ways in which operant conditioning has been put to practical use are behaviour modification and programmed learning.

Behaviour modification involves the setting of a specific behavioural goal and then systematically reinforcing the individual's successive approximations to this goal (Box 12.4). This technique has been used in places such as classrooms, mental hospitals, factories and prisons. One of the most common forms of behaviour modification is the *token economy*. In this system, individuals are rewarded for desirable behaviour by being given tokens. The tokens can later be cashed in for items or activities that the person wants, such as sweets or the right to watch a favourite television programme. Token economies have been used successfully with severely

Box 12.4   Behaviour modification

Most behaviour programmes follow a broadly similar pattern, involving a series of steps. First, the behaviour to be changed is specified as precisely as possible and this behaviour is monitored for several days before treatment commences. This monitoring process provides a baseline behaviour which may be used to assess the effectiveness of the therapy. Second, a reinforcement or punishment (or both) strategy is decided upon, and the treatment is planned. Finally, the treatment begins and progress is closely monitored (the programme may be changed if necessary).

One example of behaviour modification, using positive reinforcement, was described by Gross and McIlveen (1996). The case in question was a 40-year-old male schizophrenic who had not spoken to anyone for nineteen years. One of the therapists discovered that the patient was very keen on chewing gum, and decided to use it as a positive reinforcer to encourage the man to speak. The behaviour modification process used in this case is outlined below.

Therapist held up a piece of gum.
Patient received the gum for looking at it.
↓
Patient only given the gum if he moved his lips.
↓
Patient had to make a sound to receive the gum.
↓
Patient given the gum for saying the word 'gum' (prompted by therapist).
↓
After 6 weeks of therapy, the patient spontaneously said, 'Gum, please', and soon afterwards began talking to the therapist.

regressed schizophrenics and autistic children (Gross & McIlveen, 1996).

Programmed learning involves the use of operant conditioning to enhance the educational process. Skinner believed that all learning takes place according to the principles of operant conditioning and he devised his 'principles of programmed instruction' to take account of this. The programme breaks down the learning task into a sequence of steps, which must be completed correctly before the student can move on to the next stage. Skinner maintained that programmed learning was both quicker and more efficient than conventional learning. Modified forms of Skinner's system are used in a variety of teaching and learning situations, particularly in distance learning and supported self-study materials.

General laws of learning

If conditioning works in the same way for all species, it should be possible to produce general laws of learning. Two such laws have been suggested.

1 The law of contiguity: Events which occur close together in time and space are likely to become associated with each other.

2 The law of preparedness: Animals are biologically prepared to learn actions that are related to the survival of their species (Seligman, 1970). These actions are learned very quickly (often in just one trial) and are highly resistant to extinction. However, other behaviours are learned with great difficulty, if at all.

Many conditioning studies appear to obey the law of contiguity. In addition, the idea of biological preparedness is supported by research evidence suggesting that most human phobias relate to fear of dangerous animals or places (Seligman, 1972). However, taste aversion experiments are an important exception to the law of contiguity (Box 12.5) and the majority of psychologists believe that we cannot apply basic principles of learning to all species in all situations (Bolles, 1980). Overall, it seems unlikely that there are any general laws of learning.

Box 12.5   Taste aversion experiments (Garcia & Koelling, 1966)

Laboratory rats were given saccharin-flavoured water (NS), which they had not previously encountered. This was followed by the administration of a drug (UCS) which, after a time delay, induced severe intestinal illness (UCR). The precise time-lapse between tasting the solution and the onset of illness ranged from five to 180 minutes. In each case, a conditioned aversive response (CR) to the saccharin-flavoured water (CS) was acquired, regardless of the time elapsed. Such taste aversion experiments represent an important exception to the law of contiguity.

Limitations of the behaviourist approach

The behaviourist approach underestimates the importance of innate (inborn) abilities. Research on biological preparedness suggests that the ability of an organism to learn a certain behaviour is partly due to the survival value of that behaviour (Seligman, 1972).

There is a story of a teenage boy who attempted to 'train' his dog to roll over and clap its front paws together. The dog was supposed to perform this act when the boy called out the name of his favourite football team (which happened to be Ipswich Town). Despite a generous reward system, consisting mainly of biscuits, and many 'trials', the dog failed to learn the trick. This may have been due to a flaw in the training regime, or to biological constraints (dogs are not 'prepared' for such behaviour). Alternatively, there may have been cognitive limitations preventing the acquisition of this complex trick (although many dogs are capable of learning more difficult tricks than the one described above). Certain behaviours, however, are acquired very readily by animals. The removal of foil milk-bottle tops by blue-tits (described in Chapter 1, page 10) is one such example. In this case there are no biological constraints and the birds seem 'prepared' to learn such behaviour. Blue-tits normally strip the bark from certain trees to feed on insects underneath. This stripping action is very similar to that used to remove milk-bottle tops, and has obvious survival value. In general, it is important to remember that conditioning theory is limited by biological constraints.

Behaviourism also emphasises single influences upon behaviour. In reality, the situation is more complex and behaviour can be modified by many factors. This makes the influence of any one factor difficult to determine.

Some psychologists believe that humans are qualitatively different from non-human animals. Therefore we cannot generalise from non-human animals to humans (a basic assumption of the behaviourist approach). Another problem with behaviourism is that a great deal of learning does not involve making any observable response. The fact that we fail to observe any change does not mean that no change has occurred. Finally, learning can occur in the absence of reinforcement

---

Box 12.6   The role of cognitive factors in learning

Mackintosh (1978) suggested that conditioning is more complex than it seems. He believed that animals learn about the *relationship between events*. They discover what it is that signals an important event, such as food or danger, and respond appropriately to this signal. Although we may describe a rat as 'learning to press a lever', the lever pressing is simply an indicator that the animal has learned the relationship between its actions and the consequent reward. Therefore, in Pavlov's classic study (see page 112), one could say that the dogs were *expecting* food to follow the bell. In other words, presentation of the bell enables the dog to retrieve a mental representation of the food from memory (a cognitive event), with salivation being caused by that representation. This idea has been supported by experimental studies. Rescorla (1968) showed that, for classical conditioning at least, the most important factor in learning is how predictably the UCS follows the CS, not how often the CS and UCS are paired.

Bandura (1977) claimed that expectation also plays a significant role in operant conditioning. The way an animal behaves is largely determined by the expectations of future events. The processes of reinforcement and punishment provide the learner with information about the likelihood of future pleasant or unpleasant outcomes by giving animals feedback about their behaviours. Similarly, the phenomenon of *learned helplessness*, described on page 117, also suggests that cognitive factors play a role in operant conditioning.

(Tolman & Honzik, 1930), and evidence described in Box 12.6 suggests that cognitive factors play a significant role in learning (Mackintosh, 1978).

Conclusions

The behaviourist approach assumes that all behaviour can be explained in terms of classical and operant conditioning. Many laboratory studies of conditioning appear to support this assumption. In addition, behaviourism has made successful contributions to both clinical and educational psychology. However, it has not been possible to produce any general laws of learning (based on conditioning) which apply equally well to all species. Furthermore, there are significant limitations to the behaviourist approach. It appears that, in addition to conditioning, both genetic and cognitive factors are important in learning.

SUMMARY

- **Behaviourism** is a scientific approach to the study of psychology, using evidence obtained by direct observation. Behaviourists believe that the basis of psychology is the **stimulus–response** relationship and that learning occurs through the processes of **classical** and **operant conditioning**.
- An **unconditioned stimulus (UCS)** will naturally elicit a reflexive **unconditioned response (UCR)**. However, if a **neutral stimulus (NS)** is paired on a number of occasions with the UCS, an animal will learn to associate the two stimuli. The previously neutral stimulus becomes a **conditioned stimulus (CS)**. Presentation of the CS alone will then trigger the automatic or reflexive response (**conditioned response** or **CR**). The process by which this new association is learned is called **classical conditioning**.
- During classical conditioning, the **order** in which the NS and UCS are paired together is very important. For conditioning to be effective, the NS should occur just before the UCS. This is known as **forward** conditioning. Other methods include **delayed**, **trace** and **backward** conditioning. These are generally less effective than forward conditioning.
- If the CS is repeatedly presented without being followed by the UCS, the CR disappears. This is called **extinction**. A CR that has become extinct is always liable to reappear suddenly under the right conditions, a phenomenon known as **spontaneous recovery**. This implies that the CR does not actually disappear during extinction, but is simply inhibited.
- If a stimulus is presented which is similar to the CS, but not identical to it, an animal will often respond as it does to the CS. This is called **stimulus generalisation**. As the stimulus becomes increasingly different from the original, the CR gradually decreases and eventually stops altogether. This is known as **stimulus discrimination**. It is possible to train animals to discriminate, such that the CR can only by evoked by the CS. If this training is excessive, it may lead to **experimental neurosis**.

- Classical conditioning has been used to explain many aspects of human behaviour, including the acquisition of **phobias**. This was demonstrated in the case of **Little Albert**. Two major ways in which classical conditioning has been put to practical use are **behaviour therapy** and **advertising**.
- **Operant conditioning** is based on three laws of learning: the **law of trial and error**, the **law of readiness**, and the **law of effect**. The law of effect states that behaviour which is reinforced tends to be repeated and behaviour which is not reinforced tends to be extinguished. In other words, **behaviour is reinforced and maintained by its consequences**.
- **Reinforcement** is anything that increases the probability that a given behaviour will occur again. **Positive reinforcers** strengthen behaviours which result in their presentation. **Negative reinforcers** strengthen behaviours which result in their removal or avoidance. **Punishment** is anything that decreases the probability that a given behaviour will arise. **Positive punishers** weaken behaviours which result in their presentation. **Negative punishers** weaken behaviours which result in their removal or avoidance.
- Punishment can be effective in suppressing a behaviour if it immediately follows the undesirable action. However, it is not considered as effective as reinforcement in regulating behaviour. Punishment may also have unpleasant emotional side-effects, such as the development of **learned helplessness**. The most effective way of changing behaviour is to use a combination of reinforcement and punishment.
- There are five major **schedules of reinforcement**, each of which is associated with a characteristic pattern of behaviour. In general, **continuous reinforcement** schedules produce rapid initial learning, a slower response rate and rapid extinction. **Partial reinforcement** schedules (**fixed interval**, **variable interval**, **fixed ratio** and **variable ratio**) produce slower initial learning, faster rates of responding and slower extinction.

- Operant conditioning has been used to explain many aspects of human behaviour, such as the **acquisition of language by shaping** and **superstitious learning**. Two major ways in which operant conditioning has been put to practical use are **behaviour modification** and **programmed learning**.
- Two **general laws of learning** have been suggested: the **law of contiguity**, which is contravened by taste-aversion experiments; and the **law of preparedness**, which suggests that species-specific factors are important in learning. Most psychologists believe that it is not possible to apply basic principles of learning to all species in all situations.
- There are significant limitations to the behaviourist approach to psychology. It is generally considered to be too simple and it ignores the influence of **genetic** and **cognitive** factors in learning.

FORAGING AND HOMING BEHAVIOUR

Introduction and overview

The previous chapter outlined the behaviourist approach to psychology and introduced classical and operant conditioning as explanations of learning. However, the basis of many of these ideas was the laboratory experiment, conducted using only a very few species. While this investigative method has the advantages of a controlled environment and precise measurement of variables, it has been accused of artificiality and lack of generalisability. This has led to studies of learning using a wide variety of species in their natural environments, an approach known as *ethology*. In addition to the different research methods used, ethology and behaviourism are also distinguished by the emphasis they place upon the role of learning in the acquisition of behaviour. In contrast to their behaviourist counterparts, ethologists such as Niko Tinbergen and Konrad Lorenz argued that many behaviours are innate, not learned.

Ethologists study behaviour in an evolutionary context and are particularly interested in instinctive behaviour in animals and how this behaviour is adapted to their particular ecological niche. This chapter examines explanations of learning in the natural environment, concentrating on two major examples: foraging and homing behaviour.

Foraging

Foraging is a term used to describe the ways in which animals satisfy their nutritional requirements. As mentioned in Chapter 3, many animal behaviours are concerned with eating and/or avoiding being eaten. The particular foraging strategy employed depends upon a number of factors, including the type of food consumed and the distribution of food resources.

According to Ridley (1995), an animal's diet is the key to understanding its behavioural adaptations for feed-

ing. A summary of the different foraging strategies is shown in Box 13.1. Foragers exhibit behavioural adaptations for the locating of food. For example, fringe-lipped bats (*Trachops cirrhosus*) locate their prey – tungara frogs (*Physalaemus pustulosus*) – by the calls made by the frogs (Figure 13.1). Once potential foods have been located, foraging animals may still benefit from selecting carefully what to eat. This was described in Chapter 3 for carnivores avoiding unpalatable

---

> **Box 13.1   Foraging strategies**
>
> The main division of foraging types is into *herbivores* (which consume plants) and *carnivores* (which feed on other animals). The behavioural adaptations of the two types exhibit significant differences. Herbivores generally have little difficulty in 'catching' food, but need to avoid carnivores. The carnivores require adaptations for catching prey and, depending on the species, may also have to avoid being preyed upon by other carnivores. (See Chapter 3 for a detailed account of predator–prey relationships.) In addition to these two types, there are also *omnivores* (which eat a mixture of plants and animals) and *detritivores* (which consume dead organic matter).
>
> Foragers are also classified according to the effects on the organism consumed. If the prey is killed and eaten, this is known as *predation*. If part of a prey organism is consumed, but it is not killed, it is called *parasitism*. (Note that, according to this classification, a sheep would be considered to be a parasite of grass!)
>
> A final classification is based on the mode of activity of the foragers. *Searchers* actively move through their environment and may be grazers, whose food is abundant, or hunters, whose food is more patchily distributed. *Ambushers* remain in one location and wait for prey to come to them. The latter strategy often involves the use of traps or lures (see Chapter 3, page 25).

Figure 13.1   A fringe-lipped bat, about to prey upon a tungara frog (*Physalaemus pustulosus*)

species of prey, but also applies to herbivores. Leaf-cutter ants (*Atta cephalotes*), for example, select foods that are low in terpenoids, a toxin that many plants incorporate into their leaves to repel consumers (Howard, 1987). Similar behaviour has also been observed in howler monkeys, as described in Box 13.2.

Box 13.2   Food selection by Costa Rican howler monkeys (Glander, 1981)

Howler monkeys tend to avoid foraging from common tree species and spend a great deal of time searching out scarcer varieties. Glander (1981) showed that the monkeys avoided species whose leaves contained high concentrations of poisonous alkaloids. Even when foraging from the less common species, howlers are very selective about which individual trees they feed upon. This selectivity mirrors variations in toxin concentration between the trees, with monkeys choosing those which are low in alkaloids. When feeding from a tree, howlers generally prefer the scarcer, smaller, new leaves to the more abundant, large, mature leaves. These smaller leaves tend to contain more water and less indigestible fibre than the larger ones. Even when the monkeys do eat the mature leaves, they usually select specimens containing the highest protein levels. Therefore, although surrounded by trees, howler monkeys forage very carefully, avoiding toxic leaves and those low in nutritional value.

Optimal foraging theory

BACKGROUND

According to optimal foraging theory (OFT), animals will adopt feeding strategies which maximise their energy intake from the food available. Animals must weigh up the costs of foraging, such as the time and energy spent searching for food, against the benefits (energy gained from the food). If food supplies are plentiful, animals tend to restrict their foraging to areas where food has previously been found. OFT suggests that an animal will stay in an area as long as the net gain (benefits minus costs) it can expect from that area in the future is greater than the net gain it could expect elsewhere.

Individuals of some species may have to choose between a feeding location that supplies a moderate, but constant, supply of food and one that fluctuates between a rich and a poor food supply. If energy requirements are less than the average expected reward, it pays to choose the less variable option (*risk-aversive behaviour*). However, if energy requirements are greater than the average expected reward, it usually pays to gamble on the more variable supply (*risk-prone behaviour*). Species which are 'risk sensitive' alter their feeding patterns in order to reduce the chance of failing to obtain enough energy for survival or reproduction (Goodenough et al., 1993).

OFT, like other optimality models of behaviour, has the advantage that it can make predictions about the way that individuals of a given species should behave if they are maximising their gains and minimising their losses in any particular situation. These predictions can then be tested against observations in the field.

CASE STUDIES OF OPTIMAL FORAGING THEORY

Starlings

Starlings (*Sturnus vulgaris*) feed their young mainly on leatherjackets (*Tipula maxima*) and other soil invertebrates. At the height of the breeding season, a parent may make up to 400 round trips per day from its nest to feeding sites, carrying food for its offspring. The reproductive success of birds like the starling is often limited by their ability to feed their young, resulting in a strong selective pressure on parents to deliver food efficiently. In terms of OFT, the question to ask is:

how many leatherjackets (or similar invertebrates) should a parent bring home on each trip?

Given that a starling is capable of carrying several leatherjackets, it seems obvious that bringing one insect at a time is a poor strategy. However, it would also be disadvantageous for a bird to bring back the largest load it can carry on each trip. This is because, as its beak becomes loaded with leatherjackets, a starling becomes less efficient at foraging (a case of diminishing returns). This necessitates longer searching times, when it could fly home, unload and start again. If a bird takes too few leatherjackets, it spends a lot of time travelling for a small load. If it takes too many, it wastes time in inefficient searching. Between these two options is the optimal strategy, representing the maximum rate of delivery of food to the chicks (maximising offspring survival). OFT also predicts that load sizes would vary with travelling times, smaller loads being carried if the travel time is short (Krebs & Davies, 1993).

Alex Kacelnik (1984) tested the prediction of the relationship between load size and travel time and found that the observed results fitted very closely to the theoretical model (Figure 13.2).

Bees

A similar problem to that of the starling is faced by the worker honey bee (*Apis mellifera*) foraging for nectar. The reason for diminishing returns in these animals is that the weight of nectar being carried adds a signifi-

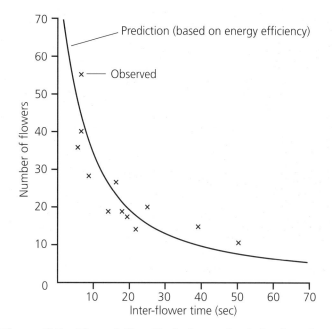

Figure 13.3   The relationship between load size (number of flowers visited) carried home by worker bees and flight time between flowers

cant energetic cost to flight. This results in bees returning home with smaller loads when they have to fly greater distances between flowers (Schmid-Hempel et al., 1985). However, in this case it is not the net rate of energy delivery which influences a bee's behaviour, but energetic efficiency (Figure 13.3). It has been shown that the life expectancy of bees depends on work load, with the hardest workers surviving for the shortest time (Wolf & Schmid-Hempel, 1989).

Shore crabs

The same approach described above for starlings and bees can also be used to account for prey choice among predators. Shore crabs (*Carcinus maenas*) prefer to eat mussels which provide them with the highest rate of energy return (Figure 13.4). Larger mussels require a lot of energy to crack open and smaller ones contain too little flesh to justify the effort. However, these crabs still eat a range of mussel sizes, centred around the optimum. This is probably due to the influence of search time upon profitability. If it takes a long time to find a profitable mussel, the crab may be able to achieve a higher rate of energy intake by eating some of the less profitable sizes (Krebs & Davies, 1993).

THE INFLUENCE OF COMPETITION

Salmon (*Salmo salar*) alter their foraging strategy in the presence of competitors, taking greater risks to acquire

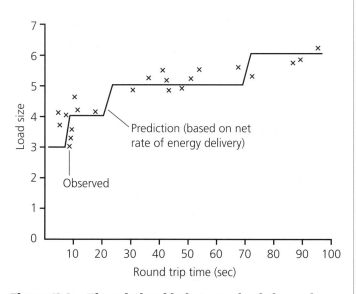

Figure 13.2   The relationship between load size and travel time for starlings (*Sternus vulgaris*) foraging on leatherjackets

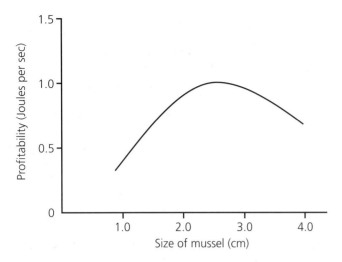

Figure 13.4   Shore crabs (*Carcinus maenas*) prefer to eat mussels which provide them with the highest rate of energy return. The curve shows the energy yield per second of time taken by the crabs to break open the shell

food. Other animals appear to adjust their behaviour according to their competitive ability. For example, sticklebacks (*Gasterosteus aculeatus*) infected with parasites cannot compete with their unparasitised peers. As a result of this, the infected fish select smaller prey (ignored by their healthy rivals), rather than competing unsuccessfully for larger, more profitable prey (Alcock, 1993).

THE INFLUENCE OF PREDATORS

Many studies have shown that predator risk can affect foraging decisions. For example, juvenile hoary marmots (*Marmota caligata*) are very reluctant to wander far from their burrows in search of food. They tend to feed mainly on the heavily grazed areas close to home. This behaviour does not fit the energy-maximising hypothesis and means that we must take into account predation risk when examining foraging behaviour (Holmes, 1984).

NUTRIENT CONSTRAINTS

In addition to maximising their energy intake, animals have specific nutritional requirements. For example, the Canadian moose (*Alces alces*) has a minimum daily requirement for sodium. This means that the moose has to compromise between satisfying its energy needs (by consuming energy-rich, low-sodium land plants) and its sodium requirements (by consuming energy-poor, high-sodium aquatic plants). A moose balances these needs by eating a mixture of plants, such that

energy intake is as high as possible but sufficient sodium is still obtained (Belovsky, 1978).

Criticisms of optimal foraging theory

The predictions made by OFT sometimes fail to match observed behaviour and some of the criticisms of OFT are outlined in Box 13.3.

Homing behaviour

Homing is a term used to refer to the navigation of an animal toward its home base. Many different species have been shown to exhibit impressive navigational skills, including wasps, fish and birds. In this section, the principles of migration are considered, followed by

---

Box 13.3   Criticisms of optimal foraging theory

When the predictions made by OFT fail to match observed behaviour, it is difficult to know whether it is the model or the animal which best demonstrates optimality. It is important to remember that the strategies used by animals may be influenced by competition, predation or specific nutrient requirements. Furthermore, other behaviours necessary for survival and/or reproduction may affect foraging behaviour. In this case, optimal foraging may be sacrificed so that a more generally optimal balance of different behaviours is achieved. For example, great tits (*Parus major*) attempt to combine foraging and territorial defence in the best possible way (Kacelnik, 1979).

When OFT models fail in their predictions, it is often difficult to establish the reason. It is not clear which of the assumptions or constraints employed are invalid. Furthermore, many animals may simply not forage optimally. A particular strategy could be successful without being optimal. In the absence of strong selection pressure, such as that imposed by competition or predation, suboptimal foraging may be relatively common. However, in the long run, species which forage suboptimally may be more likely to become extinct.

Figure 13.5   A herd of wildebeest (*Connochaetes* sp.) migrating across the Serengeti Plains in East Africa

Box 13.4   Why migrate?

One reason why species migrate is that local environments change and the optimum place to live varies with time. Food supplies, population density, climate and the presence of predators are all factors which may influence migration. In general, we find that the pattern of animal movements follows the pattern of environmental change. For example, the main reason for seasonal migration in ectothermic (cold-blooded) insects is probably the requirement to be in a climate that is warm enough to allow an active life. In the autumn, monarch butterflies (*Danaus plexippus*) migrate south from the USA and Canada towards the warmer climate of Mexico. In the spring, they return north.

an examination of the mechanisms by which animals navigate.

MIGRATION

Migration is a general term which usually describes the mass movement of members of a species from one location to another. This includes the movement of herds of wildebeest (*Connochaetes* sp.) across the African plains (Figure 13.5), the seasonal migration of swallows (*Tachycineta bicolor*) and the return of salmon to the stream where they hatched. In order to understand the process of migration, we need to consider the reasons for migration (see Box 13.4) and the factors involved in navigation.

How do migrating animals 'know' that they are moving towards a better environment? In the case of the wildebeest, it appears to be rain that acts as the environmental cue. Wildebeest can sense where rain is falling and then migrate in that direction. (Rain usually implies better growth of grass, the staple diet of wildebeest.) Wildebeest movements follow, at a distance of a few days, the pattern of rainfall. They only keep moving so long as rain is falling or has recently fallen within the area scanned by their senses (Ridley, 1995).

The majority of animal migrations are triggered by seasonal changes, more specifically by changing day length. The effect of day length on behaviour seems to be mediated hormonally. In the northern hemisphere, southward migration in the autumn is stimulated by falling production of sex hormones. Likewise, northward migration in the spring is triggered by the release of sex hormones.

It is not clear whether these animals are capable of true navigation (the ability to reach a goal, regardless of the starting point), or simply show a compass orientation, such as always heading north or south (Figure 13.6). In order to assess this distinction, experiments were carried out with starlings on their annual migration from their breeding grounds around the Baltic Sea to their wintering sites in southern England, Holland and northern France. The birds were caught in Holland, tagged, taken by aeroplane to Switzerland and released. Juvenile starlings continued to fly in the same direction (south-west) and wintered in southern France and Spain. However, the adult starlings flew north-west to the usual overwintering grounds. It appears that the young starlings used only compass orientation, whereas the adults were capable of true navigation.

NAVIGATION

One explanation of navigation which has been suggested is that animals memorise local landmarks and directions on their departure, and simply reverse the directions to return home. This appears to be the mechanism used by the bee-killing digger wasp (*Philanthus triangulum*). Female wasps of this species

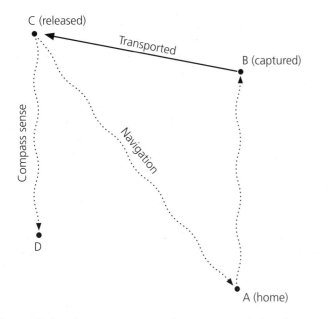

Figure 13.6   A compass sense is necessary, but not sufficient, for navigation. An animal capable of returning directly to its home (A) from C has the ability to navigate. If the animal moves to D it possesses a compass sense, but is not capable of navigation

dig burrows in sand, where eggs are laid and larvae hatch out. The female feeds the growing larvae on bees that she has captured and killed, leaving and returning to the burrow many times. However, it is not always easy to find a particular burrow because the wasps tend to nest in dense groups. In a classic experiment, described in Box 13.5, Tinbergen and Kruyt (1938) confirmed that these wasps return to their own burrows using memorised local landmarks.

Learned local landmarks may be a reasonable explanation of navigation over small distances, but longer distance homing requires other mechanisms. One such mechanism may be the recognition of the home site at a distance by some distinctive property possessed by the area. This seems to be the technique used by salmon, which have been known to travel 2000 miles out to sea, only to return to the exact stream where they hatched. Salmon appear to find their way home using their sense of smell. The odour may come from young salmon still in the stream, which have not yet migrated, and/or other characteristic odours in the stream. Experimental studies have shown that, if the salmons' olfactory (smell) sense was impaired (by plugging their nostrils), they homed less accurately than untreated controls (Harden-Jones, 1968). A third explanation of homing,

Box 13.5   Navigation in the bee-killing digger wasp

Tinbergen and Kruyt (1938) placed a circle of pine cones around the entrance of several digger wasp burrows. They left them there for a few days, checking that the wasps still kept returning to their burrows. They then waited for the wasps to leave on a foraging expedition. While the wasps were away, Tinbergen and Kruyt moved the circles of cones approximately 1 metre from the

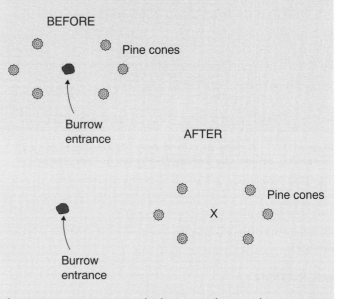

burrow entrances below. When the wasps returned, they landed where the burrow 'should' have been, in the centre of the circle of pine cones (X). It appears that the wasps recognised the burrow by its surrounding landmarks, not by any stimulus from the burrow itself.

which is most likely to be important over very long distances, is that the animal has an internal 'map sense' and can estimate both its own map reference and that of the home site (Ridley, 1995). This type of homing is referred to as true navigation and is most clearly seen in the homing pigeon.

Homing pigeons: a case of true navigation?

Humans have artificially selected pigeons for their homing ability for thousands of years. The pigeons were originally used for carrying messages, but have recently been bred for their ability to home rapidly in competitive pigeon racing. Homing pigeons appear to be able to find their way home from any starting point, whether or not they have previously seen the area. In order to do this, pigeons need the equivalent of a map (indicating the position of home and the position of the starting point) and a compass to find the direction from one to the other.

Many experiments have suggested that pigeons will initially orientate themselves using the position of the sun in the sky as a compass. The birds use an internal clock to make allowances for changes in the sun's position during the day. Evidence for the use of this internal clock has been obtained from experiments in which pigeons have their clock shifted six hours forwards. Baker (1978) found that these birds orientate themselves 90° anticlockwise away from the correct direction (Figure 13.7).

Pigeons must also possess some other compass sense in addition to the sun, because they can also navigate cor-

rectly on overcast days. Birds with magnets attached to their heads navigate incorrectly on overcast but not on sunny days. This implies that pigeons have a magnetic sense (disrupted by the presence of an external magnet) and that it may be used as a compass when the sun is invisible. Some psychologists have taken this idea one step further, suggesting that pigeons may have a magnetic map sense. However, there is not yet any evidence to support this idea.

It has been suggested that homing pigeons use olfactory cues, in a manner similar to that of the salmon. Alternatively, they may have some sort of olfactory map, which they could use to navigate. Pigeons do seem to home less accurately if their olfactory sense is experimentally removed, but the evidence is far from conclusive.

The most likely explanation for the navigation skills of homing pigeons is that they can use a large number of cues and the particular cues used depend upon local conditions. They primarily use the sun as a compass, but also have a back-up compass sense when the sun is invisible (probably the earth's magnetic field). Their map sense is unknown, but may involve magnetism and olfaction. Finally, pigeons probably also make use of memorised local landmarks and other home cues when they can be sensed.

Conclusions

Foraging is a term used to describe the ways in which animals satisfy their nutritional requirements. According to optimal foraging theory, animals will adopt feeding strategies which maximise their energy intake from the food available. If predictions are based on this theory, they should also take into account nutrient constraints and the influence of competition and predation. OFT has been criticised for being over-simplified and not taking into account the idea that some species may forage suboptimally.

Homing is a term used to refer to the navigation of an animal towards its home base. Some species find their way home by memorising local landmarks, others use olfactory cues. Many birds are capable of true navigation. In addition to the use of landmarks and olfactory cues, homing pigeons use the sun (and perhaps the earth's magnetic field) as a compass. They may also possess a map sense.

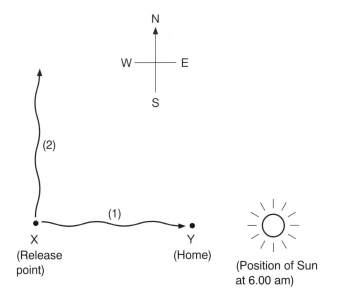

Figure 13.7   Clock-shifting and altered navigation in homing pigeons. (1) indicates the (correct) path taken by a bird kept in natural light. (2) is the path taken by a bird whose clock has been shifted forwards by six hours. The birds must fly east to return home. Pigeon 1 'knows' it is 6.00 am and therefore the sun is in the east, so it flies towards the sun. Pigeon 2 'thinks' it is noon and therefore the sun is in the south, so it flies at 90° anticlockwise to the sun (believing this to be east, when it is actually north)

SUMMARY

- **Foraging** is a term used to describe the ways in which animals satisfy their nutritional requirements. An animal's diet is the key to understanding its behavioural adaptations for feeding. The main foraging types are: **herbivores**, which consume plants; **carnivores**, which feed on other animals; **omnivores**, which eat a mixture of plants and animals; and **detritivores**, which consume dead organic matter. Foragers may be further classified into: **predators**, which kill and eat their prey, or **parasites**, which consume part of the prey but do not kill it; and **searchers**, which actively move through their environment, or **ambushers**, which remain in one location and wait for prey to come to them.
- According to **optimal foraging theory**, animals will adopt feeding strategies which maximise their energy intake from the food available. Animals must weigh up the costs of foraging, such as the time and energy spent searching for food, against the benefits (energy gained from the food).
- Individuals of some species may have to choose between a feeding location that supplies a moderate, but constant, supply of food and one that fluctuates between a rich and a poor food supply. Species which are **risk sensitive** alter their feeding patterns in order to reduce the chance of failing to obtain enough energy for survival or reproduction.
- Starlings forage in a manner which ensures **maximum rate of delivery** of food to their chicks, maximising offspring survival. A similar situation occurs in honey bees, which forage for nectar on the basis of **maximum energy efficiency**. Optimal foraging theory can also apply to prey choice among predators. For example, shore crabs select mussels which provide them with the highest rate of energy return.
- Optimal foraging theory has sometimes been criticised for failing to take into account **nutrient constraints** and the influence of **competition** and **predation**. It is also seen as being **oversimplified** and unable to explain **suboptimal foraging**.
- **Homing** is a term used to refer to the navigation of an animal towards its home base. Many different species have been shown to exhibit impressive navigational skills, including wasps, fish and birds.
- **Migration** is a general term which usually describes the **mass movement of members of a species from one location to another**. One reason why species migrate is that local environments change and the optimum place to live varies with time. **Food supplies, population density, climate**, and **the presence of predators** are all factors which may influence migration. In general, the pattern of animal movements follows the pattern of environmental change.
- The majority of animal migrations are triggered by **seasonal changes**. It is not clear whether migrating animals simply show a **compass orientation** or are capable of **true navigation** (the ability to reach a goal, regardless of the starting point).
- One method of navigation is to **memorise local landmarks** and directions on departure, and simply reverse the directions to return home. This appears to be the mechanism used by the bee-killing digger wasp. Salmon navigate to their home site over long distances using their sense of **smell**. Many species of bird seem to be capable of true navigation.
- **Homing pigeons** appear to be able to find their way home from any starting point, whether or not they have previously seen the area. The most likely explanation for the navigation skills of homing pigeons is that they can use a large number of cues and the particular cues used depend upon local conditions. They primarily use the **sun as a compass**, but also have a back-up compass sense when the sun is invisible (probably the earth's **magnetic field**). Their map sense is unknown, but may involve **magnetism** and/or **olfaction**. Pigeons probably also make use of memorised local landmarks and other home cues when they can be sensed.

ANIMAL LANGUAGE

Introduction and overview

Language, we might suppose, is a human characteristic which sets us apart from animals. Darwin's theory of the evolutionary origin of species asserts that humans differ from non-human animals only quantitatively, not qualitatively. If language is not a special characteristic of humans, research should indicate that non-human animals do have language, or at least the capacity to learn it. The aim of this chapter is to explore the nature of language and whether it is unique to humans. It describes studies of natural animal language and attempts to teach language to captive, non-human animals.

Could animals have language?

Lewin (1991) summarises the split in opinion about the existence of language in animals. The *continuity school* views language as part of a cognitive continuum, which had its roots in our ape-like ancestors. Opposing this view is the *discontinuity school*, for whom language is a uniquely human trait with no direct evolutionary connection to the brains of apes or other non-human animals. If Darwin's assertion about the evolutionary origin of species is correct (the foundation of the continuity school), animal communication systems should show some, or all, of the properties of language. By contrast, Chomsky, a member of the discontinuity school, believes that communication in non-human animals differs from human language. This is because animals cannot generate an infinite variety of utterances.

The strategy for solving this dilemma is to decide what all human languages have in common, and whether these characteristics are also demonstrated by non-human animal communication in the natural world.

Alternatively, we could investigate whether, if given training, animals could acquire language which did fulfil the chosen criteria. Evidence for either option would support the continuity school. For each animal communication system, the extent to which it can be considered to be a language is evaluated using the criteria in Box 14.1.

Animal language in the natural environment

VERVETS

Animal signalling was discussed at length in Chapter 11. One of the species described was the vervet monkey (*Ceropithecus aethiops*) which uses a 'vocabulary' of calls to indicate the presence of specific predators. Each call elicits a different response in other individuals. A loud bark, for instance, signifies the approach of a leopard (*Panthera pardus*), causing members of the troop to flee into the trees. How well does this communication system compare to the criteria for language outlined in Box 14.1?

Symbolic/semanticity

Each call is meaningful. Whether it means 'I can see a particular predator', or 'make a particular escape response' is unknown, but the semantic value of each call is indicated by the consistent response from the receivers. The calls themselves are arbitrary (the sounds are not related to the meaning that they convey) and so are symbolic.

Specialisation

The extent to which vervet calls are specialised is unclear. These alarm signals may have evolved from fear responses, but this explanation is now insufficient because they are predator specific. An animal which was merely vocalising in response to fear would be unlikely to demonstrate such reliable distinctions in its sounds, or to broadcast its fear so widely.

Box 14.1 Ten language criteria

The ten generalised features of language described below are used throughout this chapter to evaluate the existence of language in non-human animals.

Symbolic/semantic	The system uses arbitrary symbols which have shared meaning for the communicators.
Specialised	The symbols used are employed only for communication, they are not the by-product of another behavioural system.
Displacement	Language can be used to describe things which are absent in time or space (e.g. past events or hidden objects).
Generativity	Language allows for the production of an infinite variety of novel utterances.
Phonological and lexical syntax	Language is dependent on a rule-based structure. This has rules for the combination of basic units (e.g. sounds or 'phonemes'), known as phonological syntax, and for the combination of higher level units (e.g. words), known as lexical syntax.
Spontaneous acquisition	Users acquire basic language spontaneously without formal instruction or reinforcement. Only then can subsequent languages, or language elements, be learned.
Critical period	The acquisition of fluency in a first language is limited to a phase early in life.
Cultural transmission	Language, with changes accumulated by one generation, is passed to the next by its use.
Interchangeable roles	Individuals can be both transmitters and recipients of language.
Conversation	By alternating roles, individuals can exchange information about a shared understanding.

Displacement and generativity

The criterion of displacement is satisfied by vervet alarm calls in the sense that the receivers, on hearing the call, make the appropriate escape response without seeing the predator. They are not simply being alerted to look for trouble. The same displacement cannot, however, apply to the callers. There is simply no *need* to send warnings about predators which are not there in time or space. Vervet calls are not 'generative'. They can only communicate about a very limited range of events, in a restricted way.

Phonological/lexical syntax

Vervet alarm calls cannot be usefully combined. Unlike human language, a sequence of calls does not convey more information, or different meanings, than each call would individually.

Spontaneous acquisition, critical period and cultural transmission

Cheney and Seyfarth's (1990) observations of young vervets suggest that their ability to call develops as a result of both genetic and cultural factors. Young vervets will give alarm calls to a wider category of objects (both animate and inanimate) than adults. The infants do, however, display a certain logic to their calling. Things in the air (geese, falling leaves and hawks) will elicit an 'eagle' alarm. Things moving along the ground (mice, tortoises and snakes) cause them to raise the 'snake' alarm. The existence of these predispositions to respond to categories of predator suggest an innate element to the signals.

Nearby adults follow the youngster's gaze, and because they only reiterate the call when it is appropriate, the infant's calling is refined. This is a cultural element in the transmission of the signals. This pattern resembles the acquisition of human language. According to Chomsky (1965), we have an innate processing capacity, the Language Acquisition Device, which governs the way language is learned. But *what* we learn, the specific language, is determined by our environment.

Further evidence for the involvement of both nature and nurture in vervet calls is reported by Bright (1984). Comparison of calls given by vervets in Senegal and Kenya shows that they are very alike, despite the populations having been separated for thousands of generations. The degree of similarity supports an underlying genetic component, whereas experimental isolation studies suggest that cultural transmission also plays a part. Young vervets raised apart from adults, or in the company of other species, produce very different sounds from socially reared individuals. This suggests that there could be a critical period for learning variations on a theme, as with bird song (see Chapter 1, page 7).

Interchangeable roles and conversation

The roles of sender and receiver are interchangeable, although particular individuals may call more often. There is no evidence of conversation between vervets using alarm calls. The calls are only employed in response to the external stimulus of a predator.

HONEY BEES

Honey bees (*Apis mellifera*) perform dances to communicate complex information about the direction and distance of food sources (Box 14.2). The *round dance* is used to indicate food found near to the hive, the *waggle dance* for more distant sources. The waggle dance is *symbolic*; it uses angles and vigour to convey meaning about direction and distance respectively. Surprisingly, distance is indicated by *increasing* vigour (one might expect a bee who had flown a long way to be less active). These signals are *specialised*, and by communicating about something which is absent, they show *displacement*. The roles of transmitter and recipient are *interchangeable*. Therefore, the dance of honey bees satisfies at least some of the criteria of language.

The symbols used by bees may not be truly arbitrary. Although the direction of the dance does not point to the food, there is a one-to-one correspondence between the two dimensions. This would be like representing numbers with longer and longer words. The bees' signals are restricted to two fixed 'linguistic dimensions', rather than being representative in the way that we can signify *fat* with a small word, *skinny* with a longer word and *average* with a longer word still. The size of the concept and the size of the word are unrelated. Similarly, the waggle dance could be described as *generative*, as the bees can communicate about novel locations, but this is hardly creative on the same scale as human language. Perhaps bees have even less to say of interest than we do!

Griffin and Taft (1992) have investigated the sounds made by honey bees during the waggle dance. They have found that these sounds convey the same message as the waggles. The duration of the sound correlates very closely with the duration of the waggling, so the

Box 14.2 The dance of the bees (von Frisch, 1956) (Figure 14.1)

The round dance

A worker honey bee communicates that she has been successfully foraging at a nearby food source (up to 50 metres away) using the round dance. She moves in a circular path, indicated by the arrows, on the vertical face of the comb inside the hive (a). Her dance is attended by other workers, which then leave the hive to search for food in the immediate vicinity.

The waggle dance

A worker bee who returns from a successful foraging trip to a more distant food source uses the waggle dance to communicate the whereabouts of the food to other workers. The dance indicates both the distance and direction of the food and, like the round dance, is performed in darkness on the vertical face of the comb.

A returning bee dances in a figure-of-8 pattern, followed by other workers. The angle of the waggle run tells her followers in which direction to fly when they leave the hive. The direction of the food source relative to the sun is translated by the dancer into an angle relative to gravity. If the food can be found by flying directly towards the sun, she performs the waggles on a vertical run which points upwards; if the food is directly away from the sun, she waggles on a downward-pointing run (b). If the foragers must fly out of the hive at an angle of 40° clockwise from the sun (c), then the dancer tilts her waggle run at 40° clockwise from the vertical (d). Any direction can thus be encoded by the dance. The distance the bees must fly is indicated by the vigour of the dance. The number of complete cycles of the dance, and the number and duration of waggles, all increase with distance from the hive. A bee which has travelled a long way must ensure her followers know exactly where to go as they have more scope for getting lost.

The dance is symbolic in two ways. It codes the direction of the food source as an angle relative to gravity, which translates to an angle from the sun. It codes distance with increasing vigour of waggles.

two are equivalent indicators of distance. The auditory component, however, may be displaced in time by as much as a second, lagging behind the movements. This

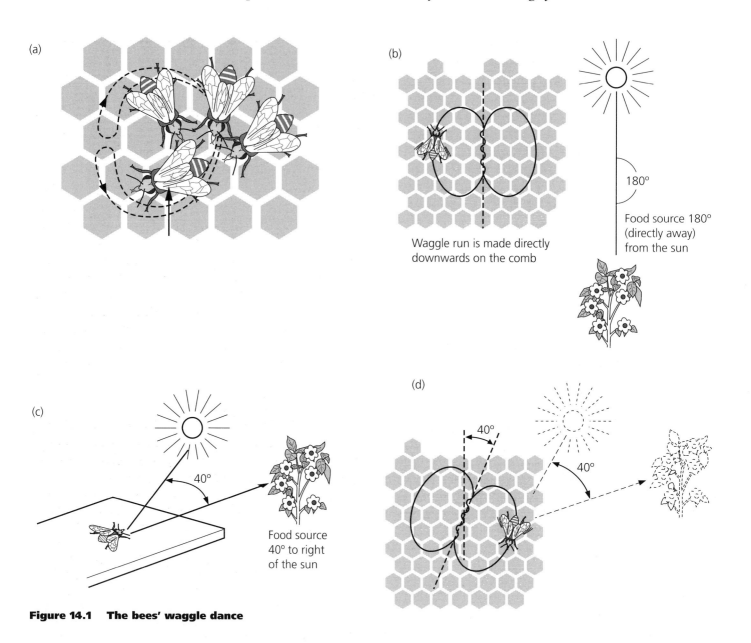

Figure 14.1   The bees' waggle dance

delay does not appear to communicate any additional information about the food source. In language we may convey the same message simultaneously, using two signalling systems – for example, saying no and shaking our heads, or asking a question and using a rising tone. Such reinforcement of the message ensures that it is not misunderstood. Whilst the waggle dance exhibits displacement by informing the other bees about a distant food source, it could be argued that the bees were not 'talking about' that distance, but giving instructions. Certainly, there is no element of *conversation*. There is also little or no evidence to suggest that honey bee dances satisfy the criteria of *phonological/lexical syntax*,

spontaneous acquisition, critical period or *cultural transmission*. It is debatable, therefore, whether honey bees have language.

BIRDS

In Chapter 1 (page 7), the development of bird song was discussed. These songs are *symbolic* in that the meanings of territoriality or courtship are shared, but they are really only elaborate signals. Bird song is, without question, a highly *specialised* form of communication. However, it conforms to Chomsky's (1965) notion of a system with a fixed number of signals which are produced in response to a specific range of triggers. Thus, bird song, whilst varied, cannot be described as *generative*. Similarly, birds lack *syntax*, as there are too few song elements to recombine meaningfully. Furthermore, birds do not demonstrate varied, alternating exchanges, which could qualify as *conversations*.

Birds do, however, illustrate clear *spontaneous acquisition* that is restricted to a *critical period* early in life. Changes in song are, as a consequence, passed on to subsequent generations as they absorb the learned element of their song, illustrating *cultural transmission*. As with bees, bird song only satisfies a few of the criteria for true language.

CHIMPANZEES

Chimpanzees (*Pan troglodytes*) use varied facial expressions, sounds and gestures to communicate (Goodall, 1965), but none seems complex or varied enough to constitute language. However, the ability of wild primates to learn complex skills, and to imagine a situation from the point of view of another individual, has been observed by Boesch (1991). These attributes could imply a capacity to learn language.

Boesch studied young chimpanzees learning to open nuts in their natural habitat. Many nuts are difficult to open, so chimpanzees use a tool (a large stone or stick) as a hammer. Adults foraging alone carry a suitable hammer, selecting nuts and cracking them deftly against an 'anvil'. When foraging with a youngster, however, a mother will supply not only nuts but also hammers to her offspring. Boesch observed mothers guiding the behaviour of their offspring when they encountered problems. One mother was seen to reposition nuts on an anvil to enable her son to use the hammer effectively. Another mother, having been handed the hammer by her daughter who had unsuccessfully attempted to open a nut, held the hammer where it was visible and rotated it in her own hand, to illustrate a more effective grasp. She then opened ten nuts and allowed her daughter to eat some of each before giving her the hammer. The daughter assumed the same grip and maintained this whilst varying other aspects of her behaviour, such as posture. She succeeded in opening four nuts in fifteen minutes. Boesch concluded that adult chimpanzees seem to have the ability to compare their offspring's performance to an internal concept of the way a behaviour should appear. From this, they can anticipate the effects of these actions and the con-

sequences of modifications in performance which are essential to language. Being able to understand that there can be a different viewpoint from one's own, and predicting the likely outcome from a change in behaviour, is indicative of complex cognitive processes. These perspective and turn-taking skills are fundamental to aspects of language such as *cultural transmission*, *displacement* and *conversation*.

Further evidence for the ability of chimps to consider the perspective of others has been provided by Povinelli et al. (1992), as described in Box 14.3. Their work supports the idea that chimps can appreciate the symbolic nature of language, its displacement quality, and that it can convey information from one individual to another (which was previously ignorant of the content of the message). So even though chimps demonstrate little by way of language in the wild, other aspects of their comprehension and behaviour suggest that they may have some skills which underlie the acquisition of language.

Box 14.3   Chimpanzees are capable of considering the perspective of others

In Povinelli et al.'s (1992) experiment, four pairs (of a chimp and a human) were divided into two conditions. In each pair one participant was an 'informant', the other an 'operator'. In two pairs, the chimp was the informant; in the other two, the chimp played the role of the operator. The pair sat opposite one another, either side of a piece of apparatus with handles at the operator's end. These handles caused pairs of food trays to move within reach of the participants (Figure 14.2). In the first stage of the experiment, the operator learned to pull the correct handle to draw a visibly baited food tray to the edge of the apparatus. This caused the other food tray to reach the informant. This behaviour was acquired rapidly. During the second stage of the experiment, the informant, but not the operator, could see which food tray was baited. The informant was required to use a spontaneous gesture to indicate to the operator which handle to pull. Pointing at the food tray or appropriate part of the apparatus was the most common technique used for this purpose. The 'informant' chimps readily learned to indicate the correct location and the 'operators' similarly learned to respond to signalling. Both informants and operators received a food reward for correct signalling and response.

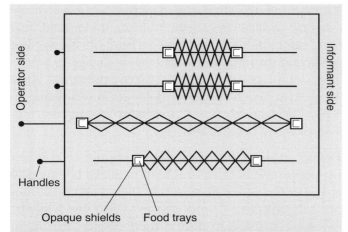

Figure 14.2   Apparatus used to test spontaneous communication in chimps (*Pan troglodytes*) (Povinelli et al., 1992)

The chimps' comprehension of the role of their partner was tested in the third stage of the experiment, in which the informant and operator swapped roles. This reversal was achieved by spinning the apparatus round so that the handles faced the ex-informant (the new operator). Three of the four chimps showed immediate transfer of skills between the two phases of the experiment. Ex-operators spontaneously pointed, and ex-informants responded accurately to pointing by using the correct handle. Povinelli et al. concluded that the chimps had learned the requirements of both roles during the training phase. Being able to comprehend the social role of another individual, and attribute intention to his or her behaviour are essential steps in the use of language as a tool for communication. This work, therefore, suggests that chimps have at least some of the cognitive requirements for language. Their pointing was *symbolic*, *specialised*, showed *displacement* and was *spontaneous*. Their behaviour also indicated their understanding of the *interchangeability of roles*.

Teaching language to non-human animals

Studies of animals in their natural habitats confirm that communication in some species shows many, although not all, the characteristics of language. Bird song and communication in cetaceans (see Chapter 11, page 106)

Box 14.4   Teaching language to birds

Birds are good potential candidates for learning language. Firstly, they use a complex form of communication in their natural habitat. Secondly, song is (at least in part) acquired (see Chapter 1, page 7). Therefore, birds are able to learn to communicate. Finally, birds use the auditory channel, making it easy to measure the success of teaching and learning. Some bird species, such as parrots, are remarkably good mimics. This further enhances their suitability for research into language acquisition. Pepperberg (1983) taught an African grey parrot (*Psittacus erithacus*), Alex, a vocabulary of about 150 spoken words. These words are used to request objects and categorise them (for instance as *same* or *different*) in response to questions about colour and shape. Alex does not respond with absolute accuracy, but the language used clearly satisfies the criteria of *symbolic/semantic*, *specialised* and *interchangeable roles*.

and primates are among the best contenders for natural language. If such animals do have a capacity for language, they would also be the most likely to display an ability to comprehend and produce human language. This section explores attempts to teach human languages to such animals. For example, the teaching of language to birds is described in Box 14.4.

TEACHING LANGUAGE TO CETACEANS

Herman et al. (1984) taught language to two bottlenosed dolphins (*Tursiops truncatus*). Akeakamai was taught a language based on visual signs and Phoenix was taught an acoustic language. Using the visual signs, Akeakamai can respond accurately to novel, four-word sentences, whose meaning depends on word order. This indicates comprehension of the grammar of the sentences. Phoenix can respond to five-word sentences, where the instruction involves a verb relating two objects, both with related modifiers such as 'surface hoop fetch bottom basket' (go to the hoop at the surface and take it to the basket at the bottom).

Herman's technique of teaching the dolphins to understand rather than to produce language has the advantage that it readily demonstrates their linguistic comprehension. It is easier to set them a task, and see if they do it (indicating that they have understood), than to sit and wait for an animal spontaneously to generate utterances in a language it may, or may not, have acquired. Herman's technique also offers greater precision, as the instructions can be rigorously controlled and the responses readily classified as correct or incorrect. Such communication does not, however, allow for *conversation*. The dolphins may comprehend, and respond correctly, on the basis of an understanding of grammar, but they cannot reply.

Herman et al. (1993) investigated Akeakamai's ability to respond to complex visual language, testing her understanding of syntax. They found evidence to suggest that she could use a rule-based language, as she could identify cases in which the experimenters were flouting the rules. When anomalous sequences of gestures were presented to Akeakamai, she sometimes rejected the signal. This indicated an awareness of an error, as she never refused normal sequences. In this sense, the dolphin's language skills not only satisfy the rules of *symbolic/semantic* and the *specialised criteria*, but also of using *syntax*.

TEACHING LANGUAGE TO PRIMATES

Kellogg and Kellogg (1933) and Hayes and Hayes (1951) attempted to teach chimpanzees, Gua and Viki, spoken English. Neither animal succeeded, as chimps simply do not have the vocal apparatus to articulate the different sounds required. Gua did, however, recognise almost 100 words, suggesting that other techniques might successfully demonstrate language skills in chimps.

Subsequent attempts to teach language to chimps have employed non-vocal techniques. The first, Gardner and Gardner's (1969) study of Washoe, used Ameslan (American sign language for the deaf), a language based on manual signs. Washoe learned the meanings of 160 signs, clearly satisfying the *symbolic/semantic* criterion. As these gestures are not part of a chimp's normal behavioural repertoire, they show *specialisation* for communication. Washoe also readily understood *displacement* – for instance asking for yoghurt even if she could not see any. She understood word strings and showed *generativity* by producing them, such as 'water-bird' when she saw a duck, and 'baby in my cup' in response to a cup with a doll inside. Gardner and Gardner claimed that Washoe understood 'sentences', strings of words whose meaning depended on word order, although this has been challenged (see below).

Washoe was able to take the role of transmitter or recipient of signs, showing *interchangeability* and, as she 'took turns', the rudiments of *conversation*. Washoe did not, however, acquire language spontaneously, even though she was very young (potentially within a *critical period*).

A different approach was later used with a chimp called Lana. Rumbaugh *et al.* (1973) taught Lana to use a typewriter, which generated different patterns (lexigrams) using a language called 'Yerkish'. She showed all the signs of language suggested by other chimps, and she was able to correct errors in her own sentences, initiate conversations and use a simple *syntax* to increase meaning.

Terrace (1979), by contrast, found no increase in meaning as his chimp's utterances increased in length. Terrace's chimp (Nim Chimpsky) used Ameslan proficiently, but Terrace raised many doubts about the validity of his own findings and those of others. He claimed that the innovative 'water-bird' generated by Washoe was nothing more than the signing of the two concepts *water* and *bird* consecutively. He argued that Washoe's ability to give the right answer in complex situations was the result of subconscious cueing by her teachers, rather than any appreciation of syntax.

Rumbaugh and Savage-Rumbaugh (1994) have suggested that the early studies made a crucial omission: they only taught the apes to speak, not to listen. This error, of focusing on production not comprehension, is a fundamental one. Children understand speech before they can produce it, yet the studies so far described expected apes to generate speech before they had a basis from which to comprehend it. If so, it is unsurprising that these demonstrations of chimp language reveal little more than sophisticated signalling. Without the underlying comprehension, it would be impossible for the chimps to be productive. Rumbaugh and Savage-Rumbaugh went on to conduct language-learning projects. In these projects, animals were reared in *language-structured* environments, in which language was used around the animals to announce and co-ordinate social activities For example, in an attempt to overcome the lack of investment in comprehension, Savage-Rumbaugh initially taught a pair of chimps, Sherman and Austin, to listen to each other. These animals could eventually use language to co-operate for mutual benefit (Anderson et al., 1996).

The Rumbaughs' more recent work has focused on the

Box 14.5   Panzee and Panbanisha, a language-reared chimp and bonobo

Rumbaugh and Savage-Rumbaugh (1994) were interested to know whether the success of teaching by immersion in language could also benefit other species which had shown lesser language skills using formal teaching methods. They reared two chimps, one *Pan troglodytes*, Panzee, and one *Pan paniscus* (bonobo), Panbanisha, of very similar ages, in the same 'language-rich' environment (Figure 14.3). Within two years, two findings were clear: that both species could learn without formal instruction, but that the bonobo was much more competent. Panbanisha and Panzee, like Kanzi, received no explicit training in language, they simply picked it up. As such, their learning fulfils the criterion of *spontaneous acquisition*, in a manner analogous to the language learning of a child. Early exposure to a language-structured environment lays the foundations for comprehension.

Figure 14.3   Panbanisha and Panzee using the lexigram keyboard

pygmy chimpanzee (*Pan paniscus*) or bonobo. (A comparison of these species is provided in Box 14.5). The first attempt to teach a bonobo language was with Matata, a wild-born animal, introduced to the laboratory at 5 years of age. The researchers spoke to the chimps in English, and used a lexigram keyboard with a matrix of 256 geometrical, coloured shapes. The shapes deliberately bore no resemblance to the items (nouns) or activities (verbs) they represented. Matata learned only eight lexigrams, and these functioned only as requests. There was no indication that the shapes had acquired any symbolic representation.

Throughout her training, Matata had Kanzi with her, a newborn infant she had kidnapped six months earlier and kept. No efforts were made to teach Kanzi, but when, at $2\frac{1}{2}$ years old, he was introduced to the language programme, it became apparent that he had learned the symbols during his mother's lessons! He spontaneously made requests, named things, and announced what he was going to do. Even at this stage, it was clear that Kanzi used language differently. He was illustrating reflexiveness without training.

Training was continued with Kanzi, but unlike the formal instruction other animals had received, he was simply exposed to people communicating with each other, and with him, about real world events via the keyboard. Kanzi was encouraged to use the keyboard, but was never denied objects or participation in activities for failing to do so. He quickly learned to communicate requests to travel around the centre to food sites, to visit other chimps, to play games and to watch television!

Lewin (1991) described Savage-Rumbaugh's findings with Kanzi, from following simple commands such as 'give the cereal to Karen', to understanding complex sentences. An instruction 'go to the colony room and get the orange' produced hesitation, but 'get the orange that's in the colony room' did not. He concluded that more complex sentences produce better comprehension, indicating a grasp of *lexical syntax*.

Kanzi picked up the rule 'action precedes object' in two-word utterances from his keepers. Children show a similar trend, from random ordering to an order preference in word pairs. Together, these observations indicate that Kanzi is using basic lexical syntax. Children use and generate such syntax spontaneously, Kanzi appeared to do the same. He also invented a rule for combining a gesture and a symbol. The lexigram always came first (for instance the symbol for chase), followed by pointing to someone. This had both generality (it was used for different verbs) and originality. The rules Kanzi uses might be called 'protogrammar' rather than grammar. If this is the case, then we should apply the same term to the early utterances of children, according to Savage-Rumbaugh.

Savage-Rumbaugh et al. (1993) conducted an experiment to compare Kanzi's comprehension of human speech with that of a child, Alia, who had also learned to use the keyboard. They were tested on over 400 novel sentences, which were specific about actions, places and objects. The required actions were not necessarily obvious, either because they were not things one normally did (putting elastic bands on balls), or because they referred to unpredictable places or situations, such as 'get the telephone that's outdoors' (when there was a telephone in sight). At 9 years old, Kanzi scored 74% correct, Alia, at $2\frac{1}{2}$, scored 65%. Clearly, Kanzi had acquired the ability to comprehend, as well as produce, language without formal teaching. He had simply responded to communication around him. As with a child, Kanzi's responses were not pure imitation to acquire meanings for symbols, but reflected an understanding of their use. Control chimps (raised without exposure to the lexigram) did not ever develop an understanding of speech, regardless of later exposure, because it had not been made accessible to them through a narrative in which they could participate. This, like the findings with Matata, suggests that chimps have a *critical period* for acquiring language skills.

Further evidence from Savage-Rumbaugh suggests that the chimps also grasped something akin to lying, at least an awareness of people tricking one another. Savage-Rumbaugh cites an example in which Panbanisha watched a person secretly substitute a bug for some sweets in a box. A second person then tried to open the box, and the first asked Panbanisha, 'What is she looking for?'. The bonobo replied that she was looking for the sweets. Apart from indicating *displacement*, this also implies that the bonobo was aware that other people's thinking was different from her own. The bonobo knew there were no sweets in the box, but was aware that the second person did not. Panbanisha added that the first person was being 'bad', a recognition of the fact that she understood that the second person had been tricked.

The language skills of the chimps discussed in this chapter are compared in Box 14.6. All of them satisfy the criterion of semanticity, but only two (Lana and Kanzi) showed all four skills of semanticity, displacement, syntax and generativity.

Box 14.6 Language skills of chimps compared on four key criteria

	Semanticity	Displacement	Syntax	Generativity
Gua	✓	✗	✗	✗
Viki	✓	✗	✗	✗
Washoe	✓	✓	✗	✓
Sarah	✓	✓	✓	✗
Lana	✓	✓	✓	✓
Koko	✓	✓	✗	✓
Nim	✓	✗	✗	✓
Kanzi	✓	✓	✓	✓

✓ criterion satisfied; ✗ criterion not satisfied.

Is language unique to humans?

Our ability to decipher whether animals are capable of language is hampered by our own inability to imagine what they are communicating *about*. Are their thoughts complex enough to *generate* an infinite variety of messages to transmit? Does their cognitive processing demand a communication system which can convey information about displaced events, about untruths or about themselves? Certainly, there is an increasing body of evidence to suggest that at least cetaceans and primates, perhaps also the parrot, have a grasp of some complex concepts. Primates seem, in addition, to be able to refer to displaced events and objects. Finally, the research of Gallup (1977) suggests that a chimpanzee has a concept of itself (see McIlveen & Gross, 1997). Perhaps this species at least has the cognitive requirements for language. It is unsurprising, therefore, that it is only in chimps that we have seen communication which closely resembles human language.

Conclusions

There are ten generalised features of language that can be used to assess its existence in non-human animals. Many animals exhibit some of these features, but it is debatable whether any non-human species satisfy them all. Attempts have been made to teach language to a variety of non-human animals, including birds, cetaceans and primates. Several species appear to be capable of grasping some of the rudiments of language, but it is only really in chimpanzees that more sophisticated aspects of language are exhibited. Despite this, language remains a special feature because no single species possesses all of the characteristics together, or to the same phenomenal extent, as human beings.

SUMMARY

- Darwin's theory of evolution states that humans differ from other species only **quantitatively**, not **qualitatively**. If **language** is not a special characteristic of humans, research should indicate that non-human animals possess language, or at least the capacity to learn it. There are ten **generalised features of language**, which can be used to assess its existence in non-human animals.
- **Honey bees** communicate complex information about the direction and distance of food sources. The **waggle dance** uses angles and vigour to convey meaning. These signals are **symbolic**, **specialised**, show **displacement**, and the roles of the transmitter and recipient are **interchangeable**. However, there is little or no evidence that these dances satisfy any other criterion of language.
- **Birds** use songs to communicate about territory and courtship. These songs are **specialised**, although they are better classified as signals than as **symbolic** communication. Bird song is **acquired spontaneously** during a **critical period** and has an element of **cultural transmission**. The songs do not exhibit any other features of language.
- **Chimpanzees** use varied facial expressions, sounds and gestures to communicate, but none seems complex or varied enough to constitute language. However, wild primates appear to have the ability to learn complex skills, and to imagine

a situation from the point of view of another individual. These attributes could imply a capacity to learn language. They are also fundamental to certain aspects of language, such as **cultural transmission**, **displacement** and **conversation**.

- Studies undertaken by Povinelli et al. suggest that chimps can appreciate the **symbolic** nature of language, its displacement quality and its ability to convey information from one individual to another. Furthermore, communication between chimps and humans was both **specialised** and **spontaneous**.

- Studies of animals in their natural habitats confirm that communication in some species shows many, although not all, the characteristics of language. **Bird song** and **communication in cetaceans and primates** are among the best contenders for natural language. If such animals do have a capacity for language, they would also be the most likely to display an ability to comprehend and produce human language. Several attempts have been made to teach language to non-human animals.

- **Birds** can use an auditory medium, making it easy to observe their language acquisition. A parrot has been taught about 150 spoken words, including concepts as well as nouns. However, these skills are simple, satisfying only **symbolic**, **specialised** and **interchangeable role** criteria.

- **Cetaceans** can learn visual or acoustic languages, which are **symbolic** and **specialised**. Dolphins have been taught to comprehend symbols for actions and objects, which could be combined into simple instructions. Their responses to sensible and nonsense messages suggest that they use a simple form of **syntax**.

- Early attempts to teach spoken English to chimps were unsuccessful because they do not have the vocal apparatus to articulate the different sounds required. Subsequent attempts have employed non-vocal techniques, such as teaching Ameslan to **Washoe**. Washoe learned over 160 signs, demonstrating **symbolism**, **specialisation**, **displacement**, **generativity** and **conversation**. However, she did not acquire language spontaneously.

- **Lana** was taught to use a typewriter, which generated different patterns (**lexigrams**) using a language called **Yerkish**. In addition to the language criteria satisfied by Washoe, Lana was able to use simple **syntax** to increase meaning. The studies involving Washoe and Lana have been criticised by Terrace.

- Rumbaugh and Savage-Rumbaugh have suggested that the early studies on chimps made a crucial omission: they only taught the apes to speak, not to listen. In their studies, animals were reared in a **language-structured** environment, where language was used around the animals to announce and co-ordinate social activities.

- **Kanzi**, a pygmy chimpanzee, **spontaneously** learned to communicate with Rumbaugh and Savage-Rumbaugh (probably during a **critical period**). He was able to understand complex sentences, indicating a grasp of lexical syntax. At 9 years old, Kanzi exhibited similar language skills to a 30-month-old human child. He had acquired the ability to comprehend as well as produce language (via a keyboard), without formal teaching.

- It is debatable whether the thoughts of many species are complex enough to generate a large variety of messages. It appears that chimpanzees have the **cognitive requirements** for language and it is only in chimps that we can see communication which closely resembles human language.

EVOLUTIONARY EXPLANATIONS OF HUMAN BEHAVIOUR

Introduction and overview

The main aim of psychology is to explain human behaviour. In Chapter 1, it was suggested that many of the behaviours exhibited by non-human animals could be explained by evolutionary processes. As humans are an evolved animal species, it seems reasonable to extend Darwinian ideas of evolution to human behaviour. This approach is known as evolutionary psychology.

It is difficult to establish the evolutionary basis of human behaviour without employing comparative psychology, in particular the sociobiological approach (see Chapter 1). Sociobiology uses evolutionary concepts to generate testable hypotheses about human behaviour, based on the assumption that individuals will act in a way which tends to propagate their genes. However, not all human behaviour represents an adaptation for survival or reproduction. A behaviour may currently raise the inclusive fitness of an individual, or it may be currently maladaptive but did promote fitness in the past in different environments. Alternatively, the behaviour in question may never have been adaptive, simply representing a by-product of some other feature of the species. Furthermore, just because a certain behaviour is considered adaptive, it does not mean that it is developmentally unchangeable or socially desirable.

This chapter considers the extent to which natural selection can explain human behaviour. It will examine four examples of behaviour in humans, drawn from different areas within comparative psychology, which may be explained (at least in part) by evolutionary processes. It will then look at the limitations of the evolutionary approach.

Darwinian medicine

Darwinian medicine is an evolutionary explanation of host–parasite relationships in disease states. It attempts to explain why humans are generally susceptible to certain diseases and not others. As such, it does not replace conventional medicine (which tends to ask 'what' and 'how' questions about disease), but complements it (by also asking 'why' questions about disease).

The principles of host–parasite relationships are very similar to the predator–prey arms races discussed in Chapter 3. However, bacteria can evolve as much in one day as humans can in 1000 years. This puts us at a significant disadvantage in the arms race, which is only partly compensated for by our large and diverse immune system. Of course, we do have the advantage of medicine on our side. However, the rapid mutation rates of many viruses, together with large increases in bacterial resistance to antibiotics, may limit the effectiveness of the medicine weapon in the arms race. Furthermore, underexposure to pathogens (disease-causing organisms), coupled with an over-reliance on medicine, reduces the selection pressure on our immune system. This may result in weakened natural defences. According to Jones (1994), the evolution of mechanisms for resisting disease represents the best example of evolution in action and most human variation is the remnant of past battles against infection.

Generally, *within-host* selection favours the increased virulence (damage caused by the disease) of pathogens. This is because the infectious organisms want to outcompete rival pathogens and reproduce as fast as possible. However, *between-host* selection acts to decrease virulence, as pathogens do not want to kill the host before they can be transmitted. Likewise, diseases spread by personal contact tend to be less virulent than those spread by insects or other vectors. It is in the

Box 15.1   The changing face of the AIDS virus

It is generally believed that the human immunodeficiency virus (HIV) is a new pathogen, perhaps originating from a monkey infected with simian immunodeficiency virus (SIV). However, recent evidence suggests that monkeys may have acquired SIV from humans infected with HIV. The original form of HIV was probably very mild and is likely to have been present in human populations for many generations.

AIDS is caused by highly virulent forms of HIV, which appear to have evolved in recent times. It has been suggested that AIDS may have arisen because of changes in social behaviour. Increased promiscuity, prostitution and intravenous drug use may have led to the rapid transmission of HIV. When this occurs, host survival becomes less important to the survival of the virus, favouring the evolution of more virulent forms. Under these conditions, even highly virulent forms of HIV may have the opportunity to disperse to new hosts before the original host dies. An interesting point about this disease is that the use of clean needles and condoms would not only reduce the transmission of HIV, it would also cause the evolution of lower virulence (as hosts would need to be kept alive longer to increase the probability of transmission) (Ewald, 1994).

interest of pathogens spread by contact to keep their host feeling reasonably well (Ewald, 1994). This will lead to greater interaction with other people and a consequent increase in transmission of the disease-causing organism (Box 15.1).

Darwinian medicine suggests that, far from being a part of the illness, many symptoms such as fever, vomiting and fussiness over food may form a vital part of the body's adaptive response towards parasitic infection (Davies, 1996). Evidence that fever is an adaptive response to infection comes from a range of studies. For example, children infected with chicken pox who were given a fever-lowering drug (acetaminophen) took longer to recover than an untreated control group (Nesse & Williams, 1996). Matt Kluger (1990) believes that using drugs to suppress fever may even kill some patients. So why do we not have more regular and severe fevers? It is important to remember that both pathogens and hosts have to devote their energies

to basic needs as well as their arms race. Higher and more frequent fevers would make us less vulnerable to pathogens, but would be more than counterbalanced by the costs of tissue damage and nutrient depletion (Nesse & Williams, 1996).

Many of the body's defences are based on expulsion, such as sneezing, coughing, vomiting and diarrhoea. In general, these are defensive adaptations, not part of the disease. However, there are exceptions. Some sneezing, for example, may be an adaptation that viruses use to disperse themselves. Similar mechanisms may be used by organisms which cause sexually transmitted diseases. These organisms may influence the sexual behaviour of their host in order to increase the rate and effectiveness of transmission.

In Chapter 7, it was suggested that 'morning sickness' and food cravings in pregnant women may be due to the fetus attempting to avoid certain food-based toxins and demanding certain essential minerals respectively (Profet, 1992). If this is true, we would expect the symptoms to begin when tissue differentiation occurs in the fetus and decrease when the fetus becomes less vulnerable. We would also expect pregnant women to avoid foods that contain substances most likely to interfere with fetal development. This certainly appears to be the case. Two nutrients which are typically avoided are iron, which bacteria require for survival (Weinberg, 1984), and certain fats, which can influence the functioning of the immune system (Clamp & Grimble, 1994).

Humans have evolved a range of strategies to reduce their susceptibility to pathogens. Some of these strategies are reviewed in Box 15.2. Finally, changes in social conditions may lead to changes in the incidence of disease. Tuberculosis became epidemic in Europe with the rise of large, crowded cities and influenza has become a major threat since mass worldwide transportation began spreading new strains to previously unexposed populations. It is important to remember that our bodies were designed over the course of millions of years for lives spent in small groups hunting and gathering on the plains of Africa. Natural selection has not had time to change our bodies to cope with fatty diets, pollution or drugs (Figure 15.1). This mismatch between our design and our environment may be the basis of many preventable modern illnesses, such as heart disease (Nesse & Williams, 1996). (Similarly, it has been argued that our psychology is not adapted

Box 15.2   Avoiding pathogens

Humans generally defecate in private and find the sight or smell of others' faeces unpleasant. This means we are unlikely to come into contact with the waste of others, avoiding infection. Another mechanism to deter invasion is the constant regeneration of human skin. The surface layers of dead cells (containing many millions of bacteria) are lost each day, removing a potential source of infection. Likewise, scratching and other grooming behaviours remove external parasites (Hart, 1990). Pain may also be seen as an adaptation that can lead to escape and avoidance of danger. Occasionally, people are born who cannot feel pain. They are nearly all dead by the age of 30 (Melzack, 1973).

Figure 15.2   Humans are an example of a mutually sexually selected species

to the modern world. Many of society's problems could be due to cultural evolution outpacing biological evolution.)

Sexual selection

Darwin (1871) believed that sexual selection was of paramount importance in human evolution. Evidence presented in Chapter 4 supports this idea, suggesting that many of our traits, such as fat distribution, hair colour and eye colour, are designed to make us appear more attractive to the opposite sex (Figure 15.2). The

Figure 15.1   Evolution has not prepared us for a modern diet

evolution of human *behaviour* may also have been influenced by sexual selection. (Evolutionary explanations of homosexuality are discussed in Box 15.3.)

One way to evaluate the role of sexual selection in human evolution is to compare our species with other primates (the comparative approach). Sexual dimorphism (the differences between the male and female sexes of the same species) is more marked among the apes and humans than among the monkeys (Crook, 1972). For example, male sexual strategy in humans involves rivalry in acquiring females and a certain amount of aggressiveness in protecting them from other men (McFarland, 1996). This may account for the man's greater size and strength, though it is more likely that this has to do with division of labour within the family (Passingham, 1982). Many of the differences between the sexes in humans can be attributed to natural selection, and to the differing roles of males and females, rather than to sexual selection. When considering sexually selected traits, we must examine those different male and female features that appear to have no direct role in survival or reproduction. Examples of such features include the beard and other body hair of the man, the change in the male voice that occurs at puberty, and the protruding and rounded breasts of the woman (Wickler, 1967). Sexual selection has a much greater effect in polygamous societies (see Chapter 6). It seems likely that humans have become progressively

Box 15.3   Evolutionary explanations of homosexuality

Homosexual behaviour presents a major puzzle for evolutionary psychology. Evidence suggests that genetic factors are involved in the development of homosexuality (Stevens & Price, 1996). However, it is difficult to account for the inclusive fitness of genes which predispose people to homosexual behaviour. Nevertheless, such genes must have some adaptive advantage, otherwise they would have been eliminated by natural selection.

One theory suggests that homosexuality is influenced by a number of genes, which are predominantly *recessive* (not expressed in the presence of other, *dominant*, genes). These genes would be dormant in heterosexuals, but could provide reproductive advantages when combined with other genes in these individuals (and so transmitted to future generations). Alternatively, the recessive genes could be passed on through the relatives of an exclusive homosexual, because he or she helps his or her relatives to raise more children.

A second theory, the *dominance failure theory*, suggests that subordinate males are unable to find female partners and consequently develop a homosexual orientation. This could have an evolutionary basis if social dominance is determined, at least in part, by genetic factors. The dominance failure theory would also help to account for the fact that there are more male homosexuals than lesbians. Another solution to the problem of failure in intermale competition is to assume a female role (*transvestism*) or identity (*transsexualism*).

One objection to evolutionary explanations of homosexuality is that they are *reductionist* arguments. In other words, they attempt to explain complex behaviour in terms of a single cause. There are many different explanations of gender role and gender identity, and the evolutionary approach ignores the influence of social, developmental and cultural factors. Similarly, an over-reliance on reductionism may be considered to be a limitation of many other evolutionary explanations.

more monogamous over time, probably in response to the increasing requirement of parental care. This implies that sexual selection would have been more effective in the past than it is now. It has been suggested that humans lost their body hair during some period in the evolutionary past when sexual selection was much more powerful than it is today (Crook, 1972).

An interesting feature of sexual activity in human males is *sperm competition*. This is based on the idea that the quantity of sperm transferred to a human female may affect the male's chance of egg fertilisation, given the possibility that his partner may also receive sperm from another male. If this is true, we would expect males to adjust the quantity of sperm donated to a partner in relation to the risk that she has received sperm from a rival male. This appears to be supported by experimental studies (Figure 15.3). Another manifestation of human male competition for mates is the greater willingness of men than women to engage in extramarital sex (Symons, 1979). This would be predicted by theoretical evolutionary cost–benefit arguments and is supported by the greater interest shown by men in prostitutes and pornography. Furthermore, in Western society the behaviour of male homosexuals is very different from that of lesbians. Not only is male homosexuality much more common than the female variety, but males (until recently) were more likely to be promiscuous (Alcock, 1993).

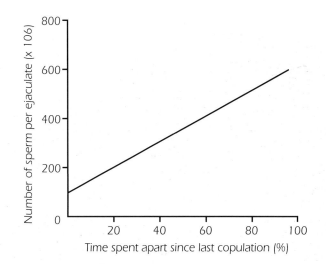

Figure 15.3   Sperm competition in humans. The number of sperm contained in an ejaculate increases as a function of the time a man and woman have spent away from each other since their last copulation (Baker & Bellis, 1989)

Sexual behaviour in humans is closely related to the high degree of parental care (see Chapter 5). Human females have evolved several mechanisms for encouraging male fidelity. These include long periods of sexual receptivity, which encourages continued attentiveness from the male, and concealed ovulation. This latter feature means that a male must copulate regularly with the same female to ensure fertilisation and that he must guard the woman against advances from other men if he is to ensure paternity (Lovejoy, 1981). It has recently been suggested that human infants have been selected not to resemble their fathers (Pagel, 1997). Concealing paternal identity in this way is advantageous as a strategy to avoid paternal neglect, abuse or infanticide when there is a risk that the domestic father is not the biological father.

These evolutionary explanations of human sexual relationships may also explain jealousy (Box 15.4) and marriage, a cultural institution (Alcock, 1993). However, it is not possible to give an entirely satisfactory account of human sexual strategy from a purely evolutionary viewpoint. As a result of cultural innovation, there is considerable variation in sexual practice among different human societies (McFarland, 1996).

Box 15.4   The evolution of a green-eyed monster

Evolutionary explanations of sexual jealousy have been proposed from both male and female perspectives (Nesse & Williams, 1996).

The main concern of males appears to be paternity. Although maternity is a certainty, paternity is always a matter of opinion. A man incapable of jealousy may have a greater risk of having an adulterous partner, with a resulting decrease in reproductive success. However, men who exhibit jealous behaviour will have an evolutionary advantage. Genes that predispose to male sexual jealousy will therefore be maintained in humans.

Although women are certain of maternity, they do face other risks. A philandering husband may lead to a loss of resources and the risk of sexually transmitted diseases. Cultural factors appear to play a greater role in female jealousy, perhaps reflecting reduced selection pressure for this behaviour (compared to males). In general, sexual jealousy is reported to be more intense for men than for women.

Figure 15.4   The formation of an attachment bond may be genetically programmed in babies and mothers. Eye-contact is a vital part of the attachment process (Stern, 1977)

Attachment

Attachment is a close emotional bond between two people, usually a caregiver and an infant, characterised by mutual involvement and a desire to maintain proximity. (This relationship was discussed in Chapter 10 in the context of bonding in altricial species.) John Bowlby (1951) argued that the formation of the attachment bond is pre-programmed into the infant. Bowlby based his ideas on imprinting research, believing that babies which stayed close to their caregiver (normally the mother) would be more likely to survive and reproduce (Figure 15.4).

Imprinting occurs in a wide range of species, including humans. For example, human infants will imprint on their mother's voice by thirty days at the latest (Lea, 1984). However, although it appears to be involved in attachment, imprinting is not a complete explanation for the development of this relationship. Stratton (1983) argued that humans inhabit a wide variety of environments where imprinting, which is an inherited response to deal with a particular environment, would be of limited use. Imprinting is also mainly applicable to precocial animals rather than altricial species like humans. Furthermore, the attachment process is more gradual than imprinting and involves parent–child interaction.

Attachment behaviour appears to be primarily instinctive, with babies being genetically programmed to behave towards their mothers in ways that ensure their survival (Hayes, 1994). These important species-specific behaviours include looking, smiling and crying. Eye-contact is a vital part of attachment formation. Infants become distressed if parents do not respond to their eye-contact (Tronick et al., 1978), and find mutual gazing rewarding. Fraiberg (1977) studied blind babies, who often turn their head away in order to hear better, and found that their mothers often felt rejected and unhappy with the infant. Human babies are also pre-programmed to smile at human-like faces (Ahrens, 1954), a response which may strengthen the inclination of the mother to care for the infant. Gewirtz (1965) found that smiling in infants is reduced if it is not reinforced, demonstrating the importance of parent–child interaction in the development of an attachment bond. Finally, it is no accident that human adults find a baby's cries uncomfortable. Only in species in which infants are immobile do they cry, using it as a sophisticated signalling system to increase their chances of survival. Wolff (1969) found that babies can produce at least three different types of cry (hunger, pain and anger) and that parents (or at least most mothers) can usually recognise the meaning of the cry.

Bowlby believed that the mother also inherits a genetic blue-print which programmes her to respond to the child (leading to attachment). Sociobiologists have suggested that the greater investment in parenting by the mother (see Chapter 5) leads to females being naturally better parents (Kenrick, 1994). Consistent with this idea is the observation that, even in communes, it is the mothers who tend to take primary childcare responsibility and that looking after children has been strictly a female job for over 90% of human history (Durkin, 1995). However, there appears to be no evidence that mothering skills are innate or instinctive (Newson, 1974) and the caregiver could just as easily be the father or, more commonly, both parents (Schaffer & Emerson, 1964).

Finally, research by Hazan and Shaver (1987) suggests that people's intimate relationships in adulthood reflect their attachments in infancy. Adults who had secure attachments found it easy to develop trusting relationships with others. Those who had been insecure (avoidant) in infancy found it difficult to get close to others and were less likely to develop intimate relationships.

Phobias

A phobia is a type of anxiety disorder in which there is a persistent and unreasonable fear of an object or situation. In Chapter 12 it was suggested that the acquisition of many phobias may occur through classical or operant conditioning. This idea is supported by the effectiveness of behavioural therapies in the treatment of phobic disorders. It is also possible that genetic factors may play a role in the development of phobias (Torgersen, 1983). However, many of the studies implicating genetic involvement have been criticised, and this area remains unclear.

One interesting observation about the development of phobic disorders is that people appear to be more likely to become phobic about some things rather than others. Many more people have phobias about spiders and snakes than about cars, in spite of their greater exposure to cars (making an association with a fearful stimulus more likely). According to Seligman (1971), the objects or situations forming the basis of most phobias were real sources of danger hundreds or thousands of years ago, and those individuals who were sensitive to these stimuli were favoured by evolution. Seligman argued that some associations are more biologically useful than others, such as taste aversion or predator avoidance. These associations are therefore learned more quickly and are more resistant to extinction (see Chapter 12). In other words, we have a psychological predisposition or 'preparedness' to be sensitive to, and become phobic about, certain (potentially dangerous) stimuli rather than others. Anxiety in general may have survival value (see Box 15.5) and human phobias, such as a fear of heights or the dark, are consistent with Seligman's theory.

The preparedness theory has been the subject of much debate in comparative psychology. McNally and Steketee (1985) studied snake and spider phobias and found that in 91% of cases the cause for concern was not a fear of being harmed, but rather a fear of having a panic attack. It has also been suggested that these phobias may be explained by social learning theory (Bandura, 1977).

Other studies have supported the preparedness theory (Hunt, 1995). Monkeys raised in the laboratory have no fear of snakes and will reach over a snake to get a banana. However, after watching a single video that

Box 15.5   The evolution of anxiety

The capacity to experience anxiety is vital to survival. It has been said that an animal incapable of fear is a dead animal. Anxiety may be thought of as a form of vigilance, which enables an animal to be alert and prepared to act. In many ways, anxiety may be considered as synonymous with arousal. Both states prepare the body for appropriate action, such as fighting, fleeing, freezing or submitting.

Nesse (1987) suggested that there are many similarities between anxiety and the immune system. Both are designed to protect an animal from harm, but both can have deleterious effects in certain circumstances. The immune system can overreact, underreact, or respond to the wrong cue or pathogen. Similarly, anxiety can be excessive, deficient, or a response to a harmless situation. Only in these cases should anxiety truly be considered as a psychological disorder.

shows another monkey reacting with alarm to a snake, the monkeys develop a lasting phobia of snakes. This observation could be explained by a preparedness argument (snakes are dangerous animals) or social learning theory (monkeys learn the fear by copying the behaviour of others). However, if the video shows another monkey demonstrating a fear reaction to a flower, no phobia to flowers is created. Monkeys readily learn a fear of snakes, but not a fear of flowers (Nesse & Williams, 1996).

In conclusion, Seligman's preparedness theory provides a very plausible account of the development of some phobias. Nevertheless, it is difficult to see how it can explain certain simple phobias and most social phobias, such as public speaking.

Limitations of the evolutionary approach

At the beginning of this chapter, it was stated that it is difficult to establish the evolutionary basis of human behaviour without employing the comparative approach. One of the main assumptions of this approach is that most of the differences between non-human animals and humans are quantitative, rather than qualitative. However, the degree to which investigations of non-human animal behaviour are applicable to humans has been questioned and there may be critical qualitative differences to be considered.

Behaviour is always an interaction between genes and the environment, never purely genetic. Evolutionary theories are highly *deterministic*, suggesting that many of our actions come from forces over which we have no control. Such theories largely ignore *free will* (the idea that people are the cause of their own actions) and the way in which we regulate most of our behaviours. The further an animal is up the phylogenetic scale (which generally places humans at or near the top), the more its behaviour is determined by experience. Furthermore, behaviour is also culturally determined, particularly in humans. Therefore, evolution can only provide a limited understanding of human behaviour.

Sociobiology has been accused of overemphasising the adaptationist approach (Gould & Lewontin, 1979). As mentioned at the start of this chapter, not every aspect of every organism is currently adaptive. It has also been suggested that sociobiologists are very selective in the examples of behaviour which they consider, ignoring numerous examples of human behaviour that do not fit the theory (Hayes, 1994).

It is difficult to identify the genes responsible for a particular human behaviour and there is currently little scientific evidence to support the theoretical arguments. However, this assumes a simple relationship between genes and behaviour, which is probably not the case. Moreover, it is entirely possible to test sociobiological hypotheses about the adaptive nature of certain human characteristics without knowing the details about the genetic basis of these characteristics (Alcock, 1993).

Finally, the evolutionary approach has been criticised for apparently supporting antisocial behaviours such as aggression and eugenics (the improvement of human society through selective breeding). There is also an ethical concern that the approach may be seen to support gender stereotypes, such as expecting males to be promiscuous. It is important to remember that sociobiology is a discipline that attempts to explain why social behaviour exists; it does not attempt to justify the behaviour.

Conclusions

Evolutionary explanations of human behaviour are based on the sociobiological approach, which assumes that humans will act in a way which tends to propagate their genes. Evolutionary arguments have been used to explain a wide range of human behaviours, including host–parasite relationships in disease states, sexual behaviour, attachment, and the occurrence of certain types of phobic disorder. However, there are a number of limitations to the evolutionary approach. These include problems with extending studies of non-human animals to humans, the influence of the environment on behaviour, maladaptive behaviour, and the small amount of supporting evidence. It seems clear that no one single approach can fully explain the complexities of human behaviour.

SUMMARY

- The main aim of psychology is to explain human behaviour. **Evolutionary psychology** applies Darwinian ideas to the behaviour of humans, based on the assumption that individuals will act in a way which tends to propagate their genes. However, not all human behaviour represents an adaptation for survival or reproduction and there are limitations to the evolutionary approach.

- **Darwinian medicine** is an evolutionary explanation of host–parasite relationships in disease states. It attempts to explain why humans are generally susceptible to certain diseases and not others. Darwinian medicine suggests that many symptoms associated with illness, such as fever and fussiness over food, may form a vital part of the body's adaptive response towards parasitic infection.

- Many of the body's defences are based on expulsion, such as **sneezing, coughing** and **vomiting**. In general, these are defensive adaptations, not part of the disease. However, there are exceptions. Some sneezing, for example, may be an adaptation that viruses use to disperse themselves.

- It is important to remember that our bodies were designed over the course of millions of years for lives spent in small groups, hunting and gathering on the plains of Africa. Natural selection has not had time to change our bodies to cope with fatty diets, pollution or drugs. This mismatch between our design and our environment may be the basis of many preventable modern illnesses, such as heart disease.

- Darwin believed that **sexual selection** was of paramount importance in the evolution of human behaviour. Evidence suggests that many of our traits are sexually selected, such as the beard and other body hair of the man and the protruding and rounded breasts of the woman.

- Human males appear to be more willing than females to engage in extramarital sex. In turn, human females have evolved several mechanisms for encouraging male fidelity. These include **long periods of sexual receptivity** and **concealed ovulation**.

- Evolutionary explanations of human sexual behaviour may also account for **jealousy** and **marriage**. However, it is not possible to give an entirely satisfactory account of human sexual strategy from a purely evolutionary viewpoint.

- **Attachment** is a close emotional bond between two people, usually a caregiver and an infant, characterised by mutual involvement and a desire to maintain proximity. Bowlby argued that the formation of the attachment bond is **pre-programmed** into the infant. Babies which stay close to their caregiver may be more likely to survive and reproduce.

- Attachment behaviour appears to be primarily **instinctive**, with babies being genetically programmed to behave towards their mothers in ways that ensure the survival of the infant. These species-specific behaviours include **looking, smiling** and **crying**.

- Sociobiologists have suggested that the greater investment in parenting by the mother leads to females being naturally better caregivers. However, there appears to be no evidence that mothering skills are innate or instinctive and the caregiver could just as easily be the father or both parents.

- According to Seligman, the objects or situations

forming the basis of most **phobias** were real sources of danger hundreds or thousands of years ago. Those individuals who were sensitive to these stimuli were favoured by evolution. We may have a psychological predisposition or **preparedness** to be sensitive to, and become phobic about, certain (potentially dangerous) stimuli rather than others. Anxiety in general may have survival value and human phobias, such as a fear of heights or the dark, are consistent with this theory.

- Seligman's preparedness theory provides a very plausible account of the development of some phobias. However, it is difficult to see how it can explain certain simple phobias and most social phobias, such as public speaking.
- There are a number of **limitations to the evolutionary approach**. These include problems with extending studies of non-human animals to humans, the influence of the environment on behaviour, maladaptive behaviour, and the small amount of supporting evidence. It seems clear that no one single approach can fully explain the complexities of human behaviour.

REFERENCES

ABELE, L.G. & GILCHRIST, S. (1977) Homosexual rape and sexual selection in acanthocephalan worms. *Science*, 197, 81–83.

AHRENS, R. (1954) Beitrag zur Entwicklung des Physiognomie und Minikerkennes. *Zeitschrift fur Experimentelle und Angewandte Psychologie*, 2, 412–454.

ALATALO, R.V., CARLSON, A., LUNDBERG, A. & ULFSTRAND, S. (1981) The conflict between male polygamy and female monogamy: The case of the pied flycatcher, *Ficedula hypoleuca. American Naturalist*, 117, 738–753.

ALATALO, R.V. & HELLE, P. (1990) Alarm calling by individual willow tits, *Parus montanus. Animal Behaviour*, 40, 437–442.

ALCOCK, J. (1984) *Animal Behavior: An Evolutionary Approach*. (3rd edition). Sunderland, MA: Sinauer.

ALCOCK, J. (1989) *Animal Behavior* (4th edition). Sunderland, MA: Sinauer.

ALCOCK, J. (1993) *Animal Behavior* (5th edition). Sunderland, MA: Sinauer.

ALEXANDER, R.D. (1974) The evolution of social behaviour. *Annual Review of Ecology and Systematics*, 5, 325–383.

ALEXANDER, R.D. & SHERMAN, P.W. (1977) Local mate competition and parental investment in social insects. *Science*, 196, 494–500.

ALTMANN, S.A. (Ed.) (1965) *Japanese Monkeys: A Collection of Translations Selected by K. Imanishi*. Edmonton: The Editor.

ANDERSON, A., HOLMES, B. & ELSE, L. (1996) Zombies, dolphins and blindsight. *New Scientist*, 4 May, 20–27.

ANDERSSON, M. (1982) Female choice for extreme tail length in widow bird. *Nature*, 299, 818–819.

ANDERSSON, M. & WICKLUND, C.G. (1978) Clumping versus spacing out: Experiments on nest predation in fieldfares (*Turdus pilaris*). *Animal Behaviour*, 26, 1207–1212.

ASKENMO, C.E.H. (1984) Polygyny and nest site selection in the pied flycatcher. *Animal Behaviour*, 32, 972–980.

AXELROD, R. (1984) *The Evolution of Co-operation*. New York: Basic Books.

AXELROD, R. (1990) *The Evolution of Co-operation*. London: Penguin.

AXELROD, R. & HAMILTON, W.D. (1981) The evolution of co-operation. *Science*, 211, 1390–1396.

BADCOCK, C. (1994) *PsychoDarwinism*. London: HarperCollins.

BAKER, R.R. (1978) *The Evolutionary Ecology of Animal Migration*. London: Hodder & Stoughton.

BAKER, R.R. & BELLIS, M.A. (1989) Number of sperm in human ejaculates varies in accordance with sperm competition theory. *Animal Behaviour*, 37, 867–869.

BALCOMBE, J.P. (1990) Vocal recognition of pups by mother Mexican free-tailed bats (*Tadarida brasiliensis mexicana*). *Animal Behaviour*, 39, 960–966.

BALCOMBE, J.P. & McCRACKEN, G.F. (1992) Vocal recognition in Mexican free-tailed bats: Do pups recognise mothers? *Animal Behaviour*, 43, 79–87.

BANDURA, A. (1977) Self-efficacy: Toward a unifying theory of behaviour change. *Psychological Review*, 84, 191–215.

BARNETT, A. (1997) The sounds that say it all as birds sing their hearts out. *New Scientist*, 2084.

BASTION, J. (1967) The transmission of arbitrary environmental information between bottlenosed dolphins. In R.G. Busnel (Ed.) *Animal Sonar Systems* (vol. 2). Jouy-en-Josas, France: Laboratoire de Physiologie Acoustique.

BATEMAN, A.J. (1948) Intra-sexual selection in *Drosophila. Heredity*, 2, 349–368.

BATESON, P.P.G. (1979) How do sensitive periods arise and what are they for? *Animal Behaviour*, 27, 470–486.

BATESON, P.P.G. (1987) Imprinting as a process of competitive exclusion. In J.P. Rauschecker & P. Marler (Eds) *Imprinting and Cortical Plasticity*. New York: Wiley.

BAYLIS, J.R. (1981) The evolution of parental care in fishes, with reference to Darwin's rule of male sexual selection. *Environmental Fish Biology*, 6, 223–251.

BECK, A.T. (1991) Cognitive therapy: A thirty year retrospective. *American Psychologist*, 46, 368–375.

BELOVSKY, G.E. (1978) Diet optimization in a generalist herbivore: the moose. *Theoretical and Population Biology*, 4, 105–134.

BENZER, S. (1973) Genetic dissection of behaviour. *Scientific American*, 229, 24–37.

BERGER, J. (1983) Induced abortion and social factors in wild horses. *Nature*, 303, 59–61.

BERTRAM, B.C.R. (1976) Kin selection in lions and in evolution. In P.P.G. Bateson & R.A. Hinde (Eds) *Growing Points in Ethology*. Cambridge: Cambridge University Press.

BERTRAM, B.C.R. (1980) Vigilance and group size in ostriches. *Animal Behaviour*, 28, 278–286.

BIGERSSON, B., EKVALL, K. & TEMRIN, H. (1991) Allosuckling in fallow deer, *Dama dama*. *Animal Behaviour*, 42, 326–327.

BIRKHEAD, T. & MØLLER, A. (1992) Faithless female seeks better genes. *New Scientist*, 4 July, 34–38.

BLACK, J.M., CARBONE, C., WELLS, R.L. & OWEN, M. (1992) Foraging dynamics in goose flocks: The cost of living on the edge. *Animal Behaviour*, 44, 41–50.

BOESCH, C. (1991) Teaching among wild chimpanzees. *Animal Behaviour*, 41, 530–532.

BOESCH, C. (1995) Co-operative hunting in wild chimpanzees. *Animal Behaviour*, 48, 653–667.

BOLLES, R.C. (1980) Ethological learning theory. In G.M. Gazda & R.J. Corsini (Eds) *Theories of Learning: A Comparative Approach*. Itaska, IL: Free Press.

BOLHUIS, J.J. & BATESON, P. (1990) The importance of being first: A primacy effect in filial imprinting. *Animal Behaviour*, 40, 472–483.

BOLHUIS, J.J. & HORN, G. (1992) Generalisation of learned preferences in filial imprinting. *Animal Behaviour*, 44, 185–187.

BORGIA, G. (1985) Bower quality, number of decorations and mating success of male satin bowerbirds (*Ptilonorhynchus violaceus*): An experimental analysis. *Animal Behaviour*, 33, 266–271.

BOWLBY, J. (1951) *Maternal Care and Mental Health*. Geneva: World Health Organisation.

BOWLBY, J. (1971) *Attachment and Loss. Vol. 1. Attachment*. New York: Basic Books.

BOYD, H. & FABRICIUS, E. (1965) Observations on the incidence of following of visual and auditory stimuli in naive mallard ducklings (*Anas platyrhychos*). *Behaviour*, 25, 1–15.

BRIGHT, M. (1984) *Animal Language*. London: British Broadcasting Corporation.

BROWER, J.V.Z. (1958) Experimental studies of mimicry in some North American butterflies. Part 1. The monarch, *Danaus plexippus*, and viceroy, *Limenitis archippus archippus*. *Evolution*, 12, 32–47.

BROWN, J.L. (1964) The evolution of diversity in avian territorial systems. *Wilson Bulletin*, 76, 160–169.

BROWN, J.L. (1969) The buffer effect and productivity in tit populations. *American Nature*, 103, 347–354.

BROWN, R. (1986) *Social Psychology: The second edition*. New York: The Free Press.

BRUCE, H.M. (1960) A block to pregnancy in the house mouse caused by the proximity of strange males. *Journal of Reproduction and Fertility*, 1, 96–103.

BURGHAM, M.C.J. & PICMAN, J. (1989) Effect of brown-headed cowbirds on the evolution of yellow warbler anti-parasite strategies. *Animal Behaviour*, 38, 298–308.

BUSS, D. (1989) Sex differences in human mate preferences. *Behavioural and Brain Sciences*, 12, 1–49.

CADE, W.H. (1981) Alternative mating strategies: Genetic differences in crickets. *Science*, 212, 563–564.

CALHOUN, J.B. (1962) Population density and social pathology. *Scientific American*, 206, 139–148.

CARO, T.M. (1986) The functions of stotting in Thomson's gazelles: Some tests of the predictions. *Animal Behaviour*, 34, 663–684.

CARPENTER, F.L., PATON, D.C. & HIXON, M.A. (1983) Weight gain and adjustment of feeding territory size in migrant hummingbirds. *Proceedings of the National Academy of Science USA*, 80, 7259–7263.

CARTWRIGHT, J. (1996) The mating game. *Psychology Review*, 2, 6–10.

CATCHPOLE, C., LEISLER, B. & WINKLER, H. (1985) The evolution of polygyny in the great reed warbler, *Acrocephalus arundinaceus*: A possible case of deception. *Behavioural Ecology and Sociobiology*, 16, 285–291.

CHENEY, D.L. & SEYFARTH, R.M. (1990) *How Monkeys See the World*. Chicago: University of Chicago Press.

CHERFAS, J. (1985) How important is the family smell? *New Scientist*, 1479, 27.

CHERFAS, J. & SCOTT, A. (1981) Impermanent reversal of filial imprinting. *Animal Behaviour*, 30, 301.

CHOMSKY, N. (1965) *Aspects of the Theory of Syntax*. Cambridge, MA: MIT Press.

CLAMP, A.G. & GRIMBLE, R.F. (1994) The effect of fatty acids on the inflammatory response to cytokines by cultured rat hepatocytes. *Proceedings of The Nutrition Society*, 53, 184A.

CLUTTON-BROCK, T.H. (1991) *The Evolution of Parental Care*. Princeton, NJ: Princeton University Press.

CLUTTON-BROCK, T.H., HIRAIWA-HASEGAWA, M. & ROBERTSON, A. (1989) Mate choice on fallow deer leks. *Nature*, 340, 463–465.

CRAIG, S.F., SLOBODKIN, L.B., WRAY, G.A. & BIERMANN, C.H. (1997) The 'paradox' of polyembryony: A review of the cases and a hypothesis for its evolution. *Evolutionary Ecology*, 11, 127–143.

CRONIN, H. (1991) *The Ant and the Peacock*. Cambridge: Cambridge University Press.

CROOK, J.H. (1964) The evolution of social organisation and visual communication in the weaver birds (Ploceinae). *Behaviour*, Supplement 10, 178pp.

CROOK, J.H. (1972) Sexual selection, dimorphism and social organisation in the primates. In B. Campbell (Ed.) *Sexual Selection and the Descent of Man*, 1871–1971. Chicago: Aldine.

CROUTIER, A.L. (1989) *Harem: The World behind the Veil.* New York: Abbeville Press.

CURIO, E. (1978) The adaptive significance of avian mobbing: Teleonomic hypotheses and predictions. *Zeitschrift fur Tierpsychologie,* 48, 175–183.

DAIL, B.E. & FITZPATRICK, L.C. (1983) Lizard tail autonomy: Function and energetics of postautonomy tail movement in *Scinella lateralis. Science,* 219, 391–393.

DARLING, F.F. (1938) *Bird Flocks and the Breeding Cycle: A Contribution to the Study of Avian Sociality.* Cambridge: Cambridge University Press.

DARWIN, C. (1859/1968) *The Origin of Species by Means of Natural Selection.* London: Penguin.

DARWIN, C. (1871) *The Descent of Man and Selection in Relation to Sex.* London: John Murray.

DAVIES, N.B. & HOUSTON, A.I. (1981) Owners and satellites: The economics of territory defence in the pied wagtail, *Motacilla alba. Journal of Animal Ecology,* 50, 157–180.

DAVIES, N.B. & HOUSTON, A.I. (1984) Territory economics. In J.R. Krebs & N.B. Davies (Eds) *Behavioural Ecology.* Oxford: Blackwell Scientific Publications.

DAVIES, N.B., BOURKE, A.F.G. & BROOKE, M. DE L. (1989) Cuckoos and parasitic ants: Interspecific brood parasitism as an evolutionary arms race. *Trends in Ecology and Evolution,* 4, 274–278.

DAVIES, R. (1995) Selfish altruism. *Psychology Review,* 1, 2–9.

DAVIES, R. (1996) *Evolutionary determinants of behaviour.* In M. Cardwell, L. Clark & C. Meldrum (Eds) *Psychology for A Level.* London: HarperCollins.

DAWKINS, M. (1971) Perceptual changes in chicks: Another look at the 'search image' concept. *Animal Behaviour,* 19, 556–574.

DAWKINS, R. (1989) *The Selfish Gene* (2nd edition). Oxford: Oxford University Press.

DAWKINS, R. & KREBS, J.R. (1979) Arms races between and within species. *Proceedings of the Royal Society (London) B,* 205, 489–511.

DE GROOT, P. (1980) Information transfer in a socially nesting weaver bird (*Quelea quelea* Ploceinae): An experimental study. *Animal Behaviour,* 28, 1249–1254.

DÉVRIES, P. (1990) Caterpillars tap-dance for an ant audience. *Science,* 248, 1104.

DIAMOND, J. (1992) *The Rise and Fall of the Third Chimpanzee.* London: Vintage.

DUDAI, Y. (1989) *The Neurobiology of Memory.* Oxford: Oxford University Press.

DUNBAR, R. (1995) Are you lonesome tonight? *New Scientist,* 145, 26–31.

DURKIN, K. (1995) *Developmental Social Psychology: From Infancy to Old Age.* Oxford: Blackwell.

EATON, R.L. (1970) The predatory sequence, with emphasis on killing behaviour and its ontogeny in the cheetah. *Zeitschrift fur Tierpsychologie,* 27, 492–504.

EDMUNDS, M. (1974) *Defence in Animals.* New York: Longman.

EKLÖV, P. (1992) Group foraging versus solitary foraging efficiency in piscivorous predators: The perch, *Perca fluviatilis,* and pike, *Esox lucius,* patterns. *Animal Behaviour,* 44, 313–326.

ELGAR, M.A. (1986) House sparrows establish foraging flocks by giving chirrup calls if the resources are divisible. *Animal Behaviour,* 34, 169–174.

EMLEN, S.T. & ORING, L.W. (1977) Ecology, sexual selection and the evolution of mating systems. *Science,* 197, 215–223.

EMLEN, S.T., DEMONG, H.J. & EMLEN, D.J. (1989) Experimental induction of infanticide in female wattled jacanas. *Auk,* 106, 1–7.

ERICKSON, C.J. & ZENONE, P.G. (1976) Courtship differences in male ring doves: Avoidance of cuckoldry? *Science,* 192, 1353–1354.

EWALD, P.W. (1994) *The Evolution of Infectious Diseases.* New York: Oxford University Press.

EWER, R.F. (1963) The behaviour of the meerkat. *Zeitschrift fur Tierpsychologie,* 20, 570–607.

FAABERG, J. & PATTERSON, C.B. (1981) The characteristics and occurrence of co-operative polyandry. *Ibis,* 123, 477–484.

FISHER, R.A. (1930) *The Genetical Theory of Natural Selection.* Oxford: Clarendon Press.

FRAIBERG, S. (1977) *Insights from the Blind: Comparative Studies of Blind and Sighted Infants.* New York: Basic Books.

FREEMAN, M.C. & GROSSMAN, G.D. (1992) Group foraging by a stream minnow: Shoals or aggregations? *Animal Behaviour,* 44, 393–403.

FRETWELL, S.D. (1972) *Populations in a Seasonal Environment.* Princeton: Princeton University Press.

GALLUP, G.G. (1977) Self recognition in primates. *American Psychologist,* 32, 329–338.

GARCIA, J. & KOELLING, R.A. (1966) Relation of cue to consequence in avoidance learning. *Psychonomic Science,* 4, 123–124.

GARDNER, R.A. & GARDNER, B.T. (1969) Teaching sign language to a chimpanzee. *Science,* 165, 664–672.

GEWIRTZ, J.L. (1965) The cause of infant smiling in four child-rearing environments in Israel. In B.M. Foss (Ed.) *Determinants of Infant Behaviour* (Vol. 3). London: Methuen.

GILL, F.B. & WOLF, L.L. (1975) Economics of feeding territoriality in the golden-winged sunbird. *Ecology,* 56, 333–345.

GITTLEMAN, J.L. & HARVEY, P.H. (1980) Why are distasteful prey not cryptic? *Nature,* 286, 149–150.

GLANDER, K.E. (1981) Feeding patterns in mantled

howling monkeys. In A.C. Kamil & T.D. Sargent (Eds) *Foraging Behavior: Ecological, Ethological and Psychological Approaches*. New York: Garland Press.

GOODALL, J. (1965) Chimpanzees of the Gombe Stream Reserve. In I. DeVore (Ed.) *Primate Behavior: Field Studies of Monkeys and Apes*. New York: Holt, Rinehart & Winston.

GOODENOUGH, J., McGUIRE, B. & WALLACE, R. (1993) *Perspectives on Animal Behavior*. New York: John Wiley & Sons.

GOSS-CUSTARD, J.D. (1976) Variation in the dispersion of redshank (*Tringa totanus*) on their winter feeding grounds. *Ibis*, 118, 257–263.

GOTTLIEB, G. (1991) Social induction of malleability in ducklings. *Animal Behaviour*, 41, 953–962.

GOULD, S.J. & LEWONTIN, R.C. (1979) The spandrels of San Macro and the Panglossian paradigm: A critique of the adaptionist program. *Proceedings of the Royal Society of London, Series B*, 205, 581–598.

GREEN, R.G., LARSON, C.L. & BELL, J.F. (1939) Shock disease as the cause of the periodic decimation of the snowshoe hare. *American Journal of Hygiene*, series B, 30, 83–102.

GRIER, J.W. & BURK, T. (1992) *Biology of Animal Behavior*. Dubuque, IA: WCB Communications.

GRIFFIN, D.R. & TAFT, L.D. (1992) Temporal separation of honeybee dance sounds from waggle movements. *Animal Behaviour*, 44, 583–584.

GROSS, M.R. & SHINE, R. (1981) Parental care and mode of fertilisation in ectothermic vertebrates. *Evolution*, 35, 775–793.

GROSS, R.D. (1996) *Psychology: The Science of Mind and Behaviour* (3rd edition). London: Hodder & Stoughton.

GROSS, R.D. & McILVEEN, R.J. (1996) *Abnormal Psychology*. London: Hodder & Stoughton.

GUBERNICK, D.J. (1990) A maternal chemosignal maintains paternal behaviour in the biparental California mouse, *Peromyscus californicus. Animal Behaviour*, 39, 936–942.

GUILFORD, T. & DAWKINS, M.S. (1991) Receiver psychology and the evolution of animal signals. *Animal Behaviour*, 42, 1–14.

GUITON, P. (1959) Socialisation and imprinting in brown leghorn chicks. *Animal Behaviour*, 7, 26–34.

HAAS, V. (1985) Colonial and single breeding in fieldfares, *Turdus pilaris* L.: A comparison of nesting success in early and late broods. *Behavioural Ecology & Sociobiology*, 16, 119–124.

HALLIDAY, T. (1976) *Sexual Strategy*. Oxford: Oxford University Press.

HALLIDAY, T. (1980) *Sexual Strategy* (2nd edition). Oxford: Oxford University Press.

HAMILTON, W.D. (1964) The genetical evolution of social behaviour I, II. *Journal of Theoretical Biology* 7, 1–52.

HAMILTON, W.D. (1971) Geometry for the selfish herd. *Journal of Theoretical Biology*, 31, 295–311.

HAMILTON, W.D. (1990) Sexual reproduction as an adaptation to resist parasites: A review. *Proceedings of the National Academy of Sciences USA*, 87, 3566–3573.

HARDEN-JONES, F.R. (1968) *Fish Migration*. London: Edward Arnold.

HARLOW, H.F. (1965) Love in infant monkeys. *Scientific American*, 200, 68–74.

HART, B.L. (1990) Behavioural defences against parasites. *Neuroscience and Biobehavioural Reviews*, 14, 273–294.

HART, B.L. & HART, L.A. (1992) Reciprocal allogrooming in impala, *Aepyceros melampus. Animal Behaviour*, 44, 1073–1083.

HAYES, K.H. & HAYES, C. (1951) Intellectual development of a house-raised chimpanzee. *Proceedings of the American Philosophical Society*, 95, 105–109.

HAYES, N. (1986) The magic of sociobiology. *Psychology Teaching*, 2, 2–16.

HAYES, N. (1994) *Principles of Comparative Psychology*. Hove: Lawrence Erlbaum Associates.

HAZAN, C. & SHAVER, P.R. (1987) Romantic love conceptualised as an attachment process. *Journal of Personality and Social Psychology*, 52, 511–524.

HEINRICH, B. (1979) Foraging strategies of caterpillars: Leaf damage and possible predator avoidance strategies. *Oecologia*, 42, 325–337.

HERMAN, L.M., RICHARDS, D.G. & WOLF, J.P. (1984) Comprehension of sentences by bottle nosed dolphins. *Cognition*, 16, 129–219.

HERMAN, L.M., KUCZAJ S.A., II & HOLDER, M.D. (1993) Responses to anomalous gestural sequences by a language-trained dolphin: Evidence for processing of semantic relations and syntactic information. *Journal of Experimental Psychology: General*, 122, 184–194.

HERTER, K. (1962) *Der Temperatursinn der Tiere*. Wittenberg, Germany: Zeinsen Verlag.

HESS, E.H. (1958) 'Imprinting' in animals. *Scientific American*, March, 71–80.

HESS, E.H. (1972) 'Imprinting' in a natural laboratory. In T. Eisner & E.O. Wilson (Eds) *Readings from Scientific American, Animal Behavior*. San Francisco: Freeman.

HINDE, R.A. (1977) Mother–infant separation and the nature of inter-individual relationships: Experiments with rhesus monkeys. *Proceedings of the Royal Society of London B*, 196, 29–50.

HOGSTEDT, G. (1983) Adaptation unto death: Function of fear screams. *American Naturalist*, 121, 562–570.

HÖLLDOBLER, B. (1971) Communication between ants and their guests. *Scientific American*, 224, 85–93.

HOLMES, W.G. (1984) Predation risk and foraging behaviour of the hoary marmot in Alaska. *Behavioural Ecology and Sociobiology*, 15, 293–302.

HOOGLAND, J.L. (1979) Aggression, ectoparasitism and other possible costs of prairie dog (Sciuridae: *Cynomys* spp.) coloniality. *Behavior*, 69, 1–35.

HOOGLAND, J.L. (1983) Nepotism and alarm calling in the black-tailed prairie dog (*Cynomys ludovicianus*). *Animal Behaviour*, 31, 472–479.

HORROCKS, J. & HUNTE, W. (1983) Maternal rank and offspring rank in vervet monkeys: An appraisal of the mechanisms of rank acquisition. *Animal Behaviour*, 31, 772–782.

HOWARD, J.J. (1987) Diet selection by the leaf-cutting ant *Atta cephalotes*: The role of nutrients, water and secondary chemistry. *Ecology*, 68, 503–515.

HRDY, S.B. (1990) Sex bias in nature and in history: A late 1980s examination of the 'Biological Origins' argument. *Yearbook of Physical Anthropology*, 33, 25–37.

HUNT, L. (1995) Why a fear of spiders is all in the genes. *The Independent*, 20 December, 17.

HURST, J.L. (1990) Urine marking in populations of wild house mice *Mus domesticus* Rutty. I. Communication between males. *Animal Behaviour*, 40, 209–222.

HUXLEY, J.S. (1914) The courtship of the great crested grebe (*Podiceps cristatus*); with an additional theory of sexual selection. *Proceedings of the Zoological Society of London*, 35, 491–562.

IMMELMANN, K. (1969) Über den Einfluss frünkindlicher Erfahrungen auf die geschlechtliche Objektfixierung bei Estrildiden. *Zeitschrift fur Tierpsychologie*, 26, 677–691.

IMPEKOVEN, M. (1969) Motivationally controlled stimulus preferences in chicks of the black-headed gull (*Larus ridibundus* L.). *Animal Behaviour*, 17, 252–270.

JONES, M.C. (1924) The elimination of children's fears. *Journal of Experimental Psychology*, 7, 382–390.

JONES, S. (1994) *The Language of the Genes*. London: Flamingo.

KACELNIK, A. (1979) The foraging efficiency of great tits (*Parus major*) in relation to light intensity. *Animal Behaviour*, 27, 237–241.

KACELNIK, A. (1984) Central place foraging in starlings (*Sturnus vulgaris*). I. Patch residence time. *Journal of Animal Ecology*, 53, 283–299.

KACELNIK, A., KREBS, J.R. & BERNSTEIN, C. (1992) The ideal free distribution and predator–prey populations. *Trends in Ecology and Evolution*, 7, 50–55.

KALELA, O. (1957) Regulation of reproductive rate in subartic populations of the vole *Clethrionomys rufacanus* (Sund.). *Annales Academiae Scientiarum Fennicae* (*Suomalaisen Tiedeakatemian Toimituksia*), ser. A (IV, Biologica) 34, 1–60.

KELLOGG, W.N. & KELLOGG, L.A. (1933) *The Ape and the Child*. New York: McGraw Hill.

KENRICK, D.T. (1994) Evolutionary social psychology: From sexual selection to social cognition. *Advances in Experimental Social Psychology*, 26, 75–121.

KENWARD, R.E. (1978) Hawks and doves: Factors affecting success and selection in goshawk attacks on wood-pigeons. *Journal of Animal Ecology*, 47, 449–460.

KESSEL, E.L. (1955) Mating activities of balloon flies. *Systematic Zoology*, 4, 97–104.

KETTLEWELL, H.B.D. (1955) Selection experiments on industrial melanism in the Lepidoptera. *Heredity*, 9, 323–342.

KIRN, J.R. & DEVOOGD, T.J. (1989) The genesis and death of vocal control neurons during sexual differentiation in the zebra finch. *Journal of Neuroscience*, 9, 3176–3187.

KLOPFER, P.H. (1959) An analysis of learning in young Anatidae. *Ecology*, 40, 90–102.

KLOPFER, P.H., ADAMS, D.K. & KLOPFER, M.S. (1964) Maternal 'imprinting' in goats. *Proceedings of the National Academy of Science USA*, 52, 911–914.

KLUGER, M.J. (1990) The adaptive value of fever. In P.A. Mackowiac (Ed.) *Fever: Basic Measurement and Management*. New York: Raven Press.

KREBS, J.R. (1971) Territory and breeding density in the great tit, *Parus major. Ecology*, 52, 2–22.

KREBS, J. (1977) The significance of song repertoires: The Beau Geste hypothesis. *Animal Behaviour*, 25, 475–478.

KREBS, J.R. & DAVIES, N.B. (1987) *An Introduction to Behavioural Ecology* (2nd edn). Oxford: Blackwell.

KREBS, J.R. & DAVIES, N.B. (1993) *An Introduction to Behavioural Ecology* (3rd edn). Oxford: Blackwell.

KRUIJT, J.P. & MEEUWISSEN, G.B. (1991) Sexual preferences of male zebra finches: Effects of early and adult experiences. *Animal Behaviour*, 42, 91–102.

KRUUK, H. (1964) Predators and anti-predator behaviour of the black-headed gull *Larus ridibundus. Behaviour* Supplement 11, 1–129.

KRUUK, H. (1972) *The Spotted Hyena*, Chicago: University of Chicago Press.

LACK, D. (1943) *The Life of the Robin*. London: Witherby.

LACK, D. (1968) *Ecological Adaptations for Breeding in Birds*. London: Methuen.

LANDE, R. (1981) Models of speciation by sexual selection of polygenic traits. *Proceedings of the National Academy of Sciences USA*, 78, 3721–3725.

LEA, S.E.G. (1984) *Instinct, Environment and Behaviour*. London: Methuen.

LESSELLS, C.M., COULTHARD, N.D., HODGSON, P.J. & KREBS, J.R. (1991) Chick recognition in European bee-eaters: Acoustic playback experiments. *Animal Behaviour*, 42, 1031–1033.

LEWIN, R. (1991) Look who's talking now. *New Scientist*, 27 April, 48–52.

LEWIS, R.A. (1975) Social influences on marital choice. In S.E. Dragastin & G.H. Elder (Eds) *Adolescence in the Life Cycle*. New York: John Wiley.

LORENZ, K. (1935) The companion in the bird's world. *Auk*, 54, 245–273.

LORENZ, K. (1952) *King Solomon's Ring*. London: Methuen.

LORENZ, K. (1958) The evolution of behaviour. *Scientific American*, 199, 67–78.

LOVEJOY, C.O. (1981) The origin of man. *Science*, 211, 341–350.

MACKINTOSH, N.J. (1978) Cognitive or associative theories of conditioning: Implications of an analysis of blocking. In S.H. Hulse, M. Fowler & W.K. Honig (Eds) *Cognitive Processes in Animal Behavior*. Hillsdale, NJ: Lawrence Erlbaum.

MAJOR, P.F. (1978) Predator–prey interactions in two schooling fishes, *Caranx ignobilis* and *Stolephorus purpureus*. *Animal Behaviour*, 26, 760–777.

MANNING, A. (1979) *An Introduction to Animal Behaviour*. London: Arnold.

MARKS, I.M. (1981) Space phobia: Pseudo-agoraphobic syndrome. *Journal of Neurology, Neurosurgery and Psychiatry*, 44, 387–391.

MAYNARD-SMITH, J. (1964) Group selection and kin selection. *Nature*, 201, 1145–1147.

MAYNARD-SMITH, J. (1982) *Evolution and the Theory of Games*. Cambridge: Cambridge University Press.

MAYNARD-SMITH, J. (1993) *Did Darwin Get it Right?* London: Penguin.

McCOMB, K.E. (1991) Female choice for high roaring rates in red deer, *Cervus elaphus*. *Animal Behaviour*, 41, 79–88.

McCRACKEN, G.F. & GUSTIN, M.K. (1987) Bat moms' daily nightmare. *Natural History*, 10, 66–72.

McFARLAND, D. (1996) *Animal Behaviour* (2nd edition). Harlow: Longman.

McILVEEN, R.J. & GROSS, R.D. (1997) *Developmental Psychology*. London: Hodder & Stoughton.

McNALLY, R.J. & STEKETEE, G.S. (1985) The etiology and maintenance of severe animal phobias. *Behaviour Research and Therapy*, 23, 431–435.

MELZACK, R. (1973) *The Puzzle of Pain*. New York: Basic Books.

MENZIES, R. (1937) Conditioned vasomotor responses in human subjects. *Journal of Psychology*, 4, 75–120.

MILINSKI, M. (1979) An evolutionarily stable feeding strategy in sticklebacks. *Zeitschrift fur Tierpsychologie*, 51, 36–40.

MILINSKI, M. (1984) Competitive resource sharing: An experimental test of a learning rule of ESSs. *Animal Behaviour*, 32, 233–242.

MILLER, D.B. & ATEMA, J. (1990) Alarm call responsivity of mallard ducklings: Multiple pathways in behavioural development. *Animal Behaviour*, 39, 1207–1212.

MØLLER, A.P. (1988) Female choice selects for male sexual tail ornaments in the monogamous swallow. *Nature*, 332, 640–642.

MOLNAR, R.E. (1977) Analogies in the evolution of combat and display structures in ornithopods and ungulates. *Evolutionary Theory*, 3, 165–190.

MOMENT, G.B. (1962) Reflexive selection: A possible answer to an old puzzle. *Science*, 136, 262–263.

NEILL, S.R. & CULLEN, J.M. (1974) Experiments on whether schooling by their prey affects the hunting behaviour of cephalopods and fish predators. *Journal of the Zoological Society of London*, 172, 549–569.

NESSE, R.M. (1987) An evolutionary perspective on panic disorder and agoraphobia. *Ethology and Sociobiology*, 8, 73–84.

NESSE, R.M. & WILLIAMS, G.C. (1996) *Evolution and Healing*. London: Phoenix.

NEWSON, J. (1974) Towards a theory of infant understanding. *Bulletin of the British Psychological Society*, 27, 251–257.

NISBET, I.C.T. (1977) Courtship feeding and clutch size in common terns *Sterna hirundo*. In B. Stonehouse & C.M. Perrins (Eds) *Evolutionary Ecology*. London: Macmillan.

NOWAK, R. (1991) Senses involved in discrimination of merino ewes at close contact and from a distance by their newborn lambs. *Animal Behaviour*, 42, 357–366.

ORIANS, G.H. (1969) On the evolution of mating systems in birds and mammals. *American Naturalist*, 103, 589–603.

PACKER, C. (1977) Reciprocal altruism in *Papio anubis*. *Nature*, 265, 441–443.

PACKER, C. & PUSEY, A.E. (1982) Co-operation and competition within coalitions of lions: Kin selection or game theory? *Nature*, 296, 740–742.

PAGEL, M. (1997) Desperately concealing father: A theory of parent–infant resemblance. *Animal Behaviour*, 53, 973–981.

PARKER, G.A. (1978) Searching for mates. In J.R. Krebs & N.B. Davies (Eds) *Behavioural Ecology: An Evolutionary Approach* (2nd edn). Oxford: Blackwell Scientific.

PARKER, G.A. (1985) Models of parent–offspring conflict. V. Effects of the behaviour of two parents. *Animal Behaviour*, 33, 519–533.

PARKER, G.A. & SUTHERLAND, W.J. (1986) Ideal free distributions when individuals differ in competitive ability: Phenotype-limited ideal free models. *Animal Behaviour*, 34, 1222–1242.

PARTRIDGE, L. (1980) Mate choice increases a component of offspring fitness in fruit flies. *Nature*, 283, 290–291.

PASSINGHAM, R.E. (1982) *The Human Primate*. New York: W.H. Freeman.

PATTERSON, I.J. (1965) Timing and spacing of broods in

the black-headed gull (*Larus ridibundus*). *Ibis*, 107, 433–459.

PAVLOV, I.P. (1927) *Conditioned Reflexes*. London: Oxford University Press.

PEPPERBERG, I.M. (1983) Cognition in the African grey parrot: Preliminary evidence for auditory/vocal comprehension of class concept. *Animal Learning and Behaviour*, 11, 179–185.

PETTIFOR, R.A. (1990) The effects of avian mobbing on a potential predator, the European kestrel, *Falco tinnunculus*. *Animal Behaviour*, 39, 821–827.

POVINELLI, D.J., NELSON, K.E. & BOYSEN, S.T. (1992) Comprehension of role reversal in chimpanzees: evidence of role reversal? *Animal Behaviour*, 43, 633–640.

POWELL, G.V.N. (1974) Experimental analysis of the social value of flocking by starlings (*Sturnus vulgaris*) in relation to predation and foraging. *Animal Behaviour*, 22, 501–505.

POWER, M.E. (1984) Habitat quality and the distribution of algae-grazing catfish in a Panamanian stream. *Journal of Animal Ecology*, 53, 357–374.

PROFET, M. (1992) Pregnancy sickness as adaptation: A deterrent to maternal ingestion of teratogens. In J.H. Barkow, L. Cosmides & J. Tooby (Eds) *The Adapted Mind: Evolutionary Psychology and the Generation of Culture*. Oxford: Oxford University Press.

PRYCE, C.R. (1992) A comparative systems model of the regulation of maternal motivation in mammals. *Animal Behaviour*, 43, 417–441.

RAFFA, K.F. & BERRYMAN, A.A. (1983) The role of host resistance in the colonisation behaviour and ecology of bark beetles (Coleoptera: Scolytidae). *Ecological Monographs*, 63, 27–49.

RAMSAY, A.O. & HESS, E.H. (1954) A laboratory approach to the study of imprinting. *Wilson Bulletin*, 66, 196–206.

READ, A.F. (1988) Sexual selection and the role of parasites. *Trends in Ecology and Evolution*, 3, 97–101.

RESCORLA, R.A. (1968) Probability of a shock in the presence and absence of the CS in fear conditioning. *Journal of Comparative and Physiological Psychology*, 66, 1–5.

RICHNER, H. & MARCLAY, C. (1991) Evolution of avian roosting behaviour: A test of the information centre hypothesis and of a critical assumption. *Animal Behaviour*, 41, 433–438.

RIDLEY, M. (1989) *Animal Behavior*. Cambridge, MA: Blackwell.

RIDLEY, M. (1993) *The Red Queen*. London: Penguin.

RIDLEY, M. (1995) *Animal Behavior* (2nd edition). Cambridge, MA: Blackwell.

RIECHERT, S.E. (1978) Games spiders play: Behavioural variability in territorial disputes. *Behavioural Ecology and Sociobiology*, 3, 135–162.

ROOD, J.P. (1978) Dwarf mongoose helpers at the den. *Zeitschrift fur Tierpsychologie*, 48, 277–287.

ROWE, M.P., COSS, R.G. & OWINGS, D.H. (1986) Rattlesnake rattles and burrowing owl hisses: A case of acoustic Batesian mimicry. *Ethology*, 72, 53–71.

ROWELL, T.E. (1991) Till death do us part: Long-lasting bonds between ewes and their daughters. *Animal Behaviour*, 42, 681–682.

ROZENFELD, F.M. & RASMONT, R. (1991) Odour cue recognition by dominant male bank voles, *Clethrionomys glareolus*. *Animal Behaviour*, 41, 839–850.

RUMBAUGH, D.M., GILL, T.V. & GLASERFELD, E. (1973) Reading and sentence completion by a chimpanzee. *Science*, 182, 731–733.

RUMBAUGH, D. & SAVAGE-RUMBAUGH, S. (1994) Language and Apes. *APA Psychology Teacher Network*, January, 2–9.

RYAN, M.J., TUTTLE, M.D. & RAND, A.S. (1981) The costs and benefits of frog chorusing behaviour. *Behavioural Ecology and Sociobiology*, 8, 273–278.

SALZEN, E.A. & MEYER, C.C. (1967) Imprinting: Reversal of a preference established during the critical period. *Nature, London*, 215, 785–786.

SALZEN, E.A. & MEYER, C.C. (1968) Reversibility of imprinting. *Journal of Comparative Physiology and Psychology*, 66, 269–275.

SAVAGE-RUMBAUGH, E.S., MURPHY, J., SEVEIK, R.A., WILLIAMS, S., BRAKKE, K. & RUMBAUGH, D.M. (1993) Language comprehension in ape and child. *Monographs of the Society for Research in Child Development*, 58, 3–4.

SAVAGE-RUMBAUGH, E.S. & LEWIN, R. (1994) *Kanzi: The Ape at the Brink of the Human Mind*. New York: Doubleday.

SCHAFFER, H.R. & EMERSON, P.E. (1964) The development of social attachments in infancy. *Monographs of the Society for Research in Child Development*, 29, Serial No. 94.

SCHALLER, G.B. (1972) *The Serengeti Lion*. Chicago: University of Chicago Press.

SCHEEL, D. & PACKER, C. (1991) Group hunting behaviour of lions: A search for cooperation. *Animal Behaviour*, 41, 697–709.

SCHJELDERUP-EBBE, T. (1935) Social behaviour of birds. In C.A. Murchison (Ed.) *A Handbook of Social Psychology*. Worcester, MA: Clark University Press.

SCHLENOFF, D.H. (1985) The startle responses of blue jays to *Catocala* (Lepidoptera: Noctuidae) prey models. *Animal Behaviour*, 33, 1057–1067.

SCHMID-HEMPEL, P., KACELNIK, A. & HOUSTON, A.I. (1985) Honeybees maximise efficiency by not filling their crop. *Behavioural Ecology and Sociobiology*, 17, 61–66.

SCHNEIDER, D. (1969) Insect olfaction: Deciphering system for chemical messages. *Science*, 163, 1031–1037.

SCHNEIRLA, T.C., ROSENBLATT, J.S. & TOBACH, E. (1963) Maternal behavior in the cat. In H.L. Rheingold (Ed.) *Maternal Behavior in Mammals*. New York: John Wiley & Sons.

SCOTT, J.P. & FULLER, J.L. (1965) *Genetics and the Social Behavior of the Dog*. Chicago: University of Chicago Press.

SEIBT, U. & WICKLER, W. (1987) Gerontophagy versus cannibalism in the social spiders *Stegodyphus mimosarum* Pavesi and *Stegodyphus dumicola* Pocock. *Animal Behaviour*, 35, 1903–1905.

SELIGMAN, M.E.P. (1970) On the generality of the laws of learning. *Psychology Review*, 77, 406–418.

SELIGMAN, M.E.P. (1971) Phobias and preparedness. *Behaviour Therapy*, 2, 307–320.

SELIGMAN, M.E.P. (1972) *Biological Boundaries of Learning*. New York: Appleton-Century-Crofts.

SEYFARTH, R.M., CHENEY, D.L. & MARLER, P. (1980) Monkey responses to three different alarm calls: Evidence for predator classification and semantic communication. *Science*, 210, 801–803.

SHEFFIELD, F.D. (1965) Relation between classical conditioning and instrumental learning. In W.F. Prokasy (Ed.) *Classical Conditioning: A Symposium*. New York: Appleton-Century-Crofts.

SHERMAN, P.W. (1981) Reproductive competition and infanticide in Belding's ground squirrels and other animals. In R.D. Alexander & D.W. Tinkle (Eds) *Natural Selection and Social Behavior: Recent Research and New Theory*. New York: Chiron Press.

SHERMAN. P.W. (1985) Alarm calls of Belding's ground squirrels to aerial predators: Nepotism or self-preservation? *Behavioural Ecology and Sociobiology*, 17, 313–323.

SHERMAN, P.W., JARVIS, J.U.M. & BRAUDE, S.H. (1992) Naked mole rats. *Scientific American*, 245, 102–110.

SHERRY, D.F. & GALEF, B.G. (1984) Cultural transmission without imitation: Milk bottle opening by birds. *Animal Behaviour*, 32, 937–938.

SHERRY, D.F. & GALEF, B.G., Jr (1990) Social learning without imitation: More about milk bottle opening by birds. *Animal Behaviour*, 40, 987–989.

SIGMUND, K. (1993) *Games of Life*. New York: Oxford University Press.

SIMMONS, L.W. (1990) Pheromonal cues for the recognition of kin by female crickets, *Gryllus bimaculatus*. *Animal Behaviour*, 40, 192–195.

SKINNER, B.F. (1938) *Science and Behaviour*. New York: MacMillan.

SKINNER, B.F. (1957) *Verbal Behaviour*. New York: Appleton-Century-Crofts.

SOLOMON, R.L. & WYNNE, L.C. (1953) Traumatic avoidance learning: Acquisition in normal dogs. *Psychological Monographs*, no. 67.

SPRINGETT, B.P. (1968) Aspects of the relationship between burying beetles, *Necrophorus spp*. and the mite *Poecilochirus necrophori*. *Journal of Animal Ecology*, 37, 417–424.

STERN, D. (1977) *The First Relationship: Infant and Mother*. London: Fontana.

STEVENS, A. & PRICE, J. (1996) *Evolutionary Psychiatry*. London: Routledge.

STINSON, C.H. (1979) On the selective advantage of fratricide in raptors. *Evolution*, 33, 1219–1225.

STIRLING, I. & LATOUR, P.B. (1978) Comparative hunting ability of polar bear cubs at different ages. *Canadian Journal of Zoology*, 56, 73–75.

STRATTON, P.M. (1983) Biological preprogramming of infant behaviour. *Journal of Child Psychology and Psychiatry*, 24, 301–309.

STUBBLEFIELD, J.W. & CHARNOV, E.L. (1986) Some conceptual issues in the origin of eusociality. *Heredity*, 57, 181–187.

SUGIYAMA, Y. (1984) Proximate factors of infanticide among langurs at Dharwar: A reply to Boggess. In G. Hausfater & S.B. Hrdy (Eds) *Infanticide: Comparative and Evolutionary Perspectives*. New York: Aldine.

SYMONS, D. (1979) *The Evolution of Human Sexuality*. New York: Oxford University Press.

TAMURA, N. (1989) Snake directed mobbing by the Formosan squirrel *Callosciurus erythraeus thaiwanensis*. *Behavioural Ecology and Sociobiology*, 24, 175–180.

TERRACE, H.S. (1979) *Nim*. New York: Knopf.

THOMPSON, J.N. (1982) *Interaction and Coevolution*. New York: John Wiley & Sons.

THORNDIKE, E.L. (1911) *Animal Intelligence: Experimental Studies*. New York: MacMillan.

THORNHILL, R. (1976) Sexual selection and nuptial feeding behaviour in *Bittacus apicalis* (Insecta: Mecoptera). *American Nature*, 110, 529–548.

TINBERGEN, N. (1951) *The Study of Instinct*. Oxford: Oxford University Press.

TINBERGEN, N. (1953) *Social Behaviour in Animals*. London: Methuen.

TINBERGEN, N. & PERDECK, A.C. (1950) On the stimulus situation releasing the begging response in the newly hatched herring gull chick (*Larus a. argentatus* Pont.). *Behaviour*, 3, 1–38.

TOLMAN. E.C. & HONZICK, C.H. (1930) Introduction and removal of reward and maze learning in rats. *University of California Publications in Psychology*, 4, 257–275.

TORGERSEN, S. (1983) Genetic factors in anxiety disorders. *Archives of General Psychiatry*, 40, 1085–1089.

TREVATHAN, W. (1987) *Human Birth: An Evolutionary Perspective*. New York: Aldine de Gruyter.

TRIVERS, R.L. (1971) The evolution of reciprocal altruism. *Quarterly Review of Biology*, 46, 35–57.

TRIVERS, R.L. (1972) Parental investment and sexual selection. In B. Campbell (Ed.) *Sexual Selection and the Descent of Man*. Chicago: Aldine.

TRIVERS, R. (1974) Parent–offspring conflict. *American Zoologist*, 14, 249–264.

TRIVERS, R. (1985) *Social Evolution*. New York: Benjamin Cummings.

TRIVERS, R.L. & HARE, H. (1976) Haplodiploidy and the evolution of social insects. *Science*, 191, 249–263.

TRONICK, E., ALS, H., ADAMSON, L., WISE, S. & BRAZELTON, T.B. (1978) The infant's response to entrapment between contradictory messages in face-to-face interaction. *Journal of the American Academy of Child Psychiatry*, 17, 1–13.

TYACK, P. (1983) Differential response of humpback whales *Megaptera novaengliae* to playback of song or social sounds. *Behavioural Ecology*, 13, 49–55.

VAN KAMPEN, H.S. & DE VOS, G.J. (1991) Learning about the shape of an imprinting object varies with its colour. *Animal Behaviour*, 42, 328–329.

VERNER, J. & WILLSON, M.F. (1966) The influence of habitats on mating systems of North American passerine birds. *Ecology*, 47, 143–147.

VIDAL, J.M. (1976) L'empteinte chez les animaux. *La Recherche*, 63, 24–35.

VON FRISCH, K. (1953) *The Dancing Bees*. New York: Harcourt Brace Jovanovich.

WAGNER, W.E., Jr (1992) Deceptive or honest signalling of fighting ability? A test of alternative hypotheses for the function of changes in call dominant frequency by male cricket frogs. *Animal Behaviour*, 44, 449–462.

WALLACE, A.R. (1889) *Darwinism: An Exposition of the Theory of Natural Selection with some of its Applications*. London: Macmillan.

WATSON, J.B. (1913) Psychology as the behaviourist views it. *Psychological Review*, 20, 158–177.

WATSON, J.B. & RAYNER, R. (1920) Conditioned emotioned reactions. *Journal of Experimental Psychology*, 3, 1–14.

WEATHERHEAD, P.J. (1983) Two principal strategies in avian communal roosts. *American Naturalist*, 121, 237–243.

WEINBERG, E.D. (1984) The sequestration of iron as a defence against bacterial pathogens. *Physiological Reviews*, 64, 65–102.

WHITHAM, T.G. (1979) Territorial behaviour of Pemphigus gall aphids. *Nature*, 279, 324–325.

WICKLER, W. (1967) Socio-sexual signals and their intra-specific imitation among primates. In D. Morris (Ed.) *Primate Ethology*. London: Weidenfeld & Nicolson.

WICKLER, W. (1968) *Mimicry*. New York: McGraw-Hill.

WICKSTEN, M.K. (1980) Decorator crabs. *Scientific American*, 242, 146–154.

WILKINSON, G.S. (1984) Reciprocal food sharing in the vampire bat. *Nature*, 308, 181–184.

WILSON, E.O. (1975) *Sociobiology: The New Synthesis*. Harvard, MA: The Belknap Press.

WOLF, A.P. (1970) Childhood association and sexual attraction: a further test of the Westermark hypothesis. *American Anthropologist*, 72, 503–515.

WOLF, T.J. & SCHMID-HEMPEL, P. (1989) Extra loads and foraging lifespan in honeybee workers. *Journal of Animal Ecology*, 58, 943–954.

WOLF, P.H. (1969) The natural history of crying and other vocalisations in early infancy. In B.M. Foss (Ed.) *Determinants of Infant Behaviour* (Vol. 4). London: Methuen.

WOOLFENDEN, G.E. (1975) Florida scrub jay helpers at the nest. *Auk*, 92, 1–15.

WOOLFENDEN, G.E. & FITZPATRICK, J.W. (1984) *The Florida Scrub Jay*. Princeton, NJ: Princeton University Press.

WOURMS, M.K. & WASSERMAN, F.E. (1985) Butterfly wing markings are more advantageous during handling than during the initial strike of an avian predator. *Evolution*, 39, 845–851.

WYNNE-EDWARDS, V.C. (1962) *Animal Dispersion in Relation to Social Behaviour*. Edinburgh: Oliver & Boyd.

YASUKAWA, K. (1981) Song repertoires in the red-winged blackbird (*Agelaius phoniceus*): A test of the Beau Geste hypothesis. *Animal Behaviour*, 29, 114–125.

YOUNG, S. (1990) Naked mole rats keep it in the family. *New Scientist*, 12 May, 38.

ZAHAVI, A. (1975) Mate selection: A selection for a handicap. *Journal of Theoretical Biology*, 53, 205–214.

ZIPPELIUS, H. (1972) Die Karawanebildung bie Feld und Hausspitzmaus. *Zeitschrift fur Tierpsychologie*, 30, 305–320.

INDEX

Page numbers which appear in **bold** refer to definitions and main explanations of particular concepts.

PICTURE CREDITS

The authors and publishers would like to thank the following copyright holders for their permission to reproduce illustrative materials in this book:

Ardea London Ltd for Figures 3.4 (p.25) © Arthus-Bertrand, 3.5 (p.26) © John Mason and 11.1 (p.101) © David & Katie Urry; **BBC Publications** for Figures 11.3 (p.105) and 11.4 (p.107) Illustrations reproduced from *Animal Language* by Michael Bright with the permission of BBC Worldwide Limited; **Blackwell Science Ltd** for Figure 9.6 (p.85); **Alan Clamp** for Figures 15.1 and 15.2 (p.144); **Bruce Coleman Ltd** for Figures 1.3 (p.6) © George McCarthy, 3.3 (p.24) © S J Krasemann and 9.2 (p.81) © Carl Roessler; **Alan Clamp** for Figures 15.1 and 15.2 (p.144); **Frank Lane Picture Agency** for Figures 1.5 (p.10) © R Wilmshurst, 2.2 (p.13) © F Polking, 2.7a (p.18) © T Whittaker, 2.7b (p.18) © A Wharton, 2.7c (p.18) © T Hamblin, 3.1 (p.21) © D Hosking, 3.7 (p.29) © M Walker, 4.1 (p.33) © J Zimmerman, 4.4 (p.37) and 5.4 (p.47) © Eric and David Hosking, 6.1 (p.54) © David T Grewcock, 81. (p.72) © Mark Newman, 11.5 (p.108) © Silvestris and 13.5 (p.127) © Eichhorn/Zingel; **Harcourt Brace** for Figures 10.3 (p.95) and 10.4 (p.96) Reprinted from *Animal Behaviour*, Vol 39, J P Blacombe 'Vocal Recognition of pups by mother Mexican free-tailed bats' (1990) and Figure 14.2 (p.136) Reprinted from *Animal Behaviour*, Vol 43, D J Povenelli et al. 'Comprehension of role reversal in chimpanzees: evidence of role reversal?' (1992) by permission of the publisher Academic Press Ltd, London; **Harlow Primate Laboratory, University of Wisconsin** for Figure 10.5 (p.97); **Katz Pictures Ltd** for Figure 12.6 (p.116); **Life File** for Figure 15.4 (p.146) © Terence Waeland; **Professor Leanne T Nash, Arizona State University** for Figure 8.3 (p.77); **Oxford Scientific Films** for Figures 7.3 (p.65) © James Robinson, 8.2 (p.75) © Raymond A Mendez, 8.4 (p.77) © Stephen Dalton and 13.1 (p.124) © Merlin D Tuttle; **Oxford University Press** for Figure 5.3 (p.46) taken with permission from T Halliday *Sexual Strategy* (1980); **Planet Earth Pictures** for Figures 5.5 (p.50) © Wendy Davies and 7.5 (p.67) © Richard Matthews; **Dr Duane Rumbaugh, Georgia State University** for Figure 14.3 (p.138); **Stuart Russell** for Figure 2.4 (p.15); **Julia Russell** for Figures 6.2 (p.59), 9.1 (p.80), 9.4 (p.83), 9.5 (p.85), 9.7 (p.86), 10.6 (p.98) and 11.2 a–d (p.103); **Science Photo Library** for Figures 5.1 (p.43) © D Phillips and 10.1 (p.89); **Springer-Verlag** for Figure 9.3 (p.82) from MJ Ryan et al. (1981) *Behav. Ecol. Sociobiol.*, 8, 273–278 © 1981 Springer-Verlag.

Every effort has been made to obtain necessary permission with reference to copyright material. The publishers apologise if inadvertently any sources remain unacknowledged and will be glad to make the necessary arrangements at the earliest opportunity.

Index prepared by Indexing Specialists, Hove, Sussex.